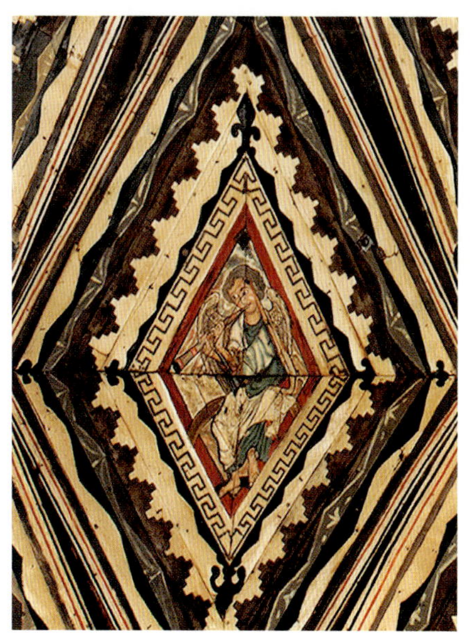

Peterborough Cathedral

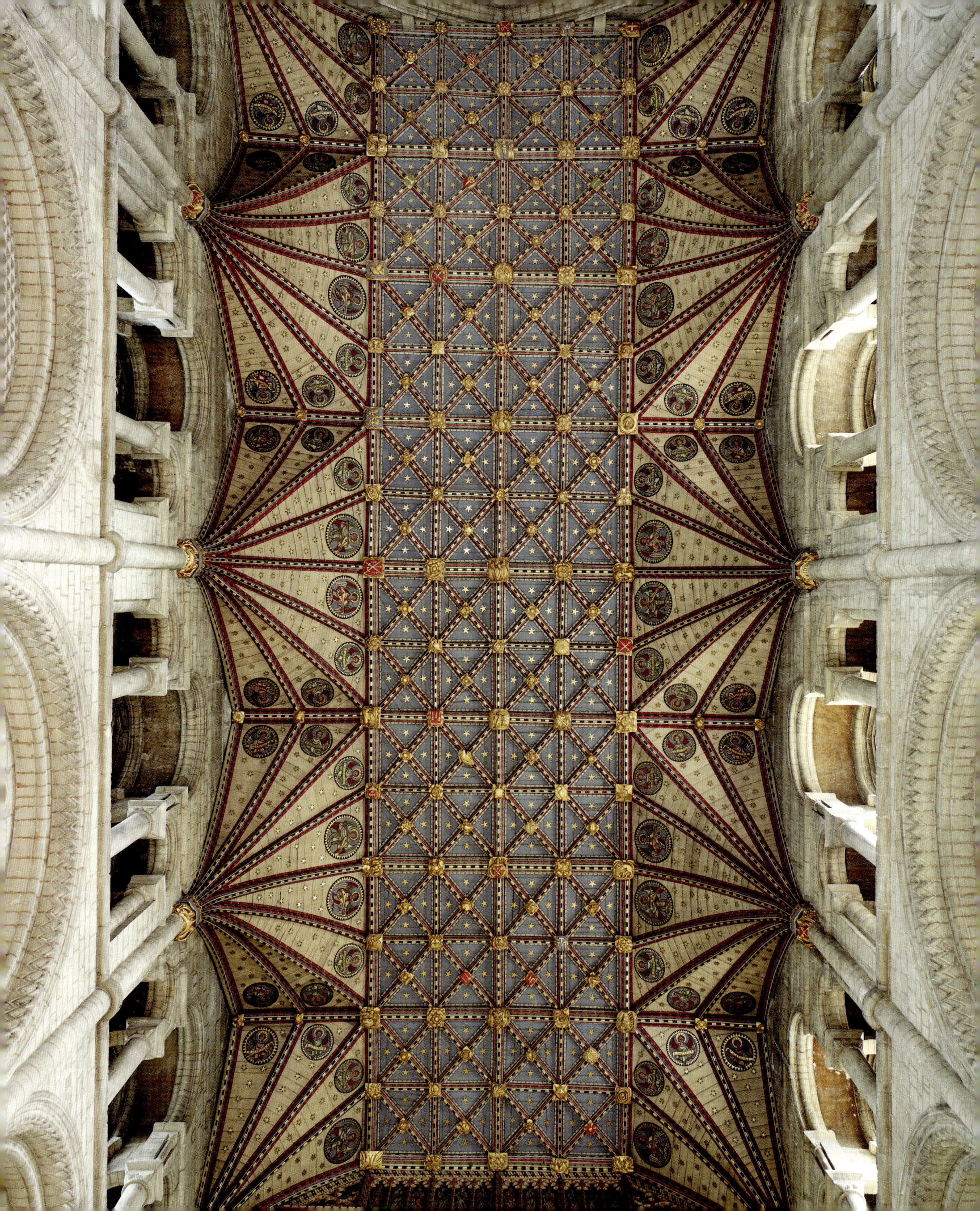

PETERBOROUGH CATHEDRAL

A GLIMPSE OF HEAVEN

JONATHAN FOYLE

SCALA

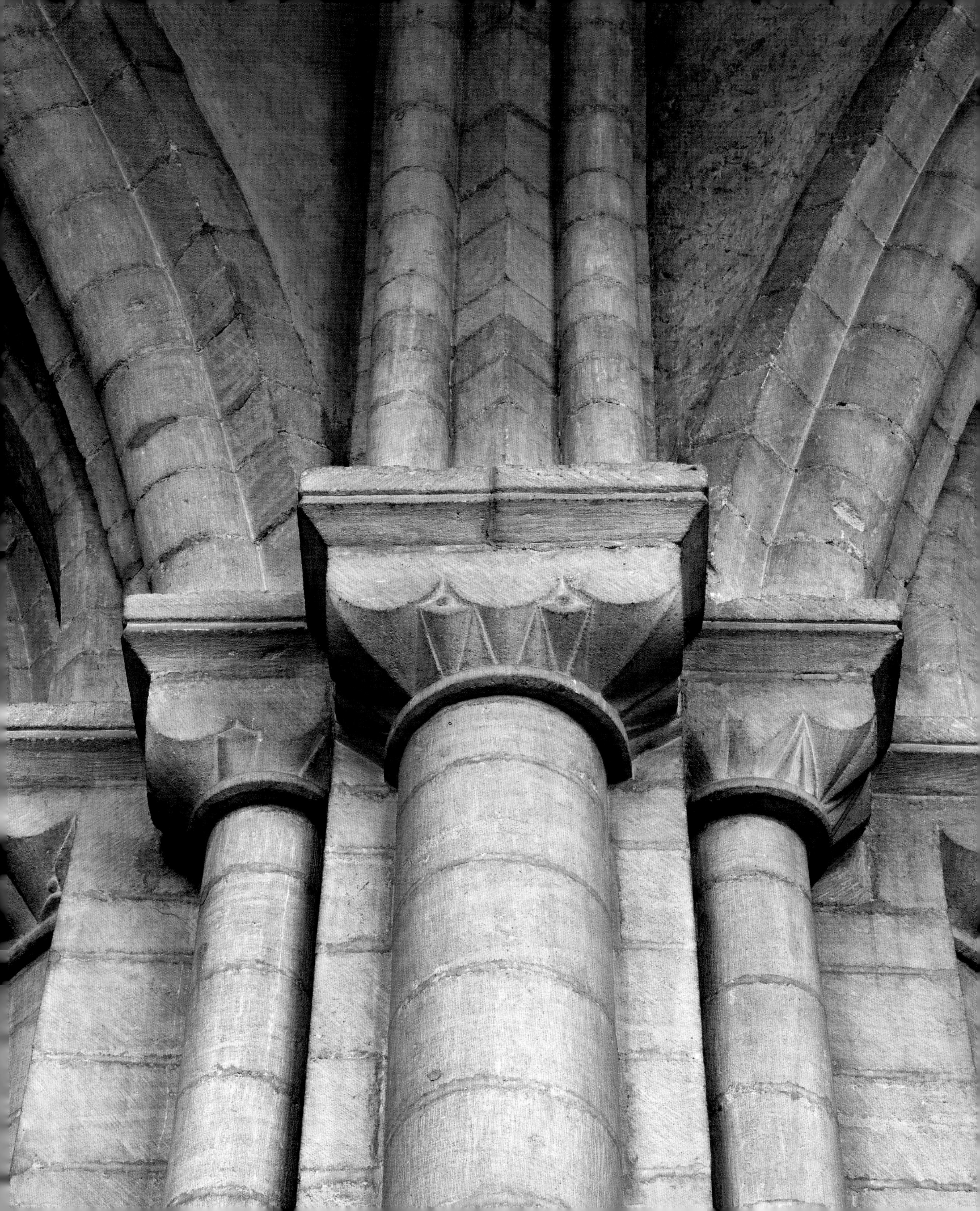

CONTENTS

INTRODUCTION 6

1

BETWEEN LAND AND WATER 10
Living on the Edge 19
The Later Anglo-Saxon Era 22

2

DESTRUCTION AND REBUILDING 28
Ransacking 31
Rebuilding 38

3

THE GREAT CHURCH COMPLETED 50
The West Front 57
Simon Magus 63

4

THE NAVE CEILING 68
The Fourteenth Century 88

5

THE END OF AN ERA 98

6

SURVIVAL AND RENEWAL 108

APPENDIX: LIST OF ABBOTS AND BISHOPS 122
NOTES 122
INDEX 126
ACKNOWLEDGEMENTS 128

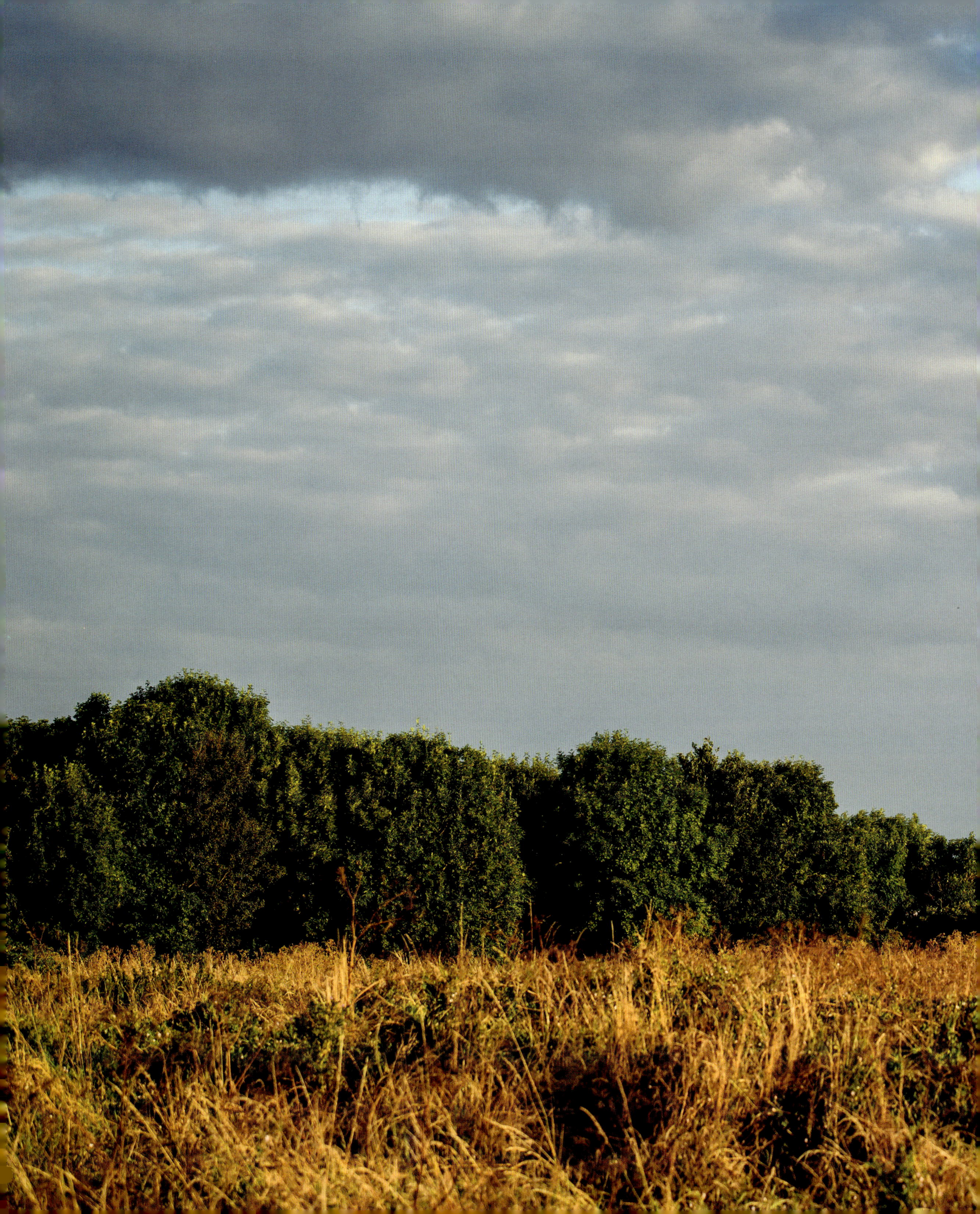

INTRODUCTION

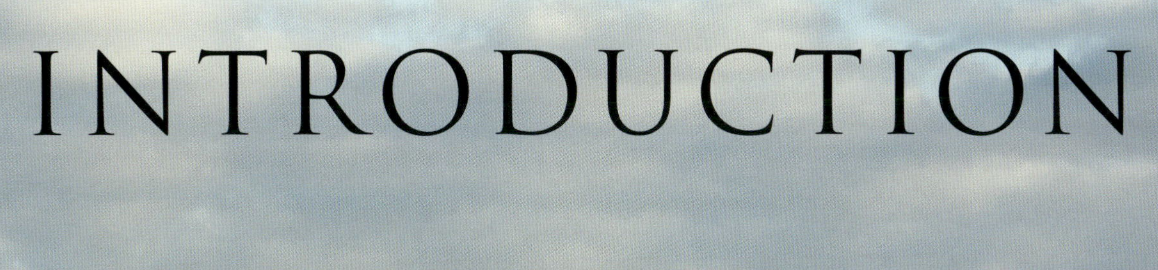

*Thou art Peter, and upon this rock I will
build my church; and the gates of hell
shall not prevail against it.*

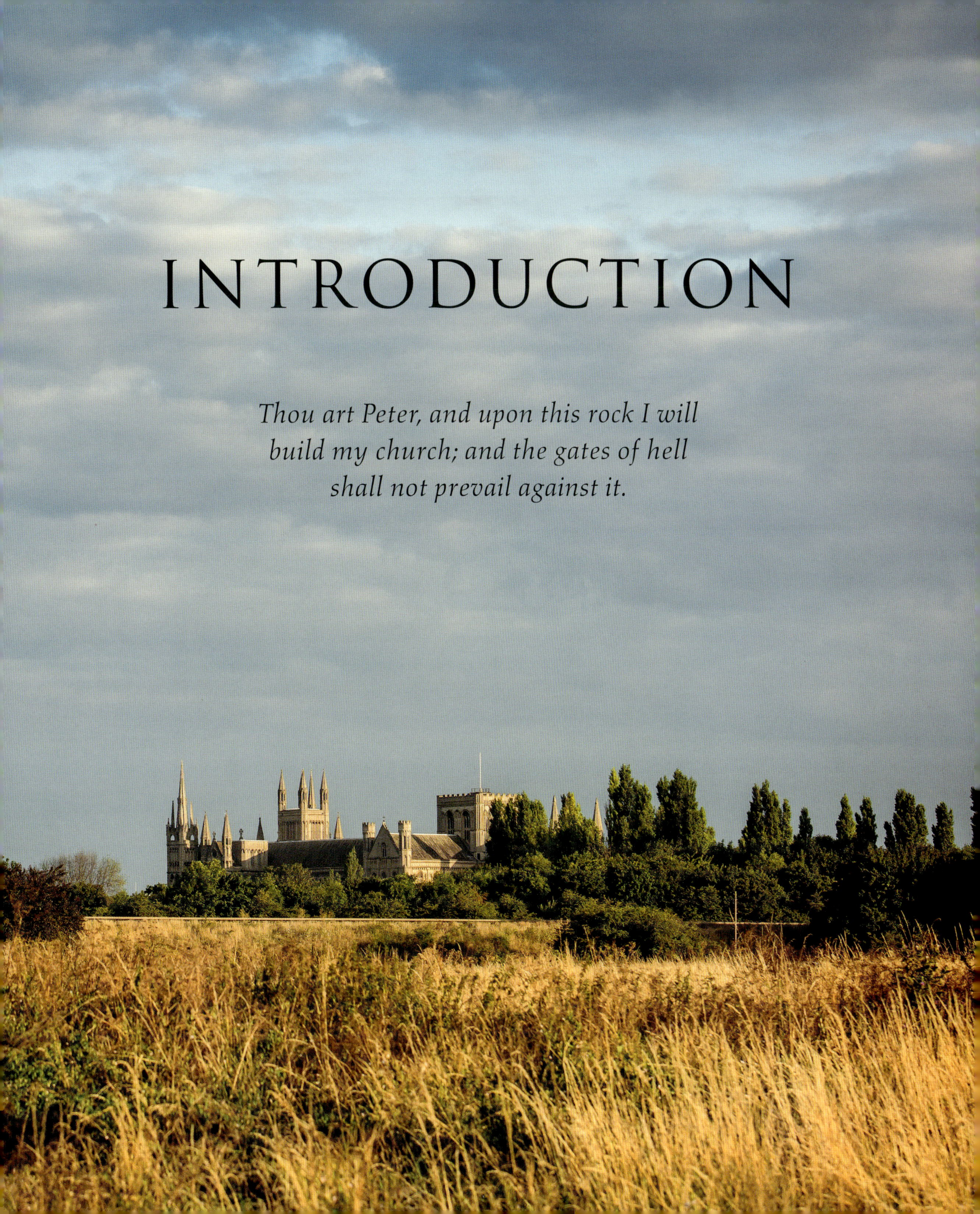

A GREAT REWARD of the 393-mile train journey between London King's Cross and Edinburgh Waverley is the parade of cathedral churches. York's magnificent white towers are best seen on axis as the train pulls out of the station's iron ribcage. Then come Durham Cathedral and its castle, grandly presiding over their ravine, as they have for almost a thousand years. Soon follows St Nicholas, Newcastle, the silhouette of its northern stone crown anticipating that of St Giles in the heart of Edinburgh. But before all these, the first great church on the line, barely fifty minutes out of London, is Peterborough Cathedral.

This intensely individual building resembles no other. Its uniquely arcaded west front presents a memorable first impression, yet the passenger is offered but a tantalising glimpse. Just visible at the far side of the city centre, rising beyond a massive late twentieth-century temple of retail, are its three stone gables with ancient wheel windows. They are studded with carving, niches framing figures best seen when afternoon sunlight throws the stones into relief. Then the shadows fall deepest within the three tall arches. What lies within?

The simple answer is that Peterborough was built to offer a glimpse of heaven, a life beyond the trodden path. The interaction of heaven and earth was the fundamental purpose of all great medieval church buildings. They occupied the meeting-place of those realms of sun and shade, creation and void, matter and spirit. Some churches make the point more obvious through a reaching spire, but the ambition was always to bridge the terrestrial and celestial realms for the living and the interred.

Peterborough's interpretations of heaven met with some hellish repercussions. They are the joint subjects of this book. This monumental church, dedicated to St Peter, with Paul and Andrew, has been built and rebuilt, furnished and stripped,

Previous page The dry, slightly elevated land chosen for the site of Peterborough Abbey faced the watery skies and marine landscape of the fens.

Above The first impression of the abbey, now cathedral, is the three arches of the west front, representing a triumphal entrance to heaven.

weathered and restored. It was not originally a cathedral but rather, for most of its existence, an abbey church in a place first known as Medeshamstede, then as Burgh. Today its founders would recognise only a stone or two. What survives, however, allows us a glimpse of the experience of generations who passed this way over the centuries, especially those who witnessed an outstanding work of architecture evolving during the twelfth and thirteenth centuries. This book draws together earlier studies of the building, reconstructs its changing shape, and reads anew its architectural design and symbolic language.

The historian of such an early building is presented with imperfect evidence. A Victorian writer on Peterborough Cathedral explained that 'there is an abundance of documentary evidence for our purpose; but recent criticism has shewn that not all is to be relied upon as authentic' while 'the absence of all reference to some works of importance (the West Front, for example), is very mysterious'. But this appeals to the historian, because reconciling conflicting ideas often generates fresh observations. Sometimes, that even allows us to glimpse a place through ancient eyes.

Below Peterborough developed slowly around its great church and monastic complex. Beneath the present crossing tower, the seventh-century abbey was similarly oriented to the building we see today. The city's market place came in the twelfth century; the church of St John (bottom left) in the early fifteenth century. The railways fuelled industry and expansion from the 1840s.

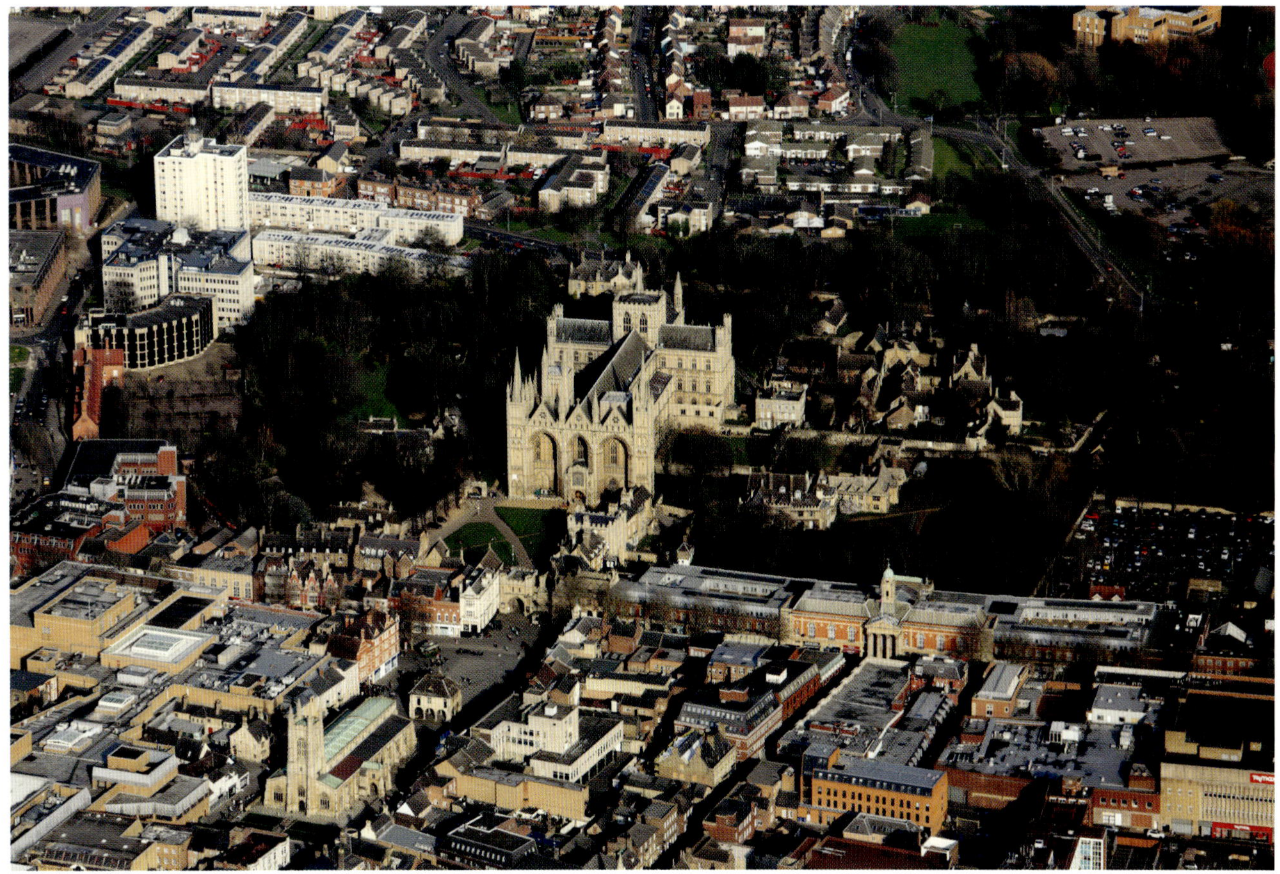

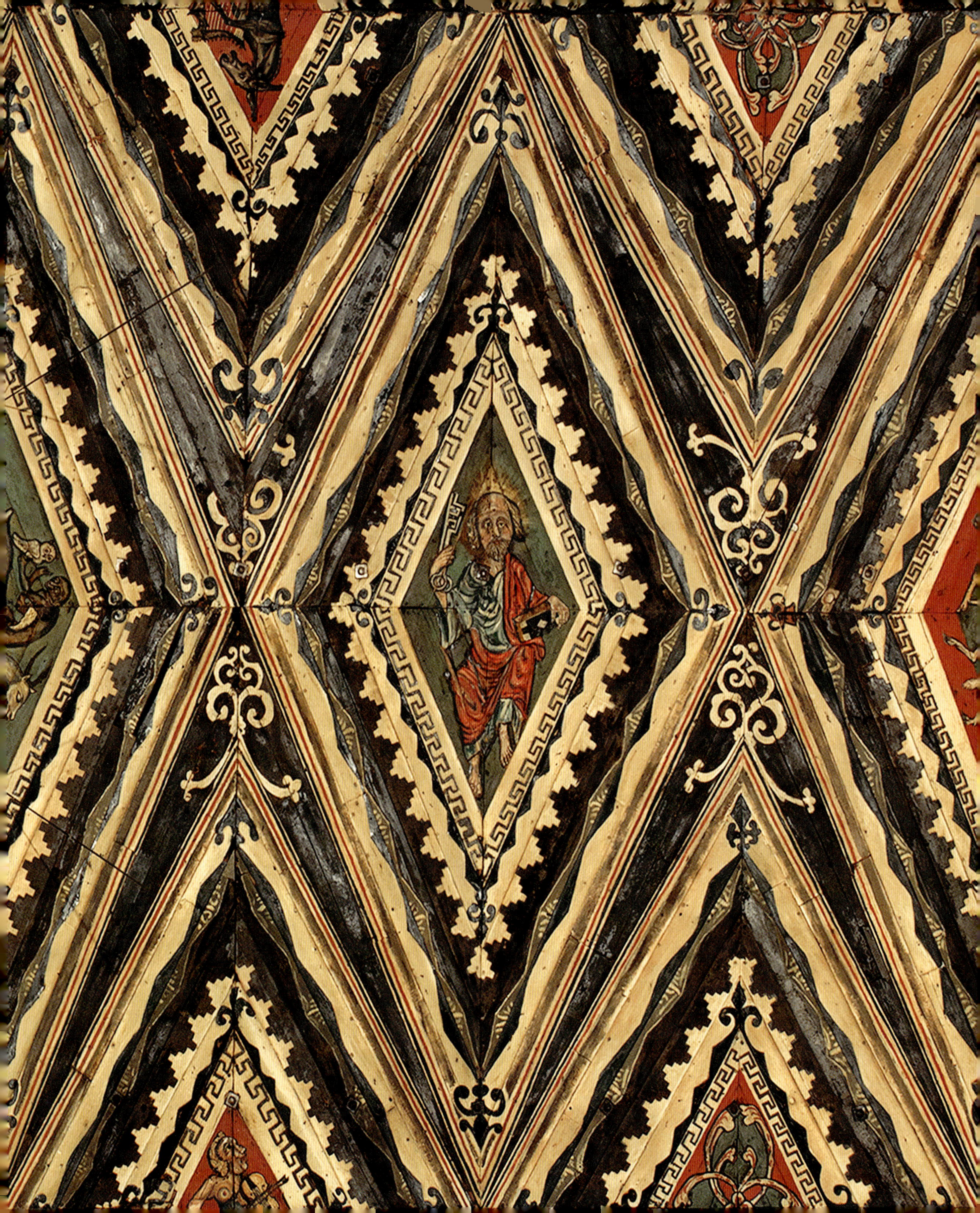

1

BETWEEN LAND AND WATER

*They wished to establish a minster in
praise of Christ and in honor of St Peter.
And they did so, and gave it the name
Medeshamstede.*

Over thirteen centuries ago, Peterborough Abbey – what would become the present cathedral – was founded on the margins of land and water. Its site linked the bustling human life of trade and travel along the Great North Road with the wilderness of the fens, its reeds and brambles teeming with fish and birds. The abbey's first dedicatee was St Peter, who eventually gave his name to the city. Peter, 'Prince of Apostles', was the biblical holder of the keys of heaven and the principal Roman saint, in tandem with St Paul. Herein lies a big question: did Peterborough Cathedral have Roman origins?

A MONK AND SCRIBE called Hugh Candidus lived at Peterborough in the twelfth century. He composed a chronicle of the abbey from its origins, and understood it to have been founded in 655. Hugh implored readers to 'regard the truth of my history', but he was at a disadvantage for he had limited sources of reference. History as written by men of the church was rarely a simple desire to record events for posterity, but usually constructed as an attempt to cultivate past glories for political advantage. Hugh had found material 'recorded in the writings of old time, or heard from the lips of faithful and ancient witnesses'.

Those lips could scarcely have been old enough to have relayed more than fifty years of experience, beyond which was hearsay and legend. Hugh's world was half a millennium later than Peterborough abbey's foundation in the mid-seventh century, which itself came over two hundred years after the Romans abandoned Britannia in *c*.410. He can have known little of the Roman environment beyond the neglected walls and gates of Britannia's once-great cities, like Lincoln, London, or Colchester. But that list does not include Peterborough. The question is whether there was any settlement here at all.

Recent scholarship offers some new answers on Peterborough's distant past.[1] For three hundred years, antiquaries and archaeologists have studied copious Roman remains near the straight military roads to the west of Peterborough, including Ermine Street, linking London to York, and King Street, running

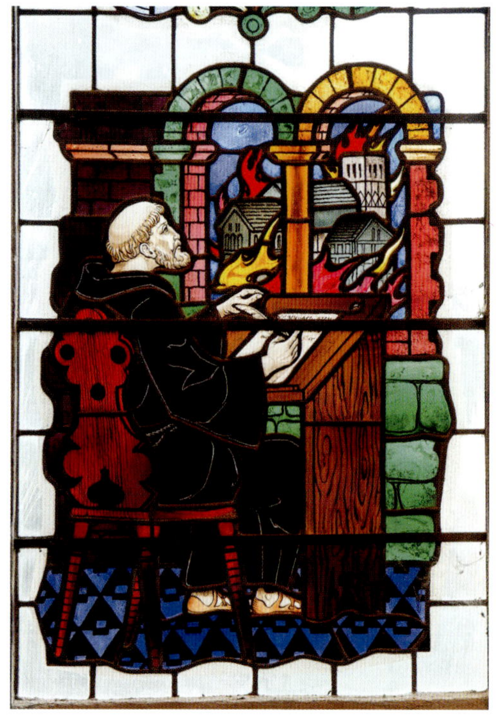

Above Stained glass panel from the 1958 Spencer Leeson memorial window by W.T. Carter-Shapland, portraying Hugh Candidus recording the fire of 1116. The chair is a typically Victorian notion, but the concept of the Anglo-Saxon western tower is probably correct.

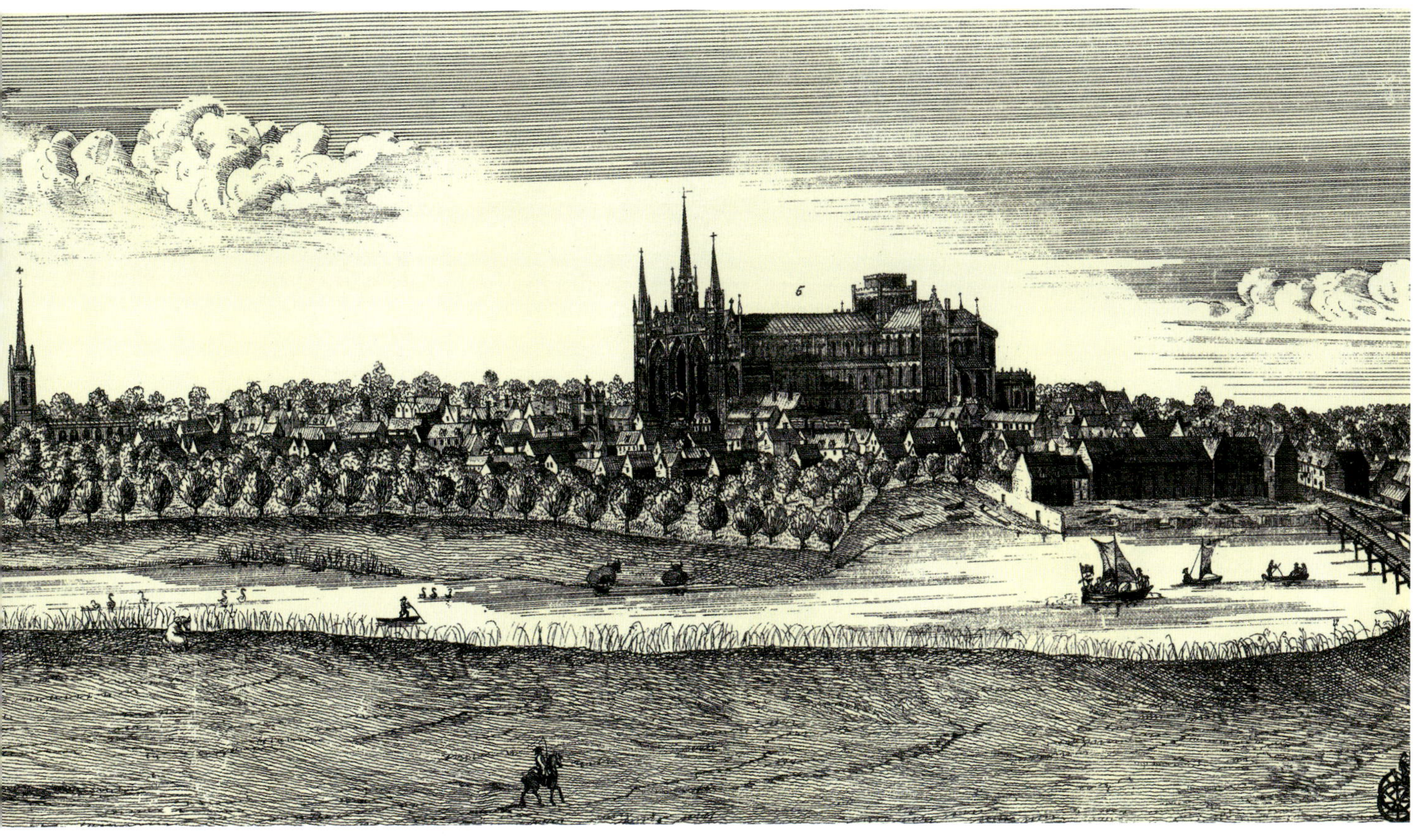

north through Maxey and West Deeping. At Longthorpe, on the western edge of the modern city, there was an early and massive 25-acre Roman fortress dating to *c*.44–48 AD, while three miles further west, a palatial third-century tax collector's compound was found at the praetorium overlooking Durobrivae (Water Newton), one of the richest small towns of Roman England and covering 5¼ acres (2 hectares).

As is common where land falls to water, the area is also a meeting-place of geological seams, which offers excellent and various building materials. Romans made ceramic roof and wall tiles from local brick earth and clay, while mines at Collyweston, west of Stamford, yielded sandy limestone slates. Excellent masonry was garnered from the open quarries of shelly silver limestone at Barnack, nine miles north-west of Peterborough. Lumber was hewn from oak, elm and ash, and willow from the wetlands, and thatch was abundant in reed or straw.

It is now becoming clear that Romans occupied a site close to the cathedral. They may have favoured this place because the fens were a state-controlled farm. In the mid-second century AD, the Car Dyke was dug through the flat lands south

Above *Prospect of Peterborough from the South* by Nathaniel & Samuel Buck, *c*.1731. The abbey occupied the angle of elevated land where the River Nene, to its south, joined the Roman canal called the 'Car Dyke' to its east. Peterborough may subsequently have become a city of spires; the octagon over the crossing may well have had a tall one.

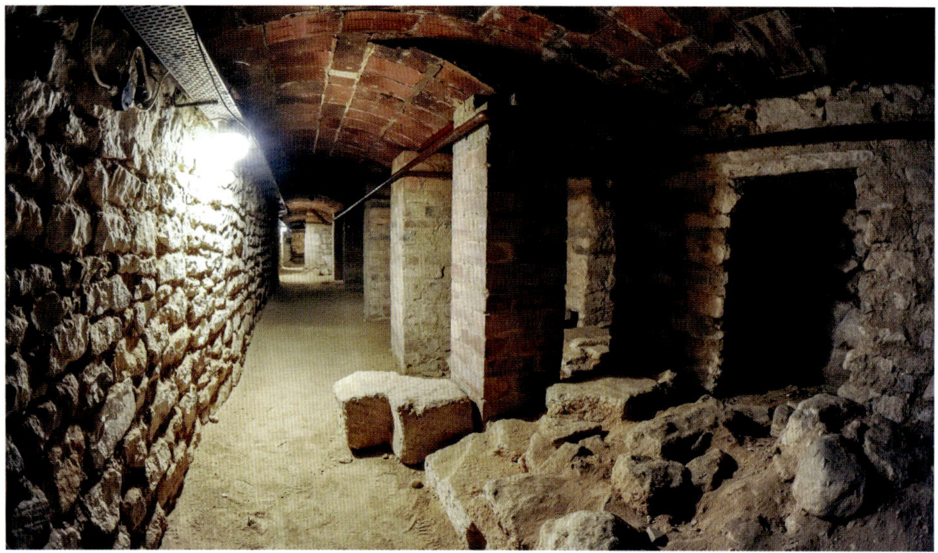

of Lincoln to serve as a major transport route and catchment channel, which after nearly sixty miles found its southern outlet into the river Nene just east of Peterborough. The ideal vantage point for this intersection was the position now occupied by the cathedral, set on gravel over beds of limestone and clay 8m above sea level, hence safe from flooding.

Recent studies by Penny Coombe, Kevin Hayward and Martin Henig have concentrated on fragments of Roman masonry in the cathedral.[2] An enigmatic carved stone embedded in the west wall of the south transept has long intrigued historians and visitors. It represents a pair of arches, each containing a figure, one bearded, the other female. They do not have haloes, as Christian saints would, but are dancing, shown with a shell, and seem to be Roman water deities. This stone must have once accompanied other monumental sculpture, which likely includes the fragment of classical pilaster and another block with part of a Roman dedicatory inscription, also in the cathedral's possession.

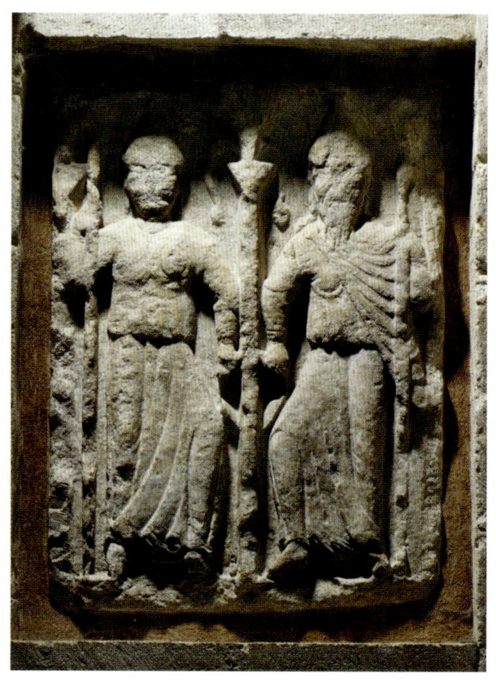

Together, these related pieces come from a local monumental building with a 'highly plausible' date of the middle of the second century. Scholarly consensus supports the 'attractive possibility' that the site of Peterborough Cathedral in the Roman period was occupied by a Roman temple, as Stephen Upex suggested.[3] The sculpted deities, with the pilaster and dedication, would all match this scenario, and the date is compatible with the creation of Car

EARLY GEOGRAPHY

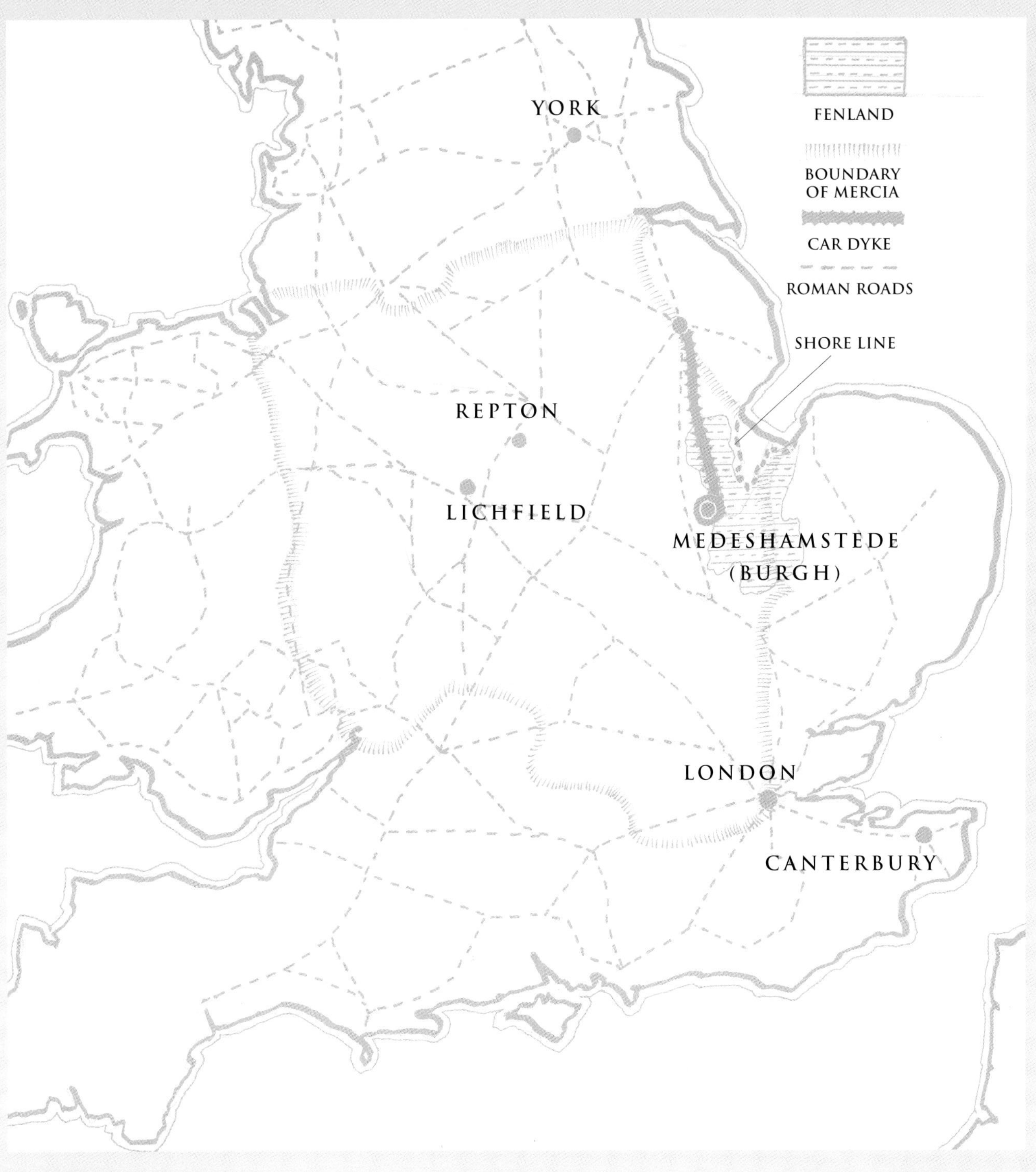

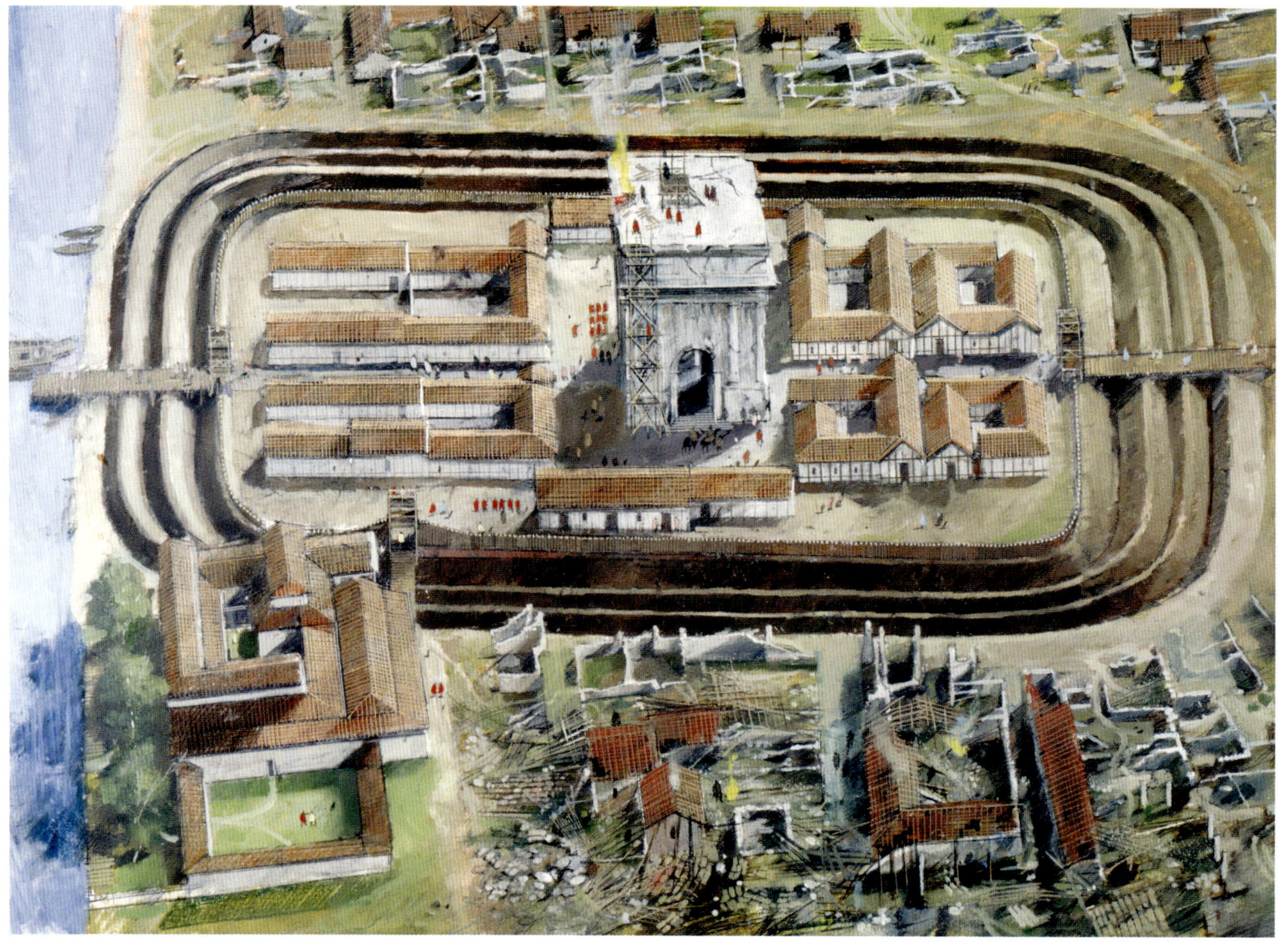

Dyke as a crucial node in the waterways of Roman England, by which cereal crops supplied the cities and troops with their daily bread.

Many Roman temples were founded on natural springs, but this aqueous intersection was much more politically important. If these fragments were from a temple, perhaps with overtones of a triumphal arch like that at Claudius' landing-place of Richborough in Kent, then its altar must have been serviced by a priest before celebrants. So did people live nearby?

In summer 2016, a dump of Roman pottery was found within the precincts. This scant evidence leaves us to wonder how large the settlement was, how many inhabitants witnessed a temple here – and whether any subscribed to Christianity. Christianity became the state religion in the early fourth century under Emperor Constantine, after his personal conversion in 312.[4] Its spread was not instant and it progressed neither smoothly nor evenly;[5] the western Latin Church based in Rome was not then expected to represent a majority religion.[6]

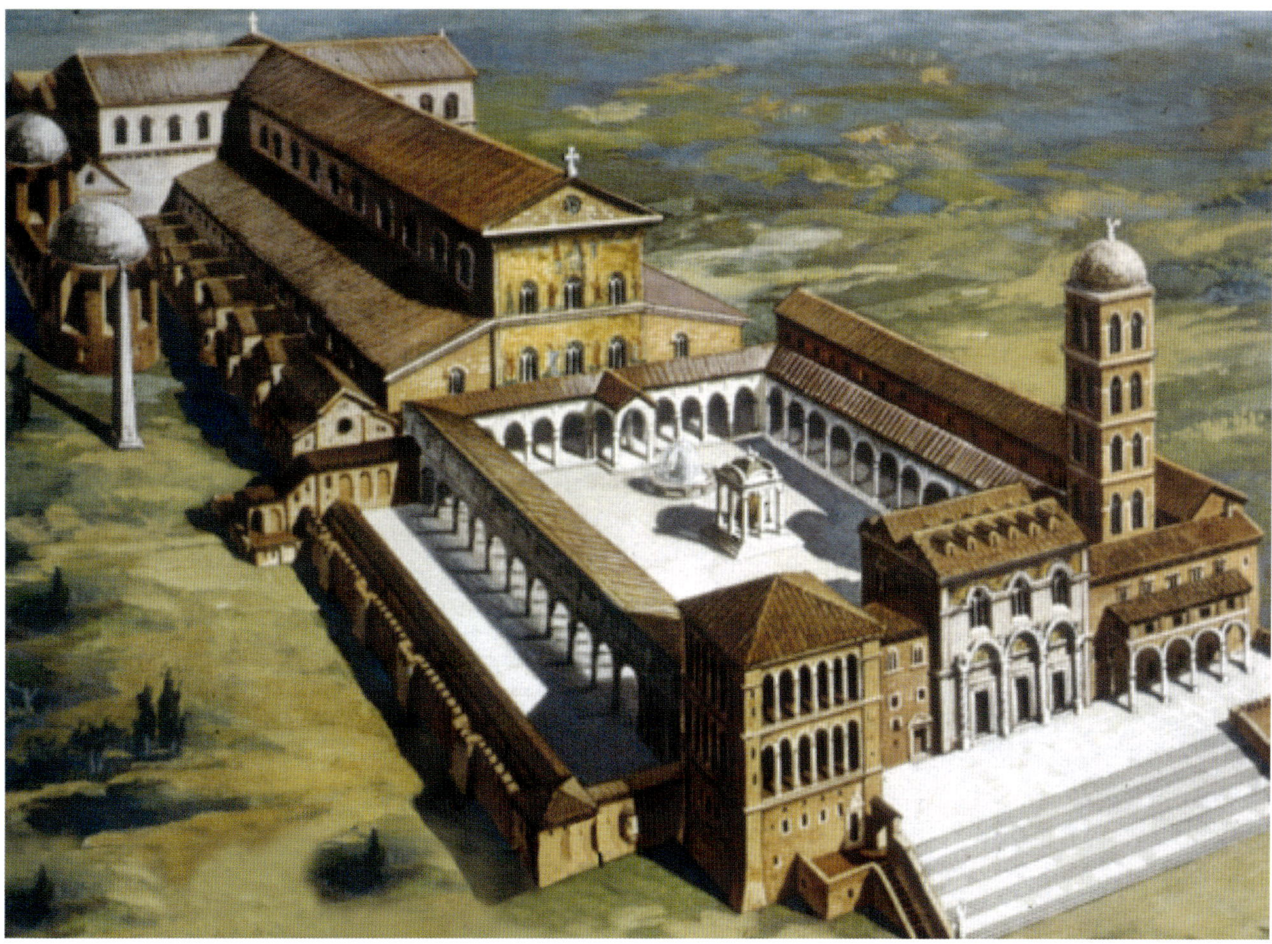

The central thrust of Christianity was thrones, stones and bones; through the convincing presentation of these in buildings of authority, the remains of the holy dead provided a bridge to heaven. The centres of authority in the western church were situated upon human remains, and provided access to them, to an extent unparalleled in other religions.

The blueprint for great churches was set in 321, when Constantine began the construction of a vast five-aisled basilica set outside the walls of Rome. Old St Peter's enclosed and made a focus of the remains of St Peter, Rome's principal saint and, like all Roman saints, a martyr. Until that time, his shrine had comprised merely an altar over a grave in a courtyard. Now enveloped within Constantine's basilica, his relics were set in a crypt beneath a baldacchino, a canopy supported on four columns.

St Peter was a fisherman, the brother of St Andrew. He is known as the keeper of heaven's gate from the biblical reference in the gospel of St Matthew,

THE WATER NEWTON TREASURE

The earliest evidence of Christianity in the Peterborough area is now displayed in the British Museum. It was revealed in February 1975, when a plough struck silver as it tore through the cold mud of a field at Water Newton by the Nene, five miles west of the cathedral. Twenty-seven silver items emerged, including nine vessels and a gold plaque. This exceptional collection proved to belong to the fourth century and is the earliest known group of Christian liturgical silver from anywhere in the Roman Empire.

One vessel reads: 'SANCTUM ALTARE TUUM DOMINE SUBNIXUS HONORO' (dependent on thee, I honour thy holy altar). Where was this altar? We are left to guess. It is possible that the collection came from the private chapel of a rich individual or a church at the settlement at Durobrivae (Water Newton) but, from its size and quality, it as plausibly belongs to a state temple, perhaps even that at Peterborough, converted to the Christian cause. Precious metal may have been hidden upriver when the empire was overthrown in the early fifth century, for it is clear that, after the Visigoths' sack of Rome in 410 and the consequent collapse of Roman authority, such a church would have ceased to function. Whatever the answer, the discovery illuminates our understanding of the earliest Christian arts in Britain and their high sophistication in the Peterborough area.

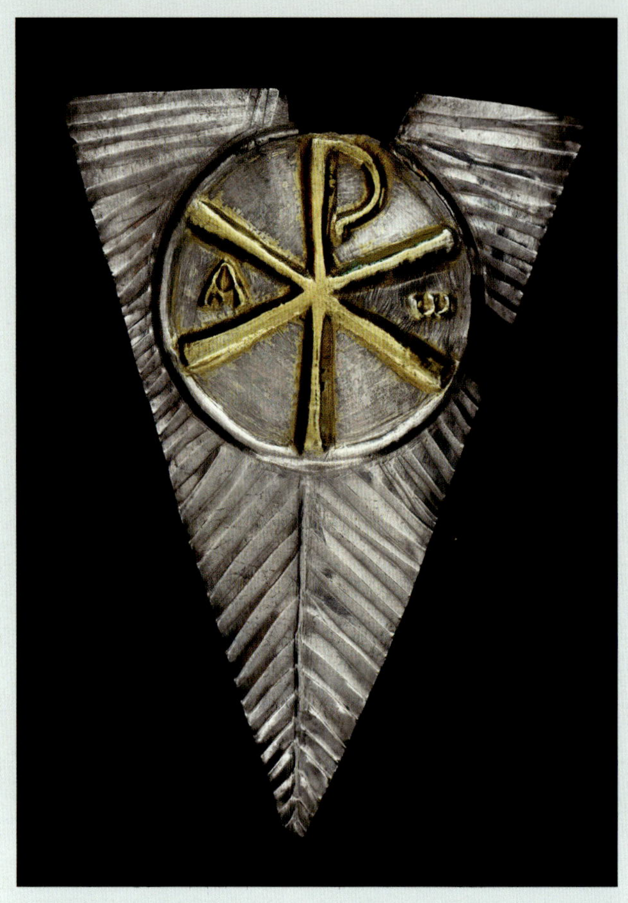

Above **The Water Newton hoard of liturgical silverware features Christian symbols such as the Chi–Rho.**

16:19: 'I will give you the keys of the kingdom of heaven, and whatever you bind on earth shall be bound in heaven, and whatever you loose on earth shall be loosed in heaven'. He enjoyed the third highest number of dedications among English churches.[8]

LIVING ON THE EDGE

The re-emergence of a church at Peterborough would have to wait until relations with Christian Rome were restored by territorial overlords in the seventh century.

Pope Gregory the Great (590–604) was a major theologian and ambitious reformer.[9] In 596 he sent St Augustine to the pagan kingdom of Kent to reconvert the Angles. Augustine's arrival at Canterbury the following year is a celebrated event in English history, but as testified by the Water Newton hoard, this was merely a re-Christianisation of part of the British Isles.[10] The northward spread of Augustine's urban, pro-Roman, Kentish church from Canterbury is a complex story, involving the establishment of the church in East Anglia and the Roman reconciliation with the more austerely monastic 'Celtic' culture at the Synod of Whitby in 664. Between the south and north divide lay the Midlands and the kingdom of Mercia.

Mercia means 'border people', referring to the margins of mountainous Wales to the west, but the eastern side of Mercia was also a border against the waterlands, with a settlement called Medeshamstede, not yet known as Peterborough. Here, among the Middle Angles, lived the North and South Gyrwe.[11] Bede explains that King Anna of East Anglia gave his daughter Æthelthryth in marriage to the leader of the South Gyrwe in 652, a year before Peada, as sub-king of the Middle Angles, brought Northumbrian Christian missionaries to the area. A foundation date of 653 for Medeshamstede sits well in the context of Peada's royal favour.

> In his time they came together, [Peada] and Oswy, brother of King Oswald and declared that they wished to establish a minster in praise of Christ and in honor of St Peter. And they did so, and gave it the name Medeshamstede, because there is a spring there called Medeswael. And then they began the

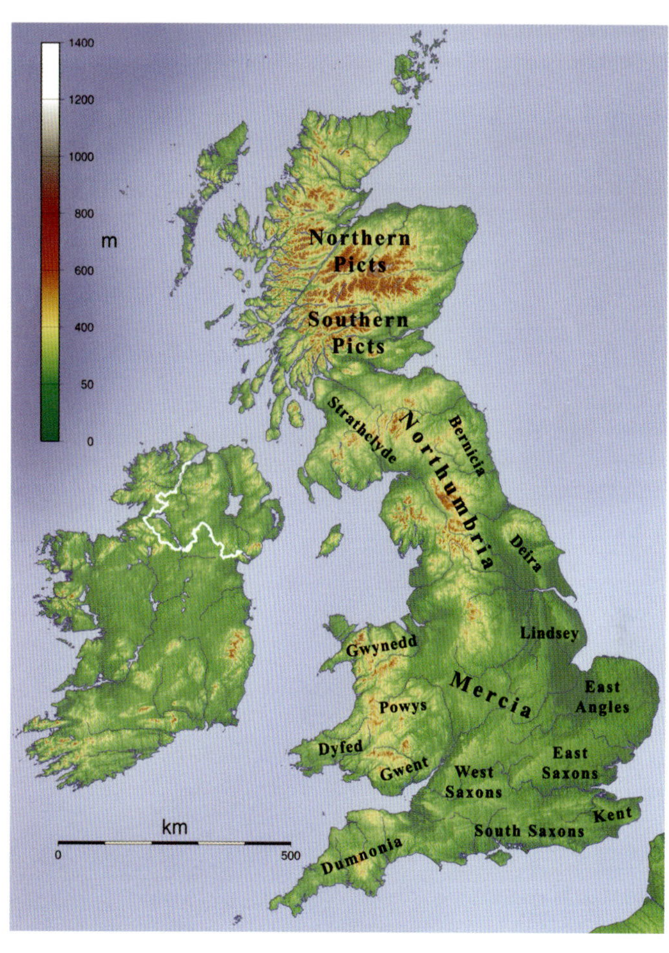

Above **The political regions of seventh-century England.**

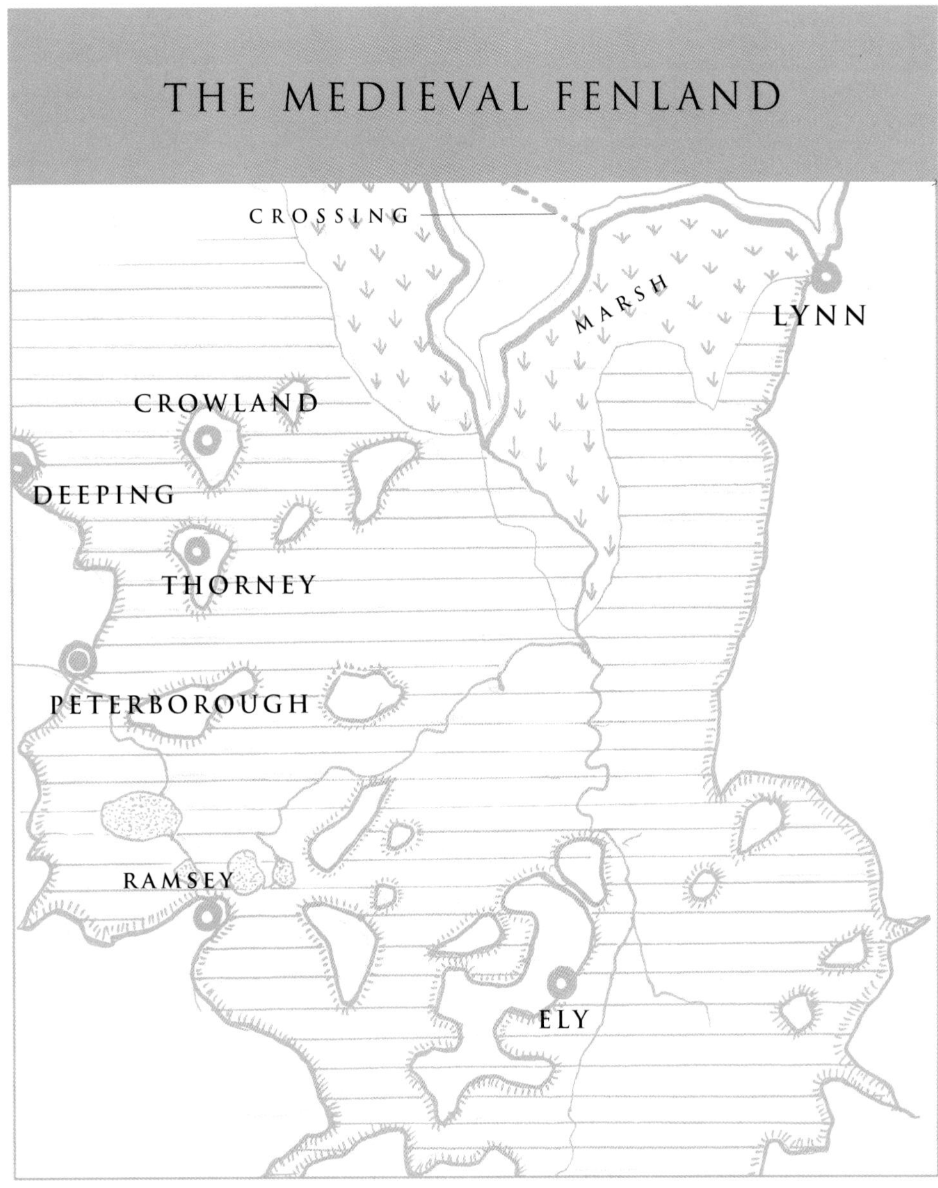

Left The River Nene runs south of Peterborough and once flowed almost immediately into the waters of the Fens, before these were drained in the seventeenth century. The remoteness of the Fenland islands suited monastic cells like Crowland and Thorney, dependents of Peterborough.

Opposite top and bottom Early Anglo-Saxon helmet cheek-piece and bracelet, just two of a collection of over 4,000 gold fragments found near Lichfield in 2009 and known as the Staffordshire Hoard. Dated to around 650 and likely of royal provenance, the metalcraft is of the highest quality, an indicator of the power and prestige of the Mercian kings under whose rule the abbey at Medeshamstede was founded.

foundations and built upon them, and then entrusted it to a monk who was called Seaxwulf. He was a great friend of God, and all people loved him, and he was very nobly born in the world and powerful. He is now much more powerful with Christ. [12]

From such humble origins, the hermits' cells at Ely, Thorney, Ramsey and Crowland developed into substantial monasteries. But Medeshamstede Abbey was very likely the first great church to have been established in the Midlands.

Medeshamstede Abbey was not intended to serve as a cathedral, the seat of a bishop. Repton (Derbyshire) was the first cathedral of Mercia, removed to Lichfield (Staffordshire) in 669. Having served as the inaugural abbot of Medeshamstede, Seaxwulf was elevated as bishop of Lichfield in around 676.[13] He presided during some fearful years. Following an eclipse of the sun on 1 May 664, a bubonic plague descended which stayed long enough to claim Abbess Æthelthryth of Ely in 680.[14] Despite this, after two decades Seaxwulf's first church was presumably complete and furnished with imagery.

There are no accounts of the building of the first Medeshamstede Abbey, nor evidence for what it looked like, and it is unclear whether any Roman structures remained standing. Saxons generally built with timber and thatch away from urban centres and although this site offered salvageable masonry, its use required mortar.[15]

The choice of dedication was not, in itself, remarkable since St Peter and St Mary were common dedicatees at this date, often represented by separate aligned churches; Lichfield's St Mary was joined by a church of St Peter. St Peter's priority at Medeshamstede, however, was fundamental to the later history of both abbey and city.

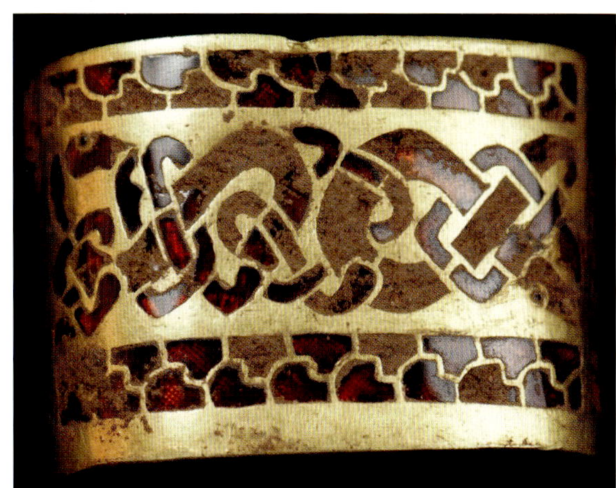

THE LATER ANGLO-SAXON ERA

The year 866 was an *annus horribilis* for Medeshamstede Abbey. The Norsemen had raided the coast for the last seven decades but late in 865 the Viking 'great heathen army' (so described in the *Anglo-Saxon Chronicle*), led by Ivar the Boneless, landed in East Anglia and wintered at Thetford just 50 miles to the east. Their conquering ambition proved alarmingly successful. Within 12 years King Burgred of Mercia had been exiled and the Danelaw had been carved out of the eastern counties, a territory that included the abbey in its southern margins. Monasteries were principal targets for the looting heathens, attracted by portable riches, and the *Anglo-Saxon Chronicle* explains that they:

> Destroyed all the monasteries they came to. In this they came
> to Medeshamstede and burnt and destroyed all they found
> there, and brought it to pass that it became nought that had
> been very mighty.

The church they plundered held an important sculpted stone shrine called the Hedda Stone, which has survived and can be found in the apse today. It shows 12 saints, signified by haloes, one of which has a cross within to identify Christ. These figures are set beneath a continuous arcade, with six arches on each side, which means the stone was freestanding. Eleven figures plus Christ leaves one of the 12 apostles unaccounted for, and this may be Peter, if the stone supplemented an altar already dedicated to him in his titular church. It is punctured by numerous holes, which Dr Janina Ramirez suggests were for embedding relics.[16]

How much else was overturned or destroyed we cannot know, for history falls silent until hearsay much later relates that, by the middle of the tenth century, there was 'nothing but old walls and wild woods'.[17] This is probably romantic overstatement but it is certain that the eyes that witnessed Peterborough's dilapidations were those of the reforming St Æthelwold, who set about rebuilding the Benedictine monastic churches as bishop of Winchester after 963. Æthelwold's was the principal voice in this cause, together with Archbishop Dunstan of Canterbury and Bishop Oswald of Worcester. Winchester was then the capital of England and the bishop was persuasive with King Edgar (959–75) and Queen Ælfthryth. By force of written argument and royal favour, the pendulum swung away from secular clergy toward the restitution of neglected Benedictine houses and their communities.

Peterborough Abbey was probably refounded in 971, receiving special favour as a second Rome and granted estates within the soke 'so freely that neither king

nor bishop nor earl nor shirereeve have any command there, nor
any one save the abbot only and him whom he shall appoint
thereunto'.[18] These were the golden years.[19] Under Abbot
Ealdwulf, the community was renewed. Ely and Thorney
were also refounded, benefiting from the stone now being
quarried on the abbey's estates near Stamford, which arose
as a burgh, a fortified town, in 919.

Wulfstan the Cantor, a monk of Winchester writing in the
tenth century, explains that Æthelwold himself gathered monks.[20]
This evidence suggests that either the existing community was
inadequate or had entirely to be restored, while consecration implies
at least some rebuilding a century after disastrous Viking raids. Wulfstan
also records that this place which 'once bore the name "Medeshamstede"
[…] is now usually called "Burh"' because it was walled around, gaining the
name of 'Burgh' as a defended settlement, like Stamford. Subsequently, Burgh
was known as 'Gildenburgh', the golden borough, after its immense riches.
Doors were opened to reveal splendid gifts of furnishing and often symbolically
charged ornamentation, trappings intended to win hearts to the Benedictine cause.
Remarkably, they are recorded; Richard Gem's research on the later Anglo-Saxon
abbey presents a fascinating list of its contents.[21]

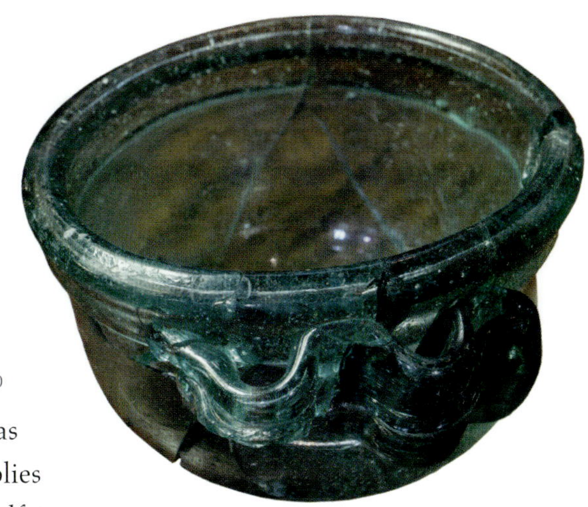

Above Saxon glass bowl found
in the cathedral precincts.

Below The so-called 'Hedda
Stone', from the eighth century
and so pre-dating the advent of
the Vikings. Such complex knot
patterns on its gabled 'roof'
were sometimes employed
to baffle evil.

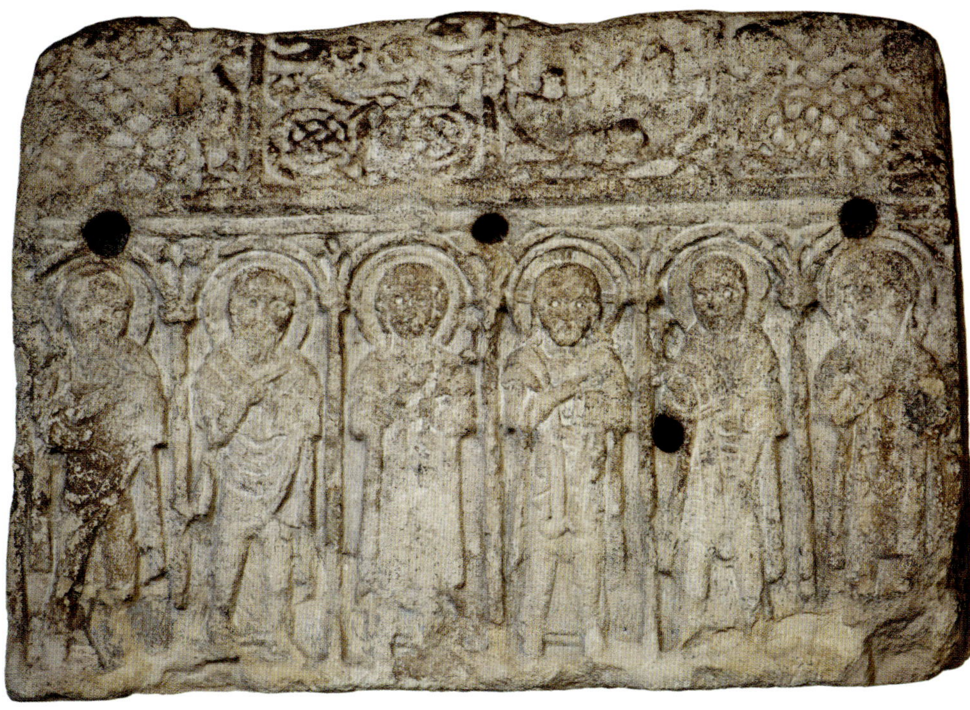

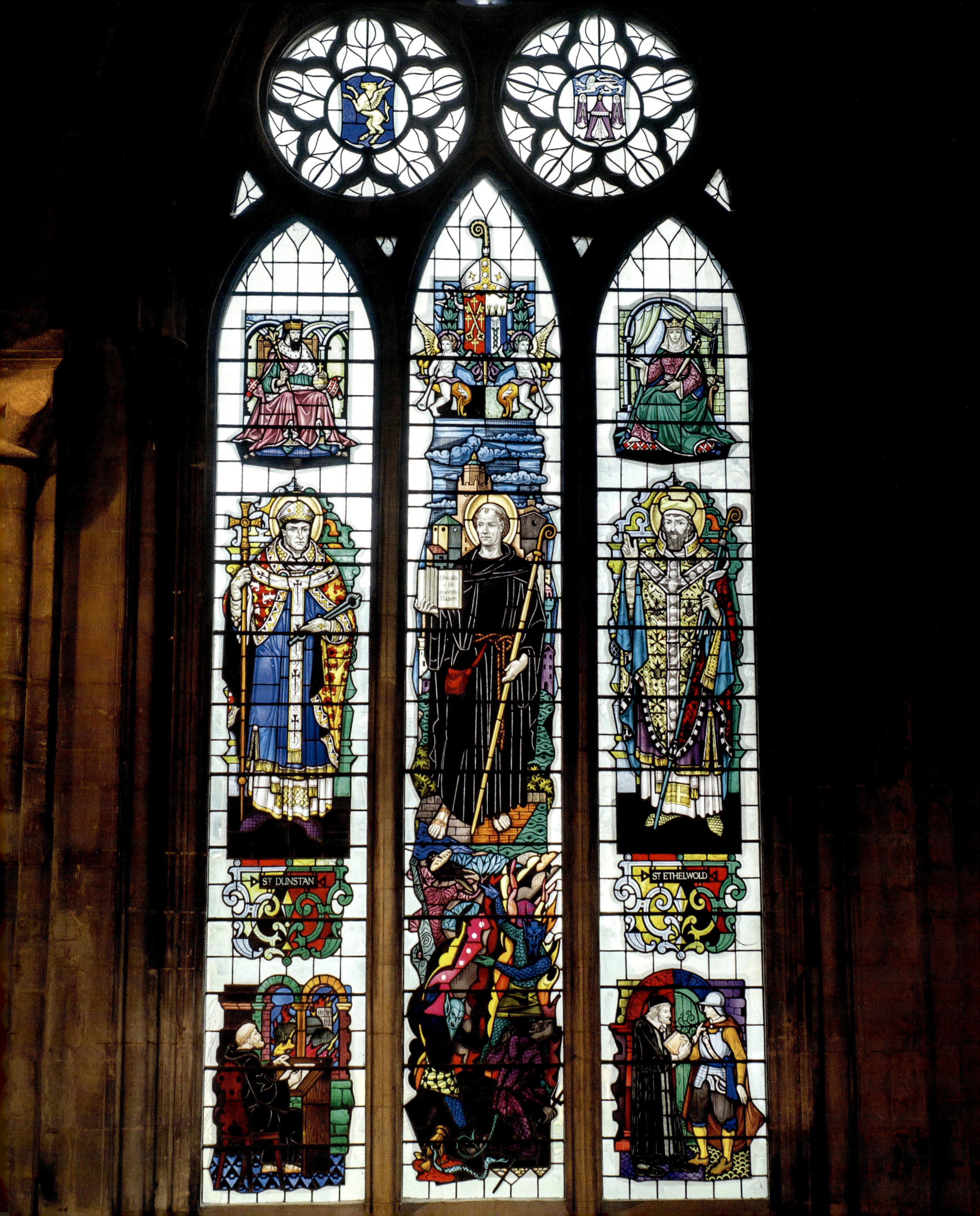
ST DUNSTAN
ST ETHELWOLD

The luxurious appointment of the abbey to which this list testifies led to a deeper culture of monastic crafts. By the 1020s, the age of Lady Godiva (born 980) and King Cnut (born *c.*995), we encounter a monk called Earnwig, who was 'expert in scribal work and whatsoever image work in colours', and produced a sacramentary and psalter, 'the principal letters of which he had embellished with gold'. Most remarkably, the books were made as a gift to be given by King Cnut and Queen Emma. Peterborough's reputation clearly attracted royal commissions and, since the recipient was in Cologne, the work of its scribes entered continental circles. Abbot Ælfsige (*c.*1006–41) seems to have been the conduit. He was abroad for the four years spanning 1013–16, when he bought a silver reliquary containing the arm of St Florentinus from Bonneval, near Chartres, its community being in disarray from famine. Having spent 500 pounds in silver, he also obtained the local relics of Kyneburga and Kyneswitha from Castor. With an existing relic of St Botolph, and Tibba (patron saint of falconers) from Ryhall, the abbey built an impressive array of holy shrines.

What form did the church take in these years? Remains of the fully-developed building can be seen beneath the south transept, its evolution the subject of much speculation since its rediscovery in 1884; see p.14.

The Anglo-Saxon church appears to be of two essential phases: an early (possibly seventh-century) nave, the eastern end of which was replaced in the late tenth century by a transept with a plaster floor, though the eastern termination of this is truncated because of the destruction required in laying the footings of the twelfth-century south transept. The transepts, only half the width of the present church, are almost certainly those built by Æthelwold. Transepts not only provided east-facing chapels but often also braced a central crossing, yet this small cruciform arrangement could hardly have supported a crossing tower. Æthelwold's gift of 10 hanging bells recorded among his treasures surely required that the church had a more substantial belfry; we might imagine this as a western tower in the German manner of *westwerk*, with an elevated throne chamber. If so, it could have influenced the unusual form of the twelfth-century front of Ely Cathedral.

Its most prized possession was reputedly stolen property. The arms of St Oswald were mounted in silver at Bamburgh in Northumberland, relics of his mutilation in battle at Heavenfield, by Penda of Mercia in the summer of 642. Oswald was brother of the abbey's founder, the Mercian Oswiu, and his incorrupted right arm, as blessed by St Aidan, was somehow taken and removed here to Burgh. It remained Peterborough's principal relic for five centuries.

The abbey's prestige grew upon the elevation of one of its monks, Æthelric, as bishop of Durham in 1041, further still by the presence of Abbot Leofric (1057–66),

THE TREASURES OF GILDENBURGH

'These are the treasures which Bishop Æthelwold gave to the monastery which is called Medeshamstede to the praise of God and St Peter, for the redemption of his soul, that is:

- 1 Gospel book adorned with silver
- 3 crosses (*rode*) likewise adorned with silver
- 2 silver candlesticks (*candelsticcan*)
- 2 [candlesticks] gilded over
- 1 silver censer (*storcille*)
- 1 [censer] made of bronze
- 1 silver water vessel (*waterfet*)
- 2 silver bells (*bellen*)
- 4 silver chalices (*calices*)
- 4 patens (*patenan*)
- 1 silver pipe (*pipe*) [eucharistic straw]
- 6 mass vestments (*masse hacelan*) [chasubles]
- 4 copes (*cæppan*)
- 1 over garment (*roc*)

- 8 stoles (*stolan*)
- 8 maniples (*handlina*)
- 11 *subumbrale* [amices?]
- 2 epistle vestments (*pistoclathas*) [tunicles]
- 3 corporals (*corporale*)
- 3 offertory cloths (*offrinc sceatas*)
- 19 albs (*albæn*)
- 4 palls (*pælles*)
- 2 linen tapestries for albs (*linen web to albæn*) [apparels]
- 2 black *regle cęesternisce* [?]
- 6 wall curtains (*uuahryst*)
- 9 seat covers (*setreil*)
- 10 hanging bells (*hangiende bellan*)
- 7 hand bells (*handbellan*)
- 4 bed covers (*bed reaf*)
- 6 horns (*hornas*), 4 of them decorated
- 8 silver cups (*cuppan*)
- 2 gilded altar cloths (*gegylde weofod sceatas*)

nephew of Earl Leofric of Mercia, who with his wife Godgifu (Lady Godiva) extended patronage to churches across the Midlands. At this time, Peterborough was chosen as a place of burial by two archbishops of York. Ælfric Puttoc (d.1051) was the first primate of York to travel to Rome to receive his pallium in 1026 and left Peterborough:

- an alb of *purpura* [shot silk taffeta] adorned with the best gold orphreys
- 2 best copes and stoles
- a white dalmatic
- a [portable] altar with relics adorned with the best gold
- 2 palls
- 2 large candelabra of silver
- his [episcopal] staff.[22]

As archbishop of a cathedral church of St Peter, did he recognise a particular piety in this rich monastery which made heaven's gate more tangible? The second York primate was Cynesige (d.1060), reputedly a former monk of Peterborough, who also gave handsomely to the abbey. But Cynesige's gifts did not stay here. They were taken by Queen Edith (*c*.1025–75), contributing to her status as England's fourth richest individual. This proved to be the start of a long dispute with royal power.

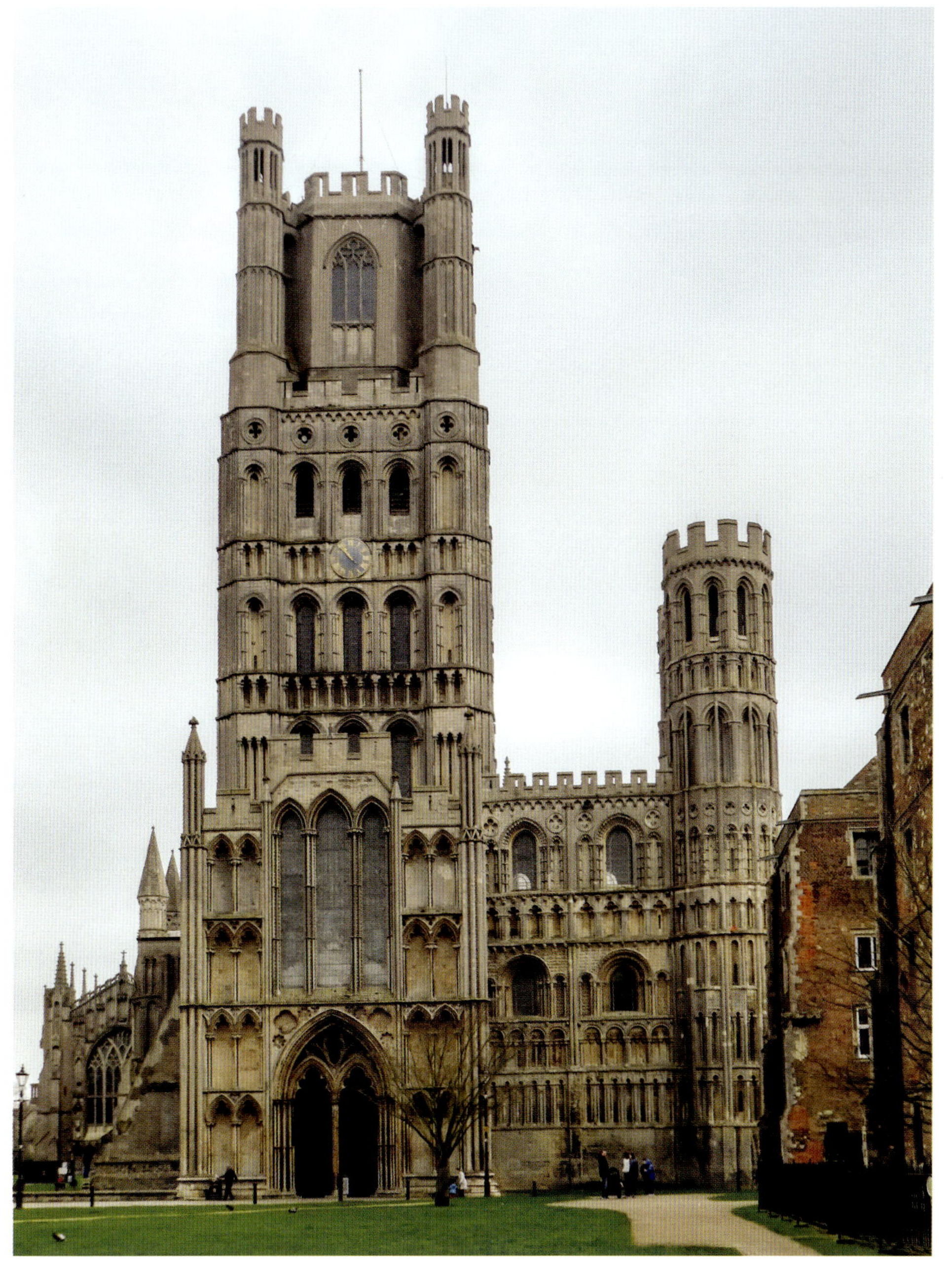

Left Ely Cathedral's exceptional twelfth-century west front probably emulated Peterborough's Anglo-Saxon western tower. The Galilee porch was added in the later twelfth century, the central tower was heightened in the early fourteenth century, and the symmetrical northern section collapsed.

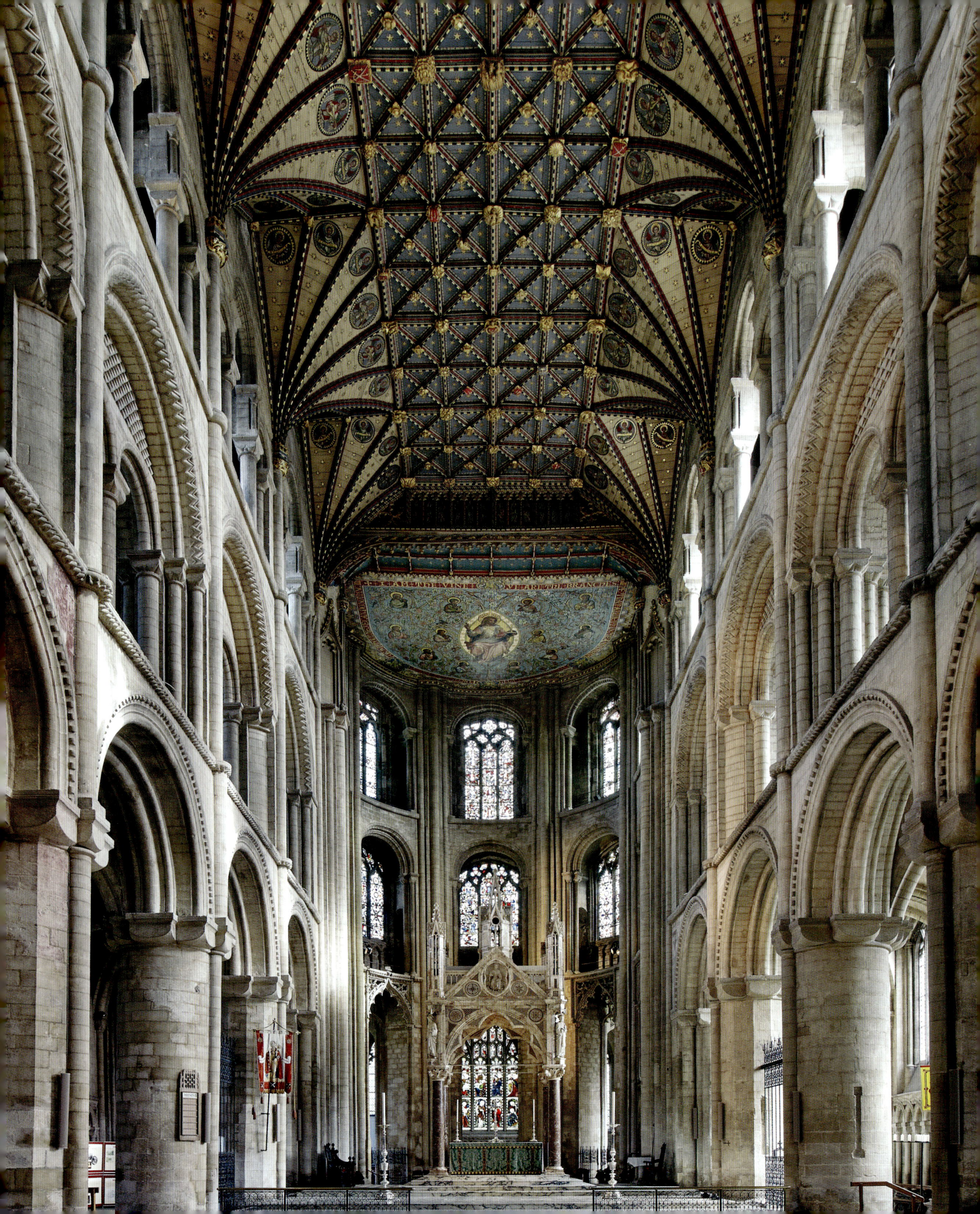

2

DESTRUCTION AND REBUILDING

*Abbot John himself began a new church
and laid the foundations on the eighth
day of March in the 1118th year after
Our Lord was made Flesh*

As the leaves yellowed and fenland birds fled the cooling air of autumn 1066, Peterborough found itself between the battlefields of the Norman Conquest. On 25 September, at Stamford Bridge near York, King Harold II famously routed the forces of his own brother Tostig Godwinson, who had allied with the Norse Harald Hardrada. Then the king turned toward Battle in Sussex, scene on 14 October of his fatal encounter with Duke William of Normandy's invading troops. Harold's archers marched along the Great North Road close to Peterborough; anxious on the way up, exhausted coming down. Though this ancient eastern highway was a little too distant for Peterborough's monks to have witnessed the passing of the last Saxon monarch and his soldiers, its penultimate Anglo-Saxon abbot Leofric joined the troops at Battle and returned to die on 1 November. The effects of those crucial weeks were long-lasting. They fostered the abbey's own anxieties and exhaustions for the next two centuries.

THE NORMAN CONQUEST was almost certainly recorded in Peterborough's compilation of the *Anglo-Saxon Chronicle*, but the volume that included these years was lost in a major fire precisely 50 years later. This was not the abbey's first post-conquest blaze – that broke out in 1070, in reaction to the new Norman regime, in a turbulent region whose access to remote fens and sea beyond bred piracy.

William I sought papal permission for his conquest, sealing a political ambition to conflate the powers of church and state, so that the heavens would seem to favour his authority. This vision was manifested through an architecture that reinterpreted ancient Roman imperialism. One by one, the Saxon great churches were pulled down, to be replaced by monumental structures, framing much larger volumes with great arcades like ancient aqueducts.

The last abbot drawn from the Anglo-Saxon community, Brand (1066–69) was soon replaced. The appointment of Norman bishops and abbots was integral to the Conqueror's political process, but some English traditions remained, or were even bolstered. Cathedral monasteries were an Anglo-Saxon tradition; the cathedrals of Canterbury, Sherborne, Winchester and Worcester had monasteries by 1066. Following this model Rochester, Durham, Norwich, and Ely were also given

Previous page Peterborough Abbey was begun at the apse, which survives to a remarkable degree. It was originally vaulted in stone, but but the architect J.L. Pearson (see p.117) removed the remains of the vault ribs in the early 1890s.

monasteries, while the existing monasteries of Chester, Bath and Carlisle became cathedrals, their bishops serving as abbots. Abbeys, then, were in no way inferior to cathedrals. Yet despite its glittering reputation, Peterborough Abbey was not rebuilt for half a century. It would be one of the last great Saxon churches to stand.

Peterborough's monks were decidedly conservative. The major obstacle to rebuilding the church, however, was financial corruption, which came with the appointment of Abbot Thorold in 1069. This priest, from Fécamp in Normandy, arrived in an unfamiliar land and met with trouble. The abbey was surrounded by territory owned by the aggrieved Saxon populace, which included Hereward the Wake, a native of Bourne in Lincolnshire, 16 miles to the north, who may have been a nephew of the deposed Abbot Brand. Lincolnshire had been part of the Danelaw and, under the banner of protectionism, Hereward allied himself with King Swein of Denmark.

RANSACKING

Late in the spring of 1070, Hereward's outlaws combined their forces with those of Swein, who had landed at Ely, and together they made their way north across the fens, approaching Peterborough Abbey on 2 June. Abbot Thorold was alerted and left the abbey to gather reinforcement, but before his return with 160 knights, the outlaws had ransacked the church.[23]

The treasure departed south to Ely, along with Prior Æthelwold who, we are told, played along by agreeing to become a Danish bishop. Winning Hereward's confidence and gaining keys to the muniment room where the riches were stashed, Æthelwold then supposedly slipped out of the refectory from among the giddily jubilant hosts and removed the irreplaceable relic of the arm of St Oswald, which he hid under his bed, to be spirited away by assistants the next day for safekeeping at Ramsey Abbey. Much of the remaining precious metal and jewels headed irretrievably for Denmark, Norway and even Ireland, 'scattered hither and thither like sheep without a shepherd'.[24]

Hereward 'swore in after times that he had done this of good intention', with the justification that he was preserving church property from the new French overlords. Hugh Candidus continued that he only 'pretended to do this out of loyalty to the church', since the monks were driven out by the raid – except for Leofwine Lang, who had lain helpless and harmless in the infirmary. Hereward's alliance with those who could have cared little for Peterborough Abbey was

LIFE IN A MEDIEVAL MONASTERY

No remains have yet been identified of Peterborough Abbey's Anglo-Saxon monastery complex. However, enough survives of the later monastic buildings that we can explore where the monks lived, worked and died from the twelfth to sixteenth centuries on the site of the lost Saxon ranges.

Each community respected the rules of their founder, and Peterborough's rule was prescribed by St Benedict. All monasteries were composed of individual buildings, serving specific functions and arranged around at least one cloister. Although this layout could be set either north or south of a great church (more usually to the south), every order had fairly standard arrangements of dormitory, refectory, library and chapter house. The Benedictine order was notable for moderation and reasonableness, but also for a culture inclined to embellishment, through which the arts flourished.

Benedictine monks served a timetable dictated by the available daylight. This might start with their rising from bed at 2.30 am, for Nocturnes at 3.00. Matins came at daybreak, then Prime, with the fourth office, Terce, at about 8.00 am followed by the Morrow Mass, the first of two daily masses. Chapter followed, where the monks met to discuss administrative matters in the chapter house, to the east of the cloister. After allotted work came Sext at noon, followed by Mass and None. Lunch might be at 2.00 pm in the refectory, on the side of the cloister opposite the church, with provision for washing hands. More work followed, concluded by Vespers at 4.15. The collation readings on the virtues of monastic life led to supper and Compline, the last prayers before an early bedtime.

Other services responded to the requirements of the liturgical calendar, with specific rituals for saints' days and Easter, for example. As Peterborough Abbey was rebuilt through the twelfth century, a Mass of the Virgin was being widely adopted, reflecting a greater emphasis on the intercessionary role of the mother of God.

The demands of co-ordinating work and worship were met by an effective management team, with the prior at its head, the precentor to manage the choir and sometimes the library, the sacrist for the care of sacred vessels, and other more workaday functionaries, for all communities required well-stocked kitchens and cellars. These administrators needed accommodation, as did visitors, according to their social status. Provision for life beyond these daily tasks of work and worship extended to sickness, for which infirmaries or hospitals were provided. These were laid out like a church, where the sick lay in the equivalent of the nave, turning their head to watch mass in the smaller chancel-like chapel at the east end.

Opposite. **This drawing of the layout of St Gallen monastery in Switzerland offers a blueprint for a Benedictine house. Traditions differed across Europe, and even specifically according to dedications, but Peterborough's essential layout of nave, transept, apse and southern cloister. with refectory parallel to the church, are directly comparable to St Gallen.**

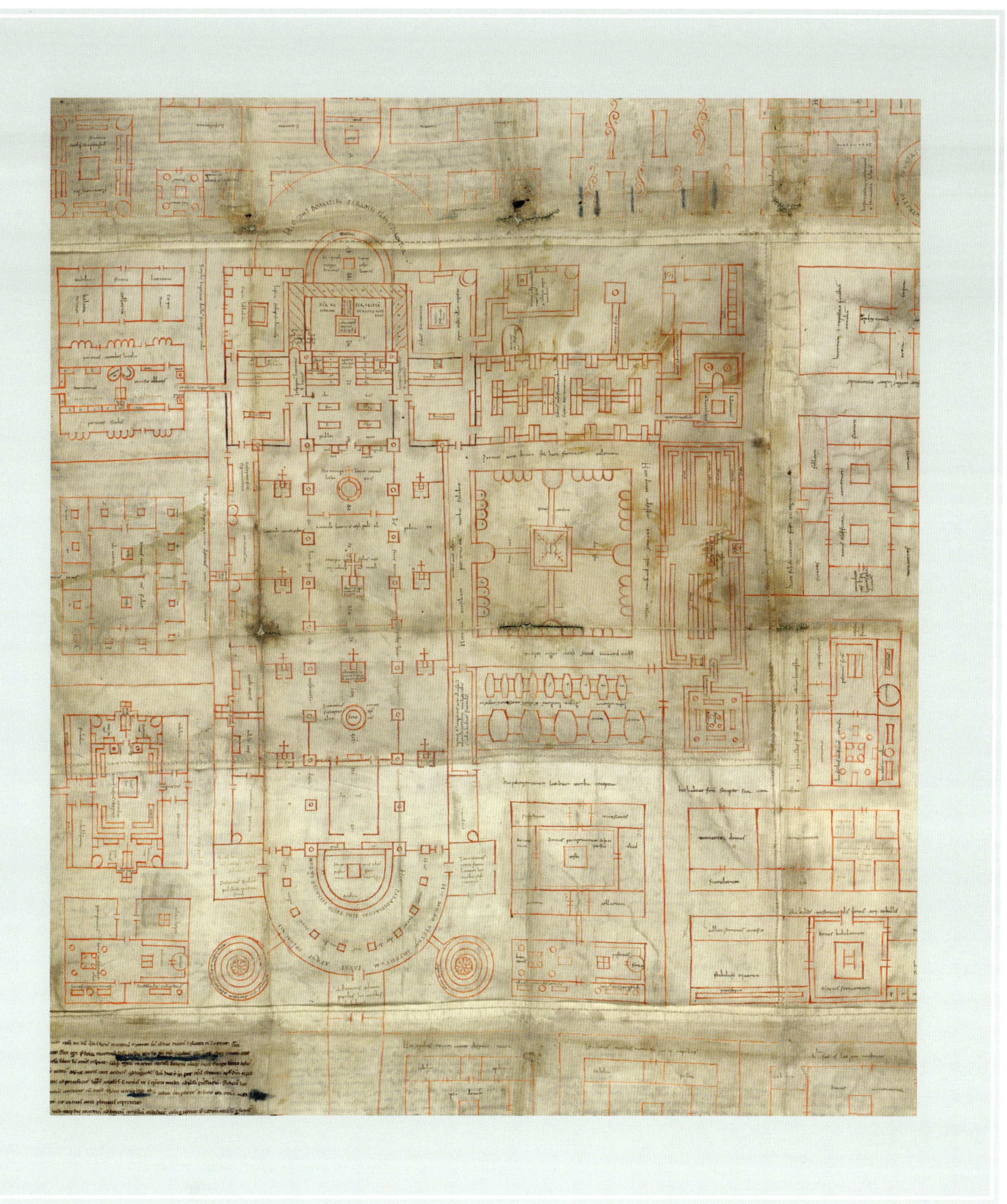

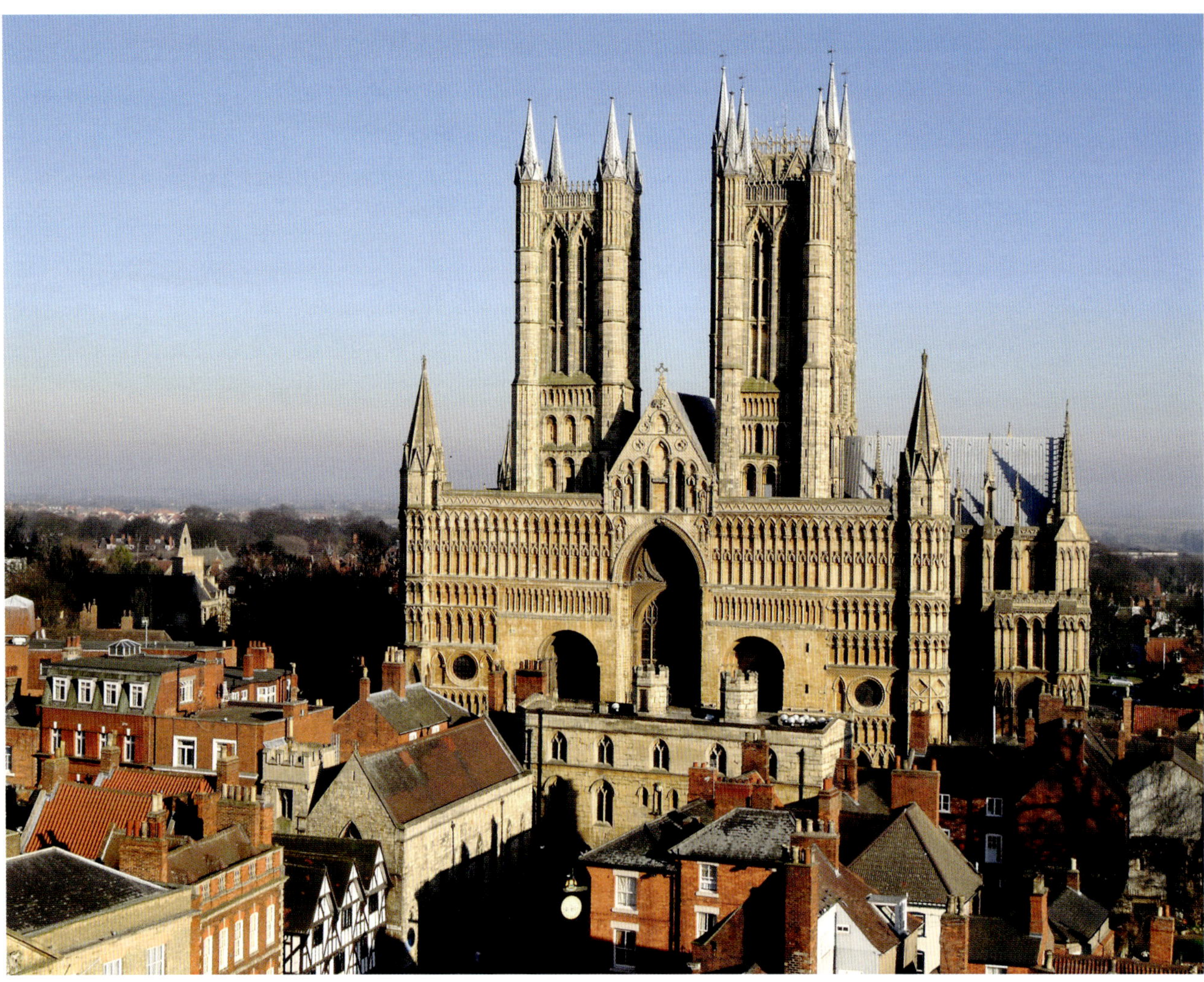

probably intended to protect his personal property, land which might otherwise have been sequestered, and granted by the new abbot to Norman knights in return for loyal service. If so, the opportunistic outlaws had nothing to lose.

Within a year of Thorold's arrival, therefore, the treasures he had inherited had largely disappeared, as Candidus lamented: once '[…] excellent in worth […] none so good remain to this day even in all England.' The monastery was 'utterly burned' except for the church, and 'the Golden Borough became the poorest of cities'. This loss could have been a moment of reform, of grand building in the manner of Bishop Rémi of Lincoln's fortified new cathedral, which arose after 1072, 60 miles north.

Yet far from replenishing the abbey's raided coffers and lost furnishings, let alone rebuilding the church, Peterborough's abbot began his own asset-stripping programme, bolstered by the presence of 60 knights – the greatest number at any English religious house – installed at the behest of King William I. The ongoing presence of this 'motley and singularly unimpressive crew'[25] gave rise to the establishment of new local landholding dynasties. It also lent Peterborough Abbey the air of a royal stronghold, although successive monarchs more often saw a financial advantage than a military responsibility.[26]

Throughout Thorold's tenure, he 'not added naught thereto but rather the lands so well acquired he evilly took away, and gave them to his relations and to the knights who had come with him, so that scarce a third of the abbey remained in demesne', wrote Hugh Candidus. The abbot reduced the income from £1050 to around £500, but maybe did at least avoid sole responsibility for the ongoing ransack. Thorold introduced 'foreign monks' as sacrists responsible for the treasures, whereupon they took the glittering chasuble bequeathed by archbishop Ælfric. 'German' robbers broke through a window and clambered down a ladder to steal the jewelled golden altar cross and candlesticks given by Ælfric. These were recovered, only to be forfeited to the king, cause of further grievance at royal advantage.

As Hereward had feared, the fenland's fertile land was a primary asset for Thorold, who traded territory for loyal support known as 'feoffdom'. Lest any further opposition arise, the abbot built a fortified conical mound on a rise to the north of the abbey, 37m diameter at the base, 10m at the top, and once surrounded by a ditch. The mound still stands in the deanery garden, known to posterity as Mount Thorold or Tout Hill. Somewhat like Durham and Lincoln Cathedrals, Peterborough was half church, half castle.

The death of Thorold in 1098 brought a collective sigh of relief for a denuded and dispirited community. After a couple of false starts under abbots Matthew

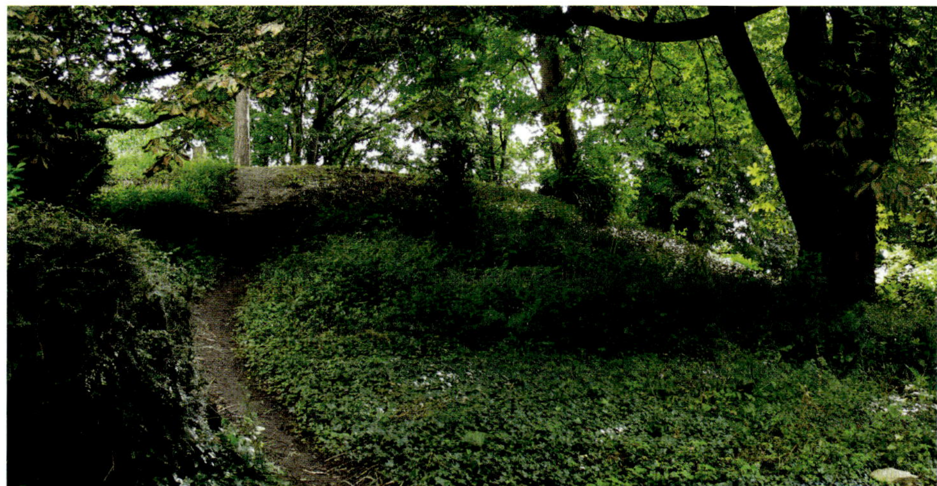

Left Tout Hill, the site of Abbot Thorold's castle to the north-east of his abbey church.

and Godric, the year 1107 heralded a period of intellectual richness under a new reforming head, Ernulf of Canterbury. There was much reforming to do, not only to recover from the catastrophic looting of the monastery's assets, but also because a small Anglo-Saxon church languished here when all around had seen monumental rebuilding. After Canterbury Cathedral arose from 1070, as the first of the Conqueror's great Anglo-Norman churches, those of the East Midlands and East Anglia were also gradually replaced.

Canterbury 1070
Lincoln 1072
Bury 1081
Ely 1083
London 1087
Norwich 1096
Southwell 1108–14?
Crowland 1114?
Peterborough 1118

Abbot Ernulf was a notable teacher (he mentored Hugh Candidus) and it was probably he who reinvigorated Peterborough's compilation of the *Anglo-Saxon Chronicle*. This needs explanation; as a Norman, he would have been championing the renowned Anglo-Saxon conservatism of these monks. Most probably, his support for the tradition of local record-keeping wisely cultivated a loyal community that would support his cause on behalf of Canterbury. To engage the monks, he helped them establish a programme of audacious forgery, planting a story of royal authority for the foundation of Medeshamstede Abbey that was 'grafted onto the framework of the Anglo-Saxon Chronicle' before 1122. This informed the earliest of Peterborough's cartularies, or collection of records, the *Liber Niger* of the 1130s, which persuaded readers of royal privileges supposedly bestowed on Medeshamstede Abbey in the seventh century, when Bede had recorded none.[27]

   If Ernulf intended that this well-embroidered narrative would help Peterborough, he also served his own agenda by bringing with him further documents for the monks' reference that supported the supremacy of the archbishopric of Canterbury over York. Peterborough represented the centre ground between them and had prominently hosted the remains of two archbishops of York. Ernulf's politics seemed to work, as Peterborough's relations turned from York in the eleventh century toward Canterbury in the twelfth.[28]

Beyond his scholarship and political skill, Ernulf was a builder. As prior of Canterbury Cathedral monastery from 1096, he had been responsible for substantial new work, notably the planning and early construction phases of the cathedral's crypt and east end, begun in 1096 and completed in about 1110 (but burned in 1174 and remodelled). This was integrated with the adjacent monastic complex, which set the pattern for his approach to Peterborough. Here his practical priority was to rebuild the monks' accommodation; 'he built a new dormitory and a necessary (latrines) and finished the chapter house which had been begun, and began the refectory and did many other good works'.

Strikingly, these claustral buildings were precisely those set ablaze in Hereward's raid of 1070. They had presumably been patched up by Thorold with flimsy structures that now needed replacement, after almost half a century. We might assume that building accommodation for the resident community took

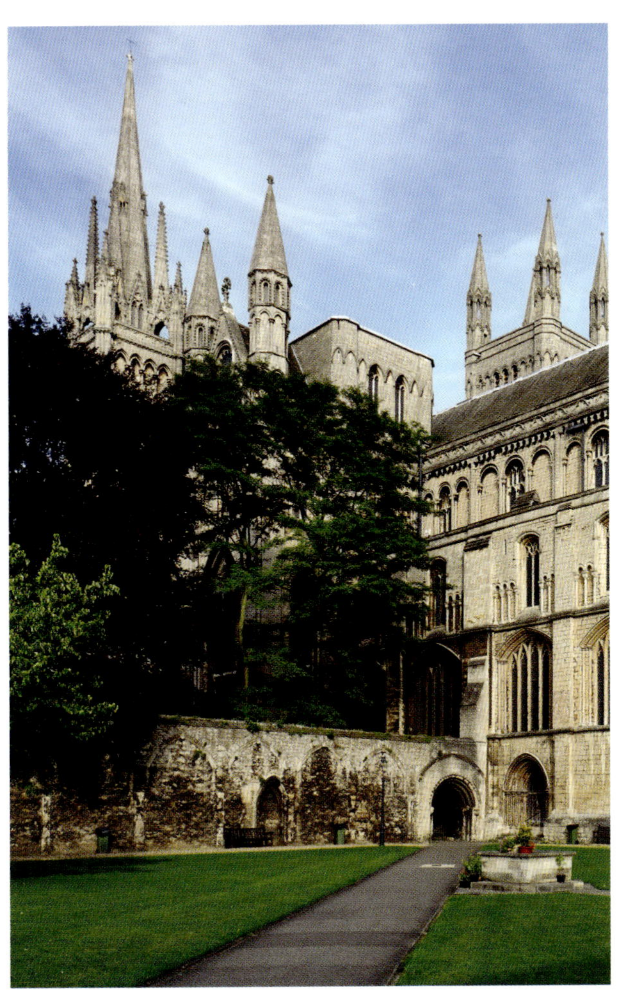

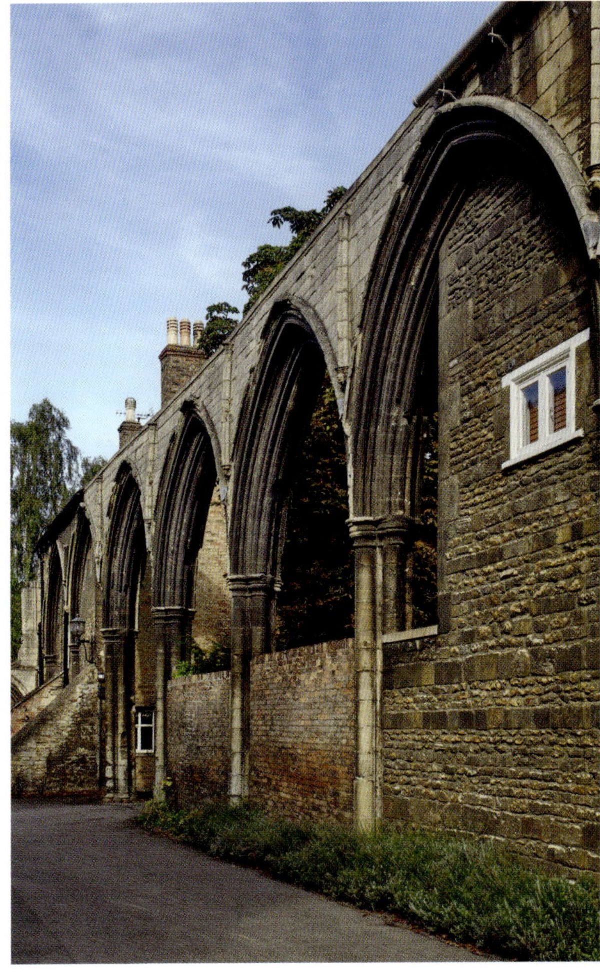

Below The remains of the infirmary hall; this grand early thirteenth-century hospital is probably on the site of its predecessor. Its roof was pulled down during Henry VIII's dissolution of the monastic buildings in 1541 and thereafter its arcades were filled by residences and offices.

Below left The west wall of the cloisters, showing blocked early twelfth-century arches.

primacy.[29] But why didn't Ernulf rebuild the church, as the focus of the monastery? Or did he? Ernulf may have envisaged a new church and even made preparations for its replacement, but the assets so heavily depleted by Thorold probably remained insufficient to fund a grand new project within the seven years of his office.

In 1114 Ernulf packed his belongings and headed south to become bishop of Rochester. He was succeeded by Abbot John de Seez, who 'straightway journeyed to Rome', returning before the feast of St Peter (29 June 1116). It would take a massive investment – or perhaps the impetus of a disaster – for a grand new church. They didn't have to wait long.

REBUILDING

Friday 4 August 1116 was a red-letter day for Peterborough. Hugh Candidus tells us that a conflagration broke out on the eve of St Oswald's feast, when Abbot John de Séez (1114–25), frustrated by the sergeant of the abbey bakehouse, muttered that the 'Devil light the fire' for the oven. Flames erupted so fiercely that they engulfed the town, and 'the whole monastery was burned by accident, save only the chapter house, the dormitory, the necessary and the new refectory...'

Whatever the true cause, the monastic buildings Ernulf had constructed were precisely those that survived the blaze. Much debate has sought to explain the fate of the Saxon abbey church, which in turn determines the credit for the present building. Did Abbot Ernulf demolish the pre-Conquest church as part of his remodelling after 1107, or did it survive, only to be burned in 1116 and wholly replaced in a new programme two years later?

It is possible that Ernulf took down the abbey church, in preparation for its replacement by the footprint of the present cathedral, before he became bishop of Rochester in 1114, and this is supported by the evidence of the fabric of the cloister. Norman monastic buildings such as those Ernulf is known to have built – refectory, chapter house, dormitory and latrines – were always arranged around a communal cloister garth. The present cloister's outer walls may therefore represent Ernulf's plan; there is Norman masonry in the west wall, and no mention during the twelfth century of later builders replacing any of Ernulf's ranges. Moreover, the present cloister is incompatible with the Saxon church.

On the other hand, Hugh Candidus recorded that a church remained two years after Ernulf's departure that was far more substantial than mere foundations. As a monk resident from 1110–70, he wrote as an eye-witness that 'the church was

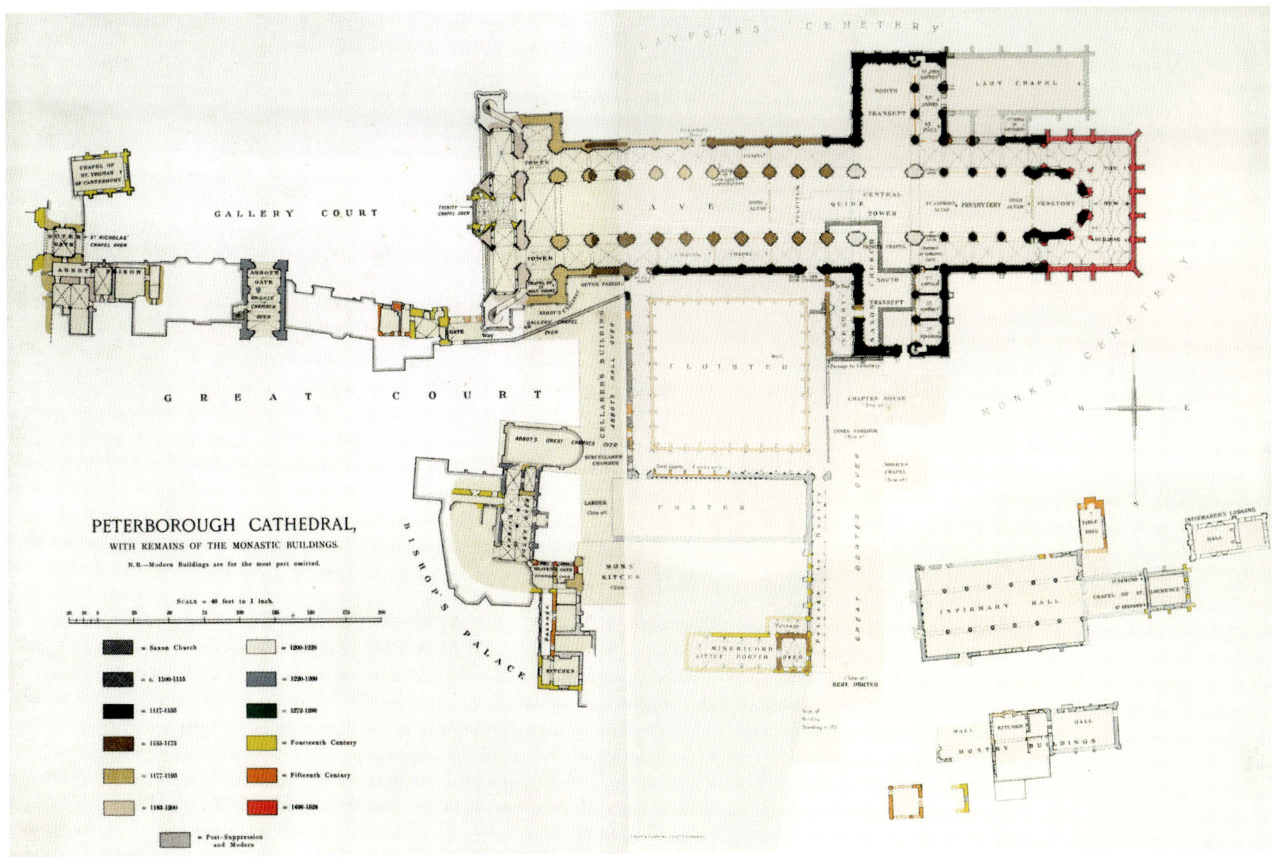

destroyed by fire' in 1116, which he reinforced by adding 'the whole church and vill was burnt' and specifically that 'the fire in the tower endured for nine days'. This is less likely to have been a crossing tower than a tall western block. It is unknown how far the nave extended to this tower, so the present cloister to its south might seem to have been built from *c*.1118 as part of the new church for Abbot John de Seez, but evidence that its layout was Ernulf's is suggested by the eastern cloister walk respecting the western line of the Saxon transepts, though his documented ranges must then have been rebuilt, leaving no trace.

The date the new abbey church was commenced is precisely recorded by Hugh Candidus: 'Abbot John himself began a new church and laid the foundations on the eighth day of March in the 1118th year after Our Lord was made Flesh.' That is, spring 1117, as the frosts subsided and allowed mortar to cure and bind the stones. Great churches were seldom realised within the life-spans of their founders, and Peterborough Abbey was no exception. From east to west, the process took over a century, and could scarcely even then be called complete. Eventually, and gradually, it took its place among the great Anglo-Norman churches of eastern England, Lincoln, Norwich, Bury St Edmunds and Ely, while further afield were the vast cathedrals of St Paul's in London, York and Durham. The builders of each drew from the others' examples, and from the lessons of history as they knew it.

Above Peterborough Abbey's monastery survives extensively, and once extended south to the river. In the late twelfth century, Abbot Benedict installed a piped water supply that ran north–south through the complex.

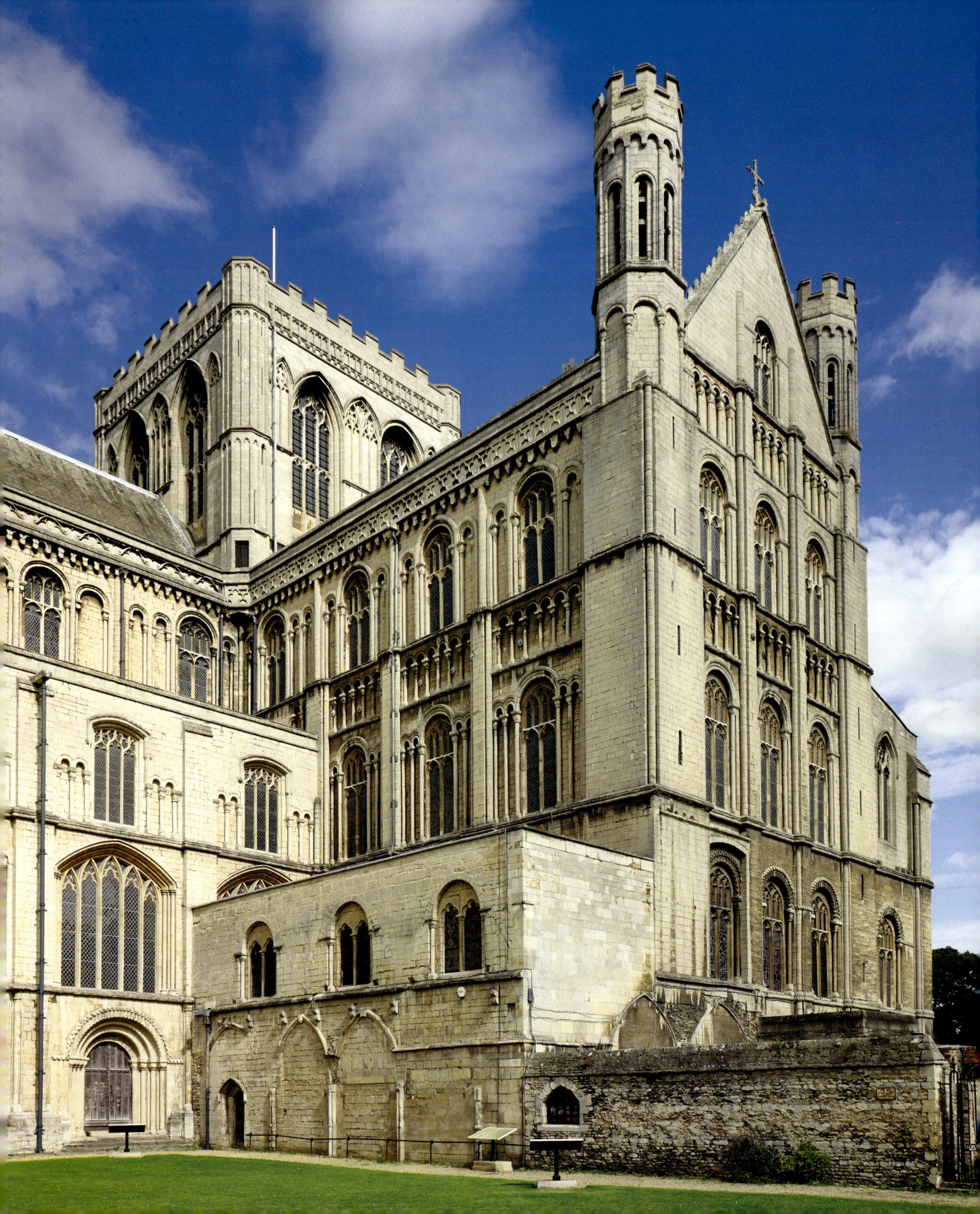

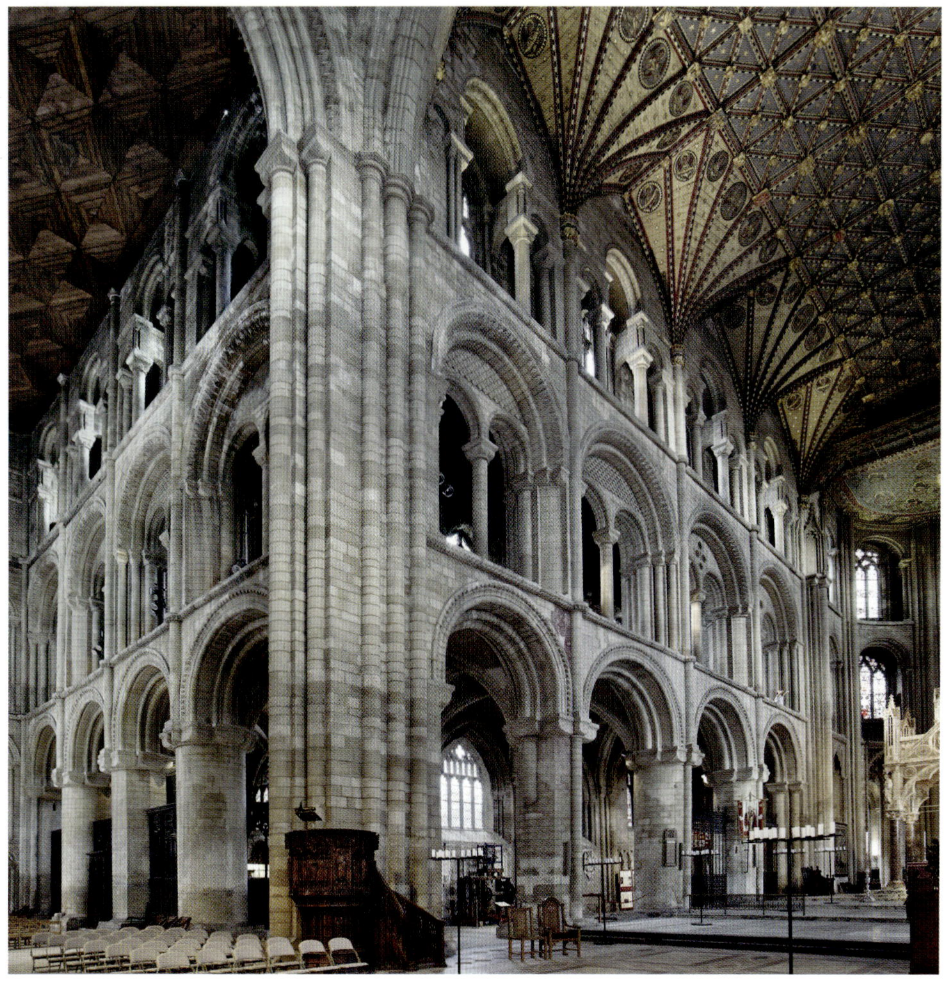

Hugh relates a telling detail about the foundation stones; some were so enormous, *'immanisimi lapides'*, that eight yoke of oxen could scarcely draw one. Their exceptional size and their positioning as buried blocks implies that these were typically massive and locally-salvaged Roman stones.[30]

Newly-quarried stone still came from the Barnack area, but was hauled from open pits rather than from the side of a scarp which provided for the great churches of Ely, Bury St Edmunds, Thorney, Ramsey, Crowland and many more fine buildings. Such a volume could not be provided within Barnack village alone, but extended through the best seams into Southorpe, as David Stocker has shown.

Partly due to the excellent durability of Barnack stone, John de Seez's church is the most complete example of an Anglo-Norman church. Paradoxically, it is also both the most consistent in its basic style and the most varied in the detail of its parts.

The new abbey occupied hallowed old ground, and its planning suggests a strong desire for continuity. The shrine of St Oswald, its watching chamber reached by a stair, was set over the eastern end of the Anglo-Saxon church, likely perpetuating its original position. The 50m-long choir was the earliest part to be built. The central triple-storeyed apse survives to a remarkable degree compared with other English examples, which in successive centuries were usually entirely replaced in favour of rectangular chapels and ambulatories. The internal face of the apse – the curved eastern wall – has vertical shafts between the arches, which rise from floor to clerestory to articulate the component ribs of a stone apse vault. That vault has long since gone, but we can reconstruct its outline.

The internal elevations of the choir are highly inventive. The apse reveals the capitals of buried arches, once set between larger windows. At the chord of the apse was a wall set behind the altar, with two doors to a reserved space typical of a shrine chapel.[31] The arches of the main arcade feature massive round and polygonal piers, two of them set so that the angles face inwards. Sometimes shafts appear halfway up these piers, to carry capitals, while others are applied up the full height. These playful details are set within sober proportions, so that the whole effect seems balanced.

What influenced Peterborough's unnamed designer? The bases of the columns and piers of the four-bay choir are closely related to Anselm's choir at Canterbury, then barely completed, with colourful paint and a glowing reputation. Peterborough's choir undoubtedly had a timber ceiling too, but we are left to guess its effect, the likeliest being some version of the diamond-set boards in all the other high roofs.

Looking to the vaults above the aisles, we see not the plain groin vaults of Canterbury (two intersecting tunnels with a seam at the junction) but the techniques of rib vaulting pioneered at Durham Cathedral after 1093, in which a principal 'X'-plan of arched ribs supports stone webs. Peterborough's designer looked across the fenlands, to the south, and also far northward.

Most interesting is the attempt to puncture the tympana (the semicircular planes of stone filling an arch) in the middle level – the tribune – of the northern

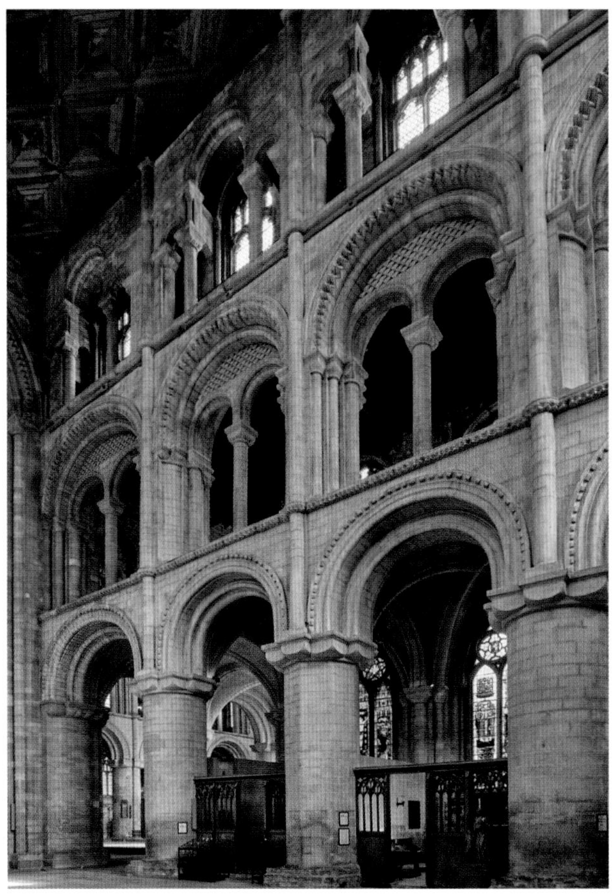

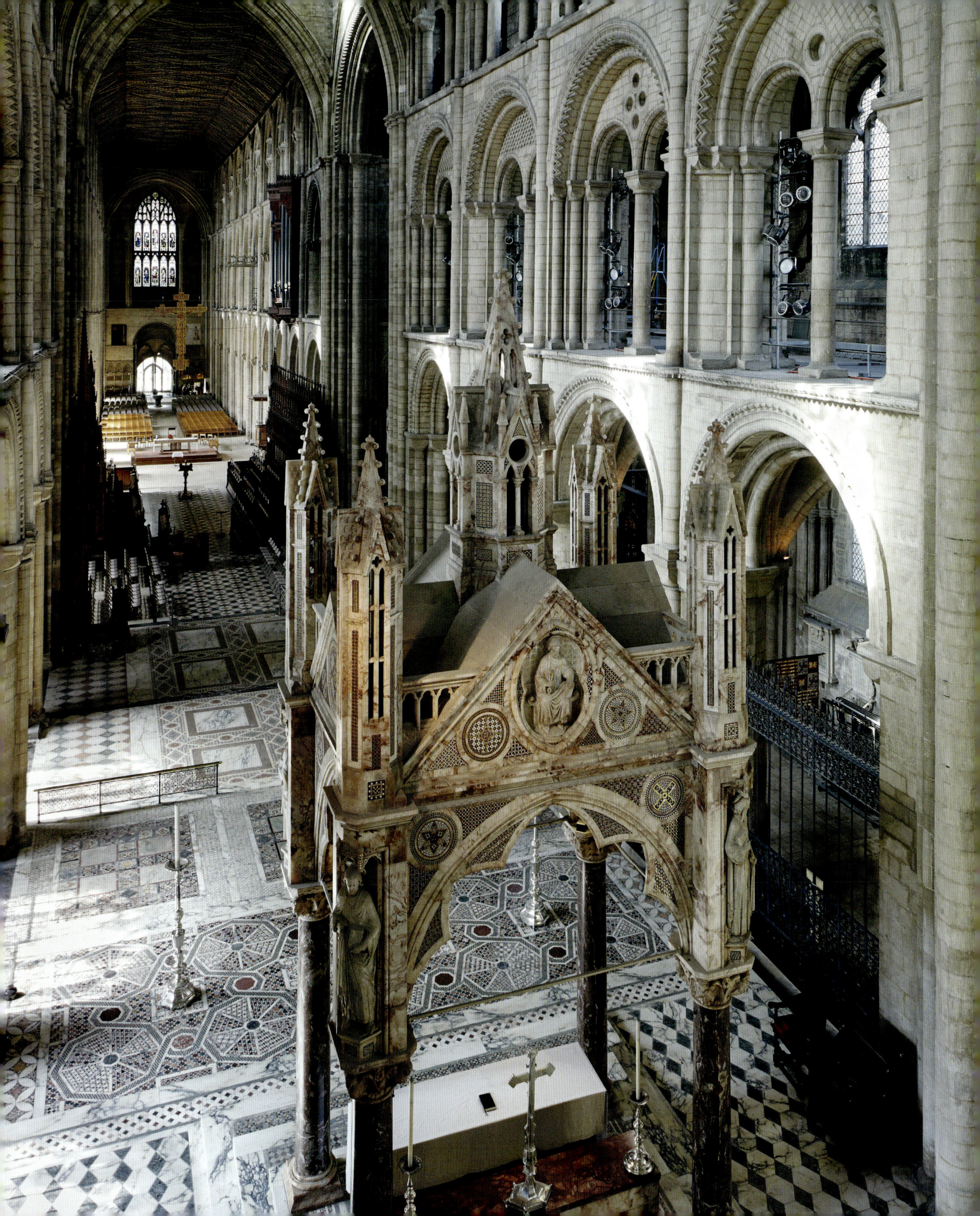

choir elevation with holes that anticipate the early window tracery of the following century. Some of these tympana feature a matrix of triangular blocks, or square ones set on an angle resembling a lattice, a Roman technique called *opus reticulatum,* still visible on the mausoleum of Hadrian near the Vatican.

The transepts were an integral part of this plan, with eastern chapels that were replaced by flat walls in the thirteenth century, and the south transept at least was intended to have a western aisle, to judge from the infilled arches at

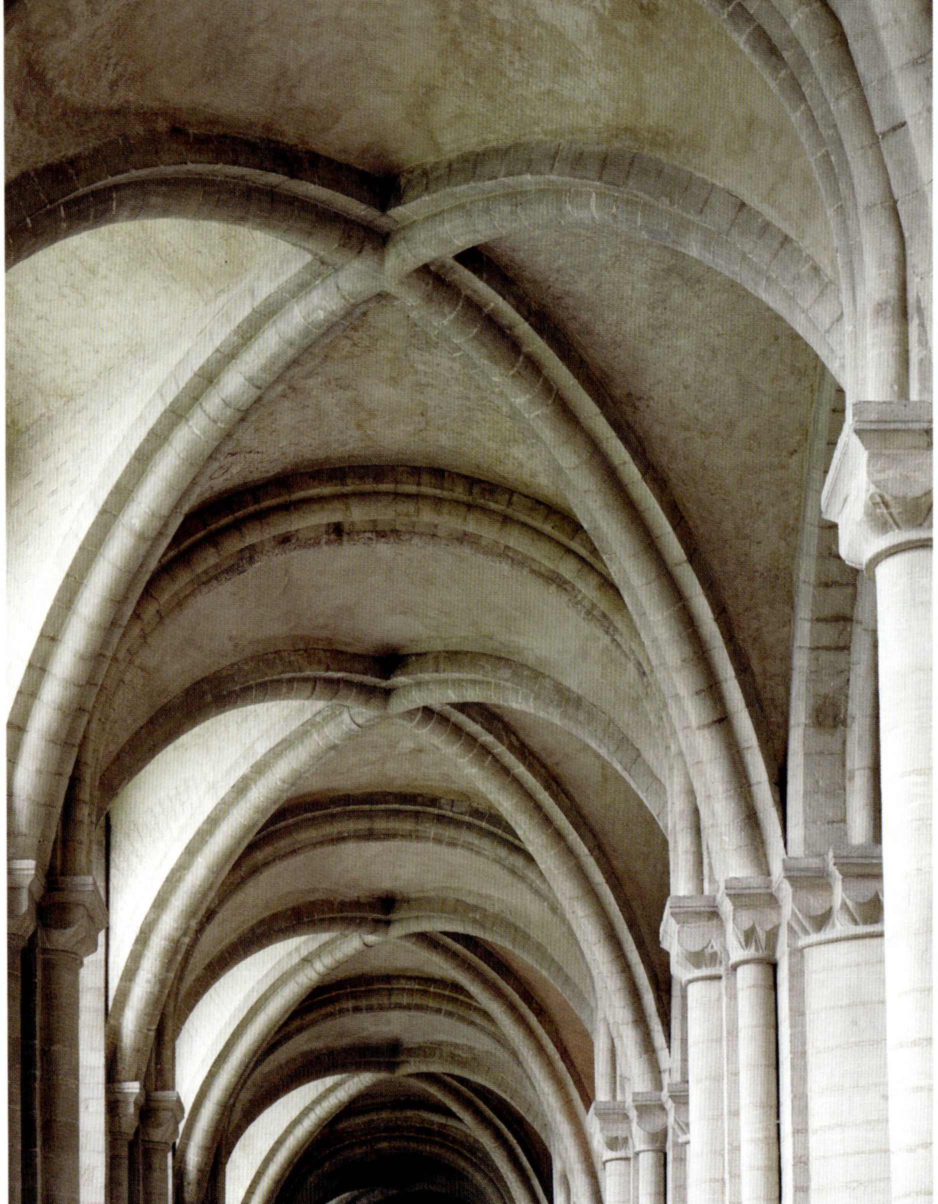

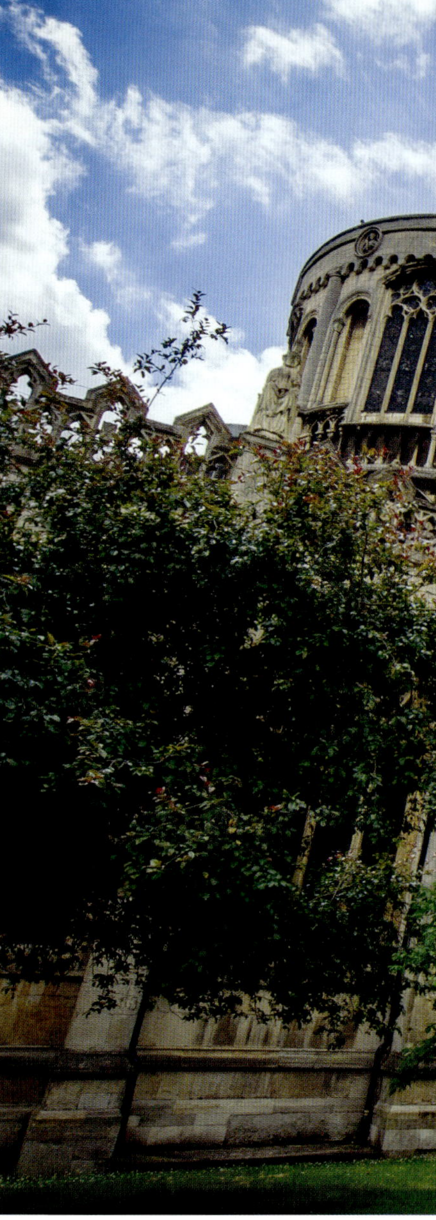

ground level in its western wall. This made way for a sacristy, which now serves as the chapter house.

The exterior design of the upper level, the clerestory, is an arcaded arrangement of a tall central arch with a window (originally round-headed but since replaced), flanked by smaller blind arches. Each bay resembles in miniature the west front of Lincoln Cathedral, or the Roman triumphal arches that Lincoln was itself based on.

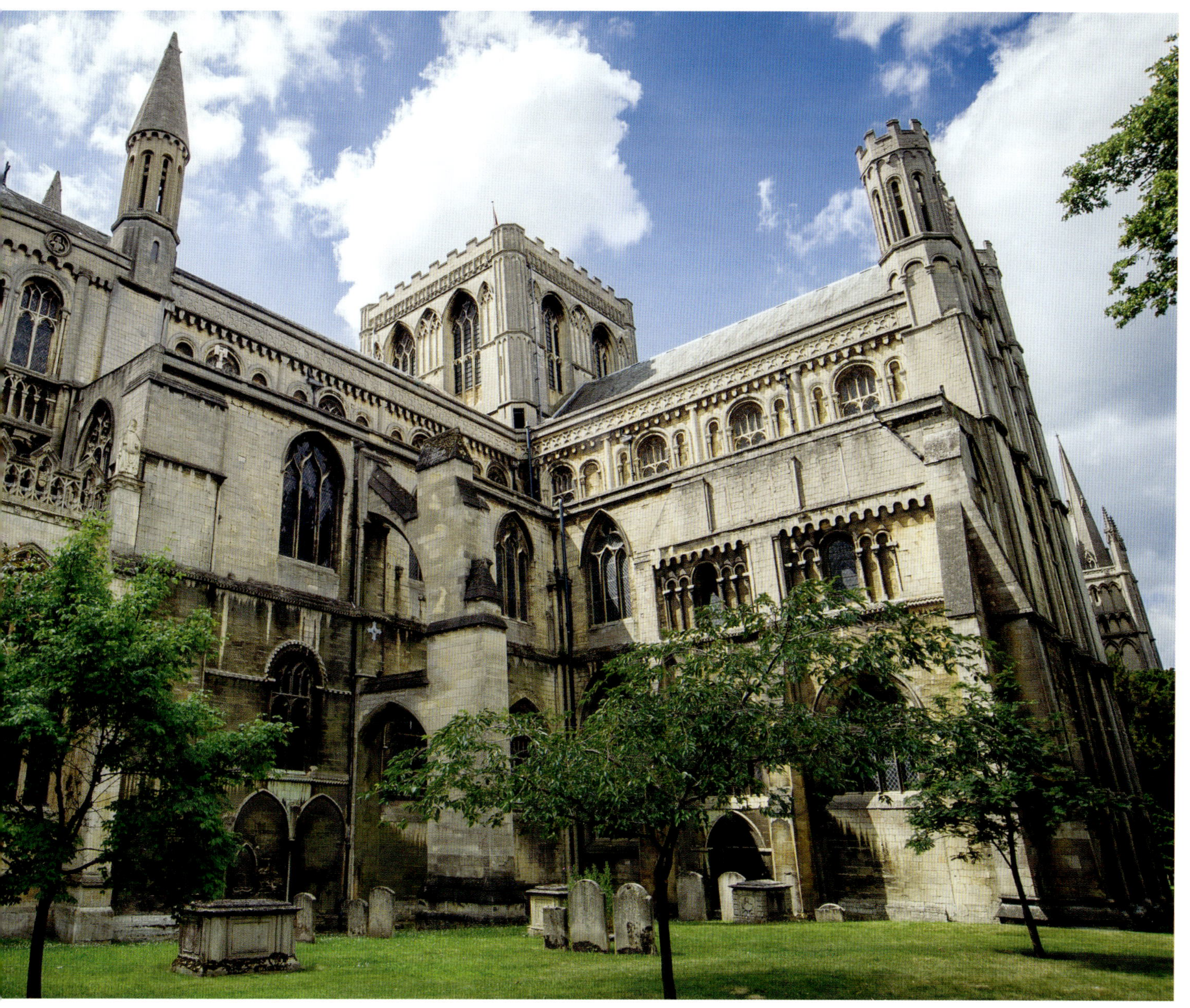

Below The exterior from the north-east, showing how the simple twelfth-century form featured variants of triumphal arches, one large arch flanked by two smaller ones. This transept was built over an infilled ditch set within the Anglo-Saxon Burgh, which may be a Roman feature like the image on p.16.

THE TWELFTH-CENTURY RENAISSANCE

The twelfth century saw a great leap in education and intellectual development in western Europe. Many have noted the classical flavour of manuscripts and sculpture, as well as a renewed scholarly interest in ancient texts. While the classical world never stopped informing philosophy and visual culture, this 'Renaissance' culture provides an essential context for many latent ideas in the maturing Peterborough Abbey.

As the early European universities took form, led by Bologna (founded 1088), classical learning moved away from the established monastic schools, dedicated to biblical disputation, writing and oration. The new curriculum revived the ancient liberal arts, divided into the *trivium* (grammar, logic and rhetoric) and the *quadrivium* (arithmetic, geometry, astronomy, music), as laid down by Plato in *The Republic*.

In England the liberal arts gained a new political currency when an influential treatise on ethics, *Policraticus*, was written in the 1150s by John of Salisbury. John was Thomas Becket's secretary at Canterbury, and it was through this connection that he and his text, which was dedicated to Becket, became familiar at Peterborough. The book would have a profound impact on the abbey's identity, informing the design of the nave ceiling. A copy is recorded in Peterborough's library in the fourteenth century.

Paradoxically, the renewed inspiration of the classical world helped the transition from the round arches of Romanesque architecture to the pointed skeletons of the Gothic era. Arabic versions of otherwise lost Latin and Greek texts were retranslated, whereupon recovered ancient scholarship could inform new ideas and designs. For example, Euclid's work refreshed the understanding of geometry, which was fundamental to a church architecture that could now evolve from dependence on the inertia of mass toward creating an equilibrium between forces through ribs and buttresses – what we call Gothic.

This was far from the only classical influence on twelfth- and thirteenth-century building: we can find Corinthian-style capitals in the earliest Gothic buildings in France and England; Roman martyrium church plans, with aisles encircling saintly remains; and ancient philosophers featuring on the portals of the great French cathedrals. Peterborough's insistent columns and round arches may represent a conscious, sober emulation of imperial Roman architecture.

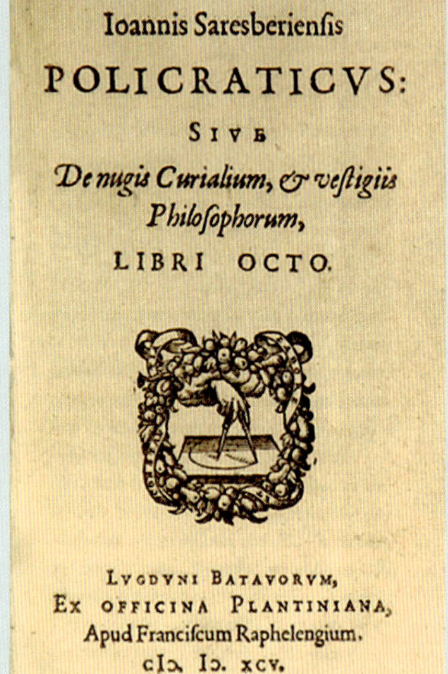

Above John of Salisbury's *Policraticus* provided encyclopedic terms of reference on issues of political ethics, championing wisdom through the Seven Liberal Arts.

Opposite Notre-Dame de Paris, built from the 1160s. We routinely call such architecture 'Gothic' yet its columns are of Roman proportions, and the west front features sculpted details evoking classical cameos.

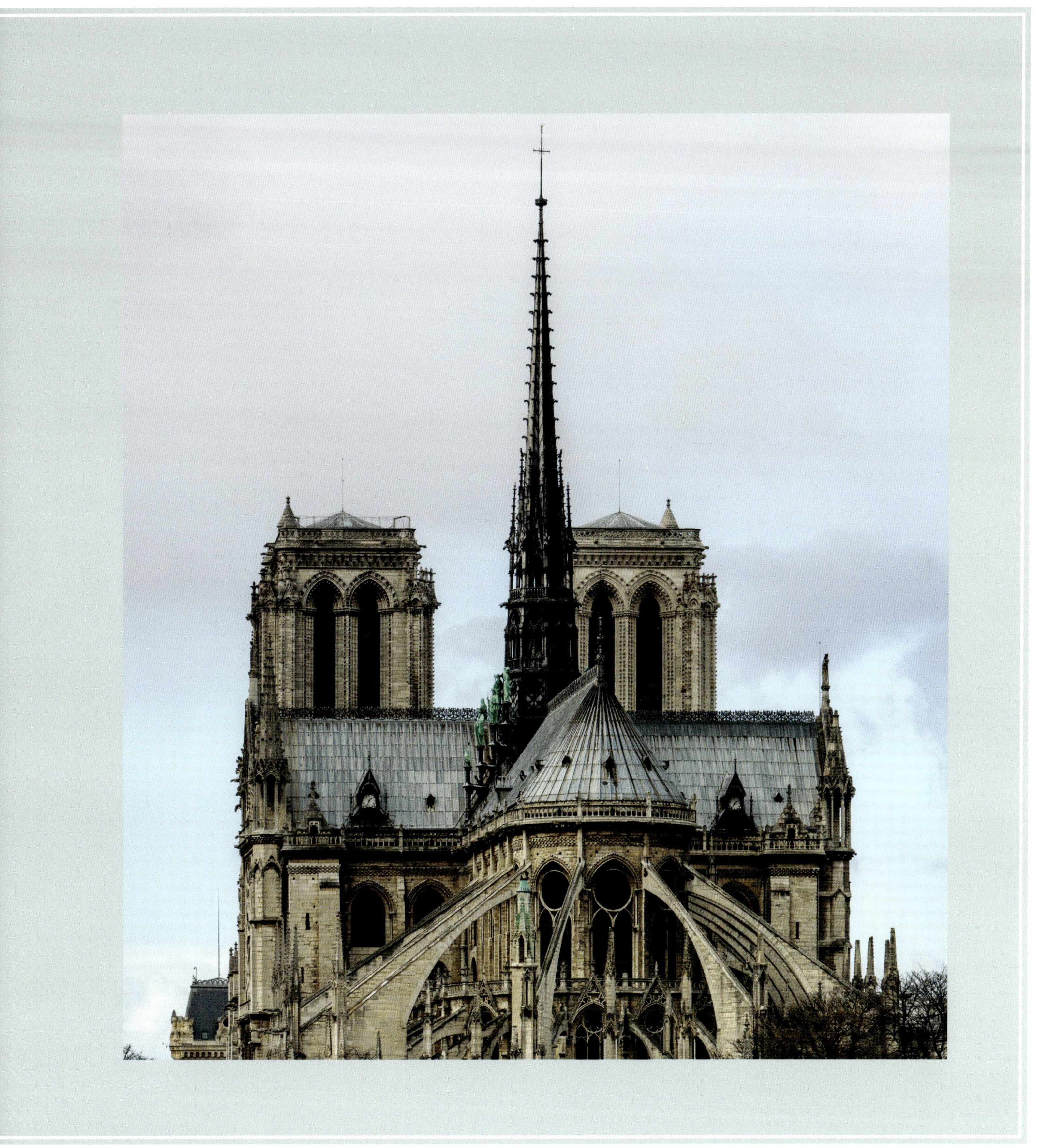

'Abbot John for eleven years ruled the church and the abbacy well, and got them lands.' His plan was for a church with transepts having aisles to east and west, and he 'worked hard at [building the church] but could not finish it'. Finally, in 1125, 'when these years were completed, he was stricken with a disease beyond remedy, to wit the dropsy, and thereof he ended his life'.

Henry de Angeli (1128–33) contributed nothing, but was happily succeeded by Abbot Martin of Bec (1133–55) who developed the transepts, the northern one featuring a door with scales; we might wonder whether this is an allusion to Peter the fisherman. He also laid out the basis for a nine-bay nave. After a decade, sufficient was completed for him to have 'brought the sacred relics and monks into the new church amid great honour, in the eleven hundred and fortieth year from the Incarnation of the Lord and the twenty-third year after the destruction of the place by fire'. If some of the Saxon church had survived the fire to offer continuity for services, it must by now have been cleared away.

Until this time, the town lay to the north-east of the abbey. New ground was now broken to its west and a market place was created, surrounded by streets that form the basis of today's city. The ensemble of new town and furnished (if not finished) abbey church was witnessed in 1154 by Henry II and his chancellor, Thomas Becket.

The accession of abbot William Waterville in 1155 led to the completion of the transepts and further work on the nave, establishing arches for its twin towers. They would never be finished.

Opposite The north transept, with inserted fifteenth-century tracery. The arches were embellished on the eastern face, for audiences facing the altars. Footings were laid for an unexecuted western aisle.

Above As builders approached the west end of the nave, the piers were thickened in preparation for towers that were never built.

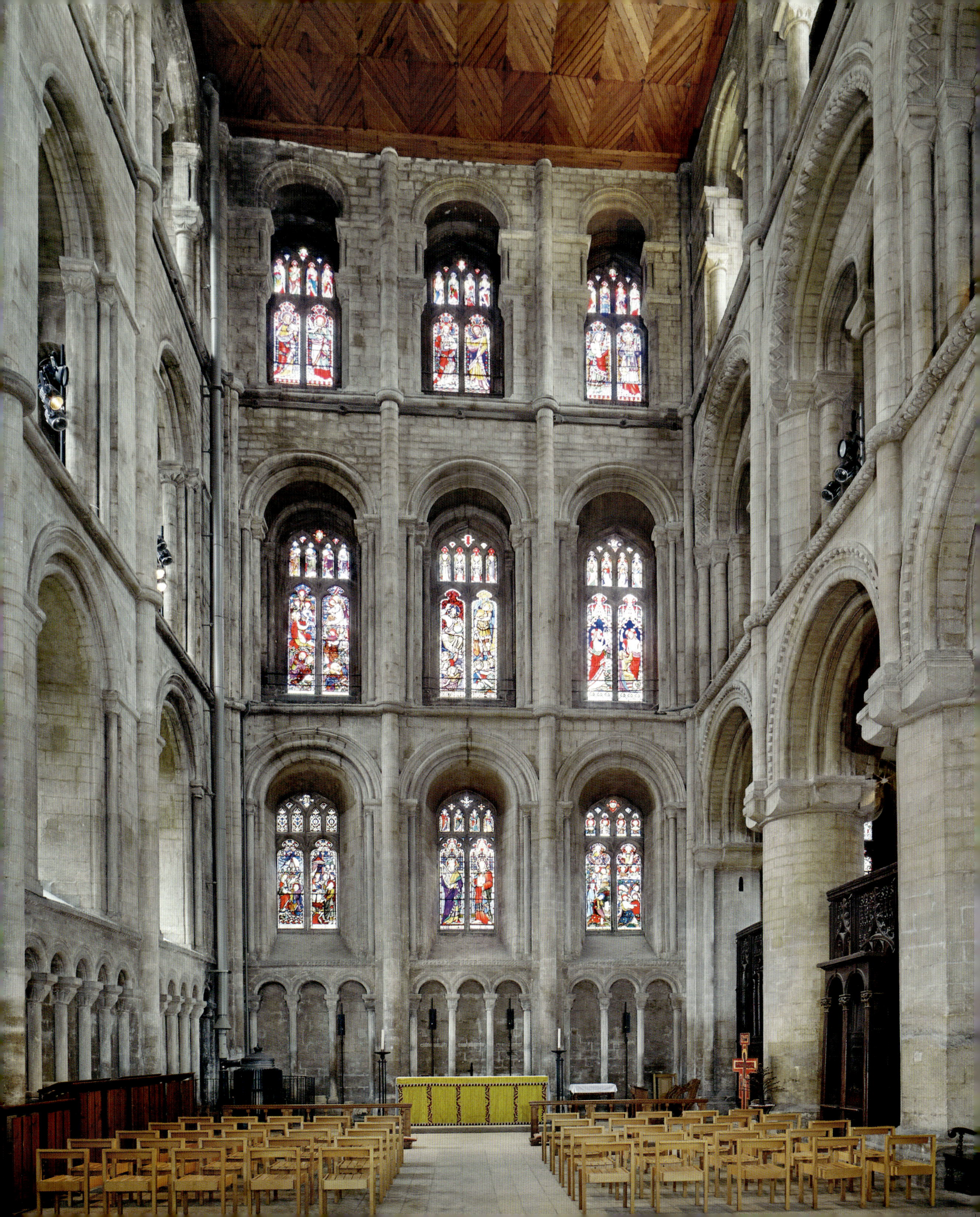

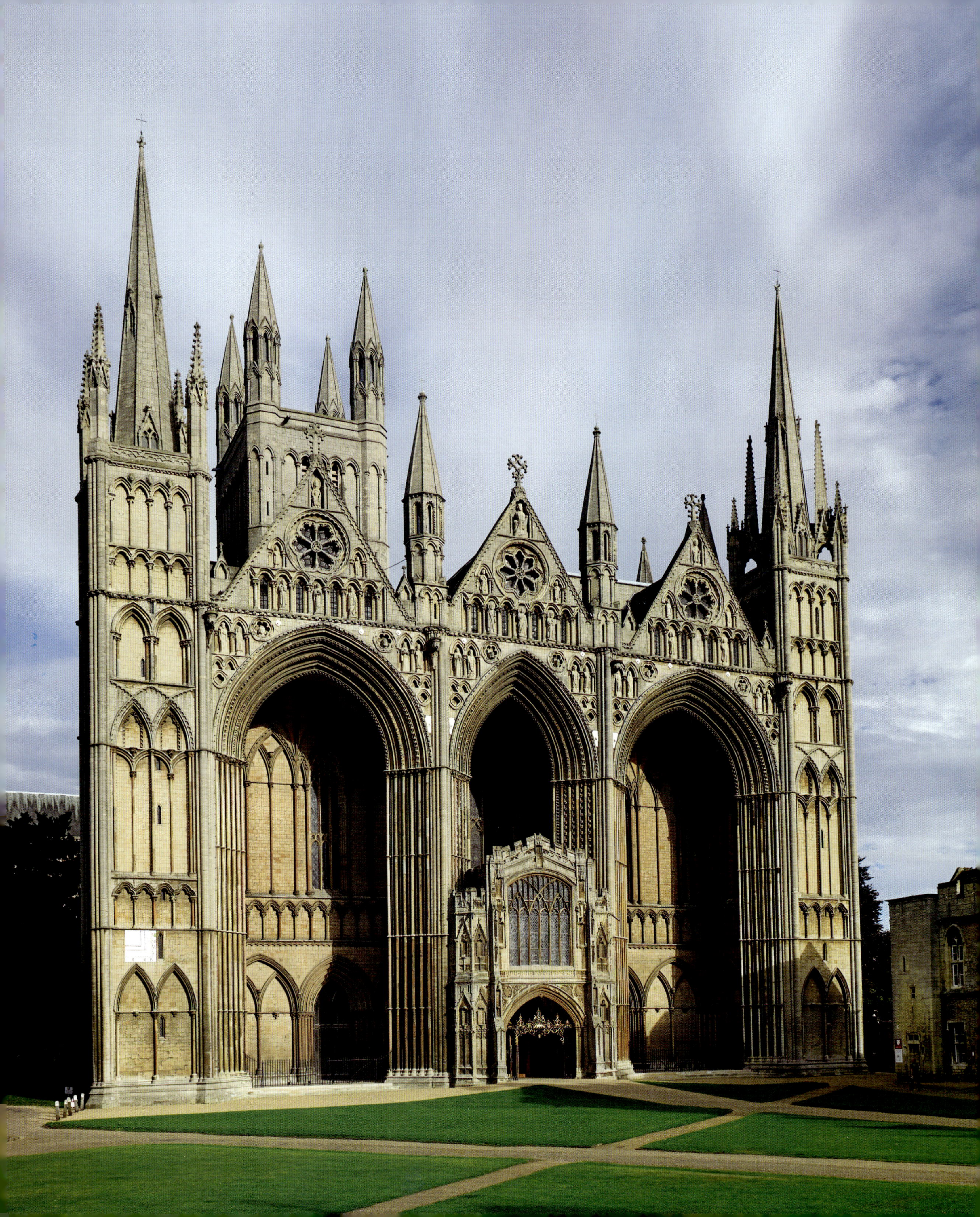

3

THE GREAT CHURCH COMPLETED

*Triumphal arches add to the
glory of illustrious men*

During the later Middle Ages, this silt zone, between sea and peat fen, seems to have been among the most prosperous parts of England. The massive parish churches of the area were – and still are – famous. Their building was no sudden effort, quickly spent, but continued for centuries. The twelfth- to fifteenth-century spires and towers that point to heaven mark everywhere the prosperity of the land.

LATE-TWELFTH-CENTURY Peterborough spans the age when the forbidding power of the 'Church Militant' era gave way to the theatre of hope in the 'Church Triumphant', a transition made here to spectacular effect. As Waterville's western towers were abandoned, the attempt to complete Peterborough Abbey's nave with western transepts gave way to a revised west front of a quite different design. The theatrical triumph of its three uneven arches opening into a great porch represents a unique creation in Europe and is the most distinctive aspect of the cathedral. Its singularity demands investigation.

Inevitably, politics played a part. The last decades of the twelfth century witnessed a shift in the relationship between English monarchs and the Church and, by extension, citizens. The fault lines split open in December 1170, when four of Henry II's knights stormed into Canterbury Cathedral and slew Archbishop Thomas Becket, apparently following the king's infamous order to 'rid me of that turbulent priest'.

The Canterbury Cathedral that Becket knew featured the famously 'glorious' choir that Ernulf had begun, completed with a *'caelum egregia pictura decoratum'* ([timber] ceiling decorated with remarkable painting).[32] The rebuilding of the east end of Becket's cathedral after a fire in 1174 extended from this choir's burned-out old walls. The design came under the control of two successive architects, William of Sens from France and William the Englishman, who held differing visions for its completion. Their unwitting collaboration introduced an architecture of breadth and spatial complexity on changing levels, where shafts of light pierce richly coloured glass, falling onto precious marble floors. Into the heart of this numinous vessel Becket's shrine was eventually installed, to the wonderment of crowds of pilgrims, so that what constituted a monumental riposte to royal trespass set the standard for popular pilgrimage churches.

Moral aspiration was sorely needed, for the same era saw a crime wave. In 1176 Henry II raised a charter for knights' rights at the assize of Northampton,

Previous pages The west front, a unique concept and an achievement of international importance. Its singularity must represent a specific expression.

Opposite Canterbury Cathedral's eastern arm, built *c*.1174–84, the glazing continued in subsequent years. In 1220 Becket's shrine was installed behind the visible throne of *c*.1200. The completed ensemble was a powerful draw to pilgrims in the Magna Carta era, still celebrated two centuries on by Geoffrey Chaucer.

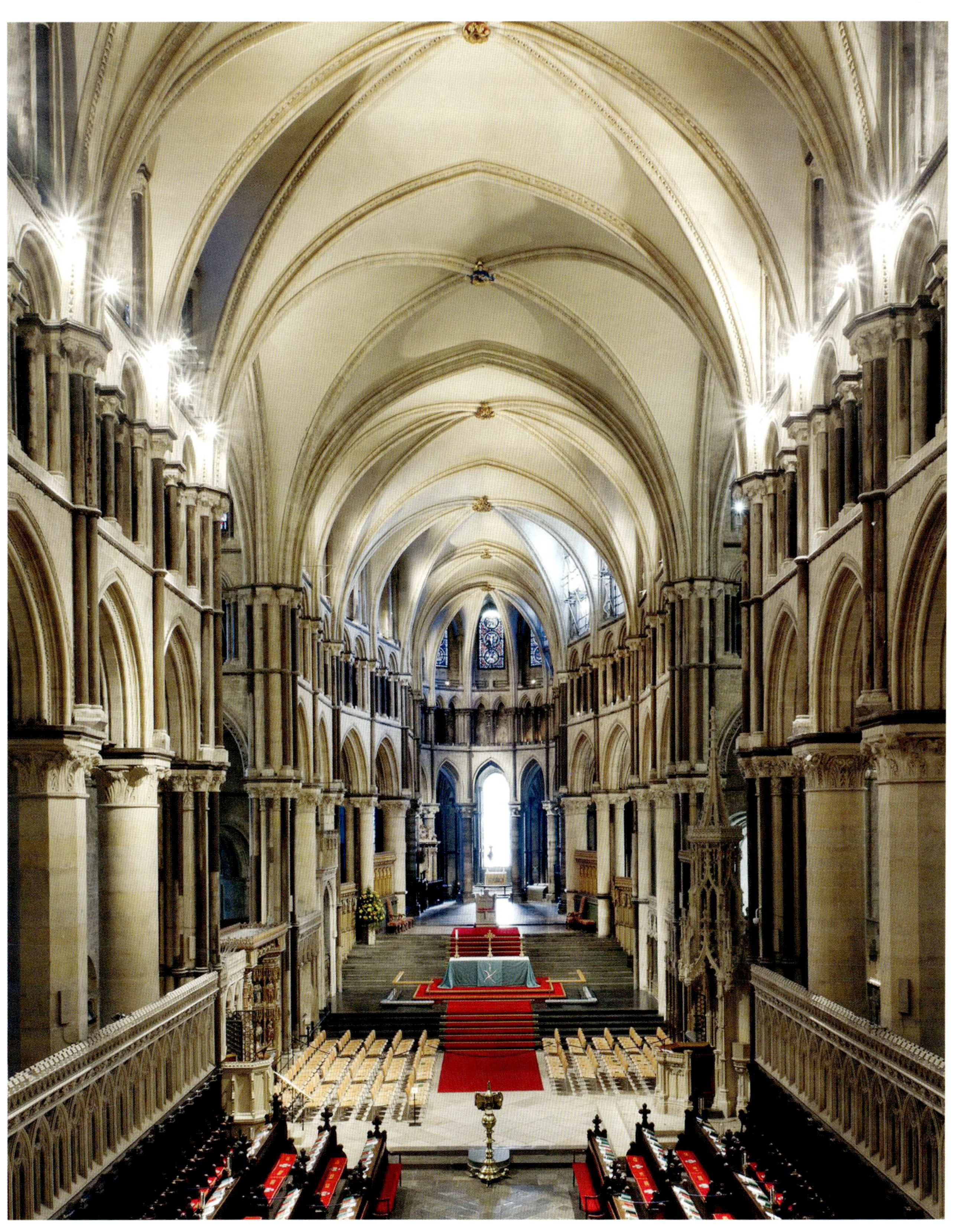

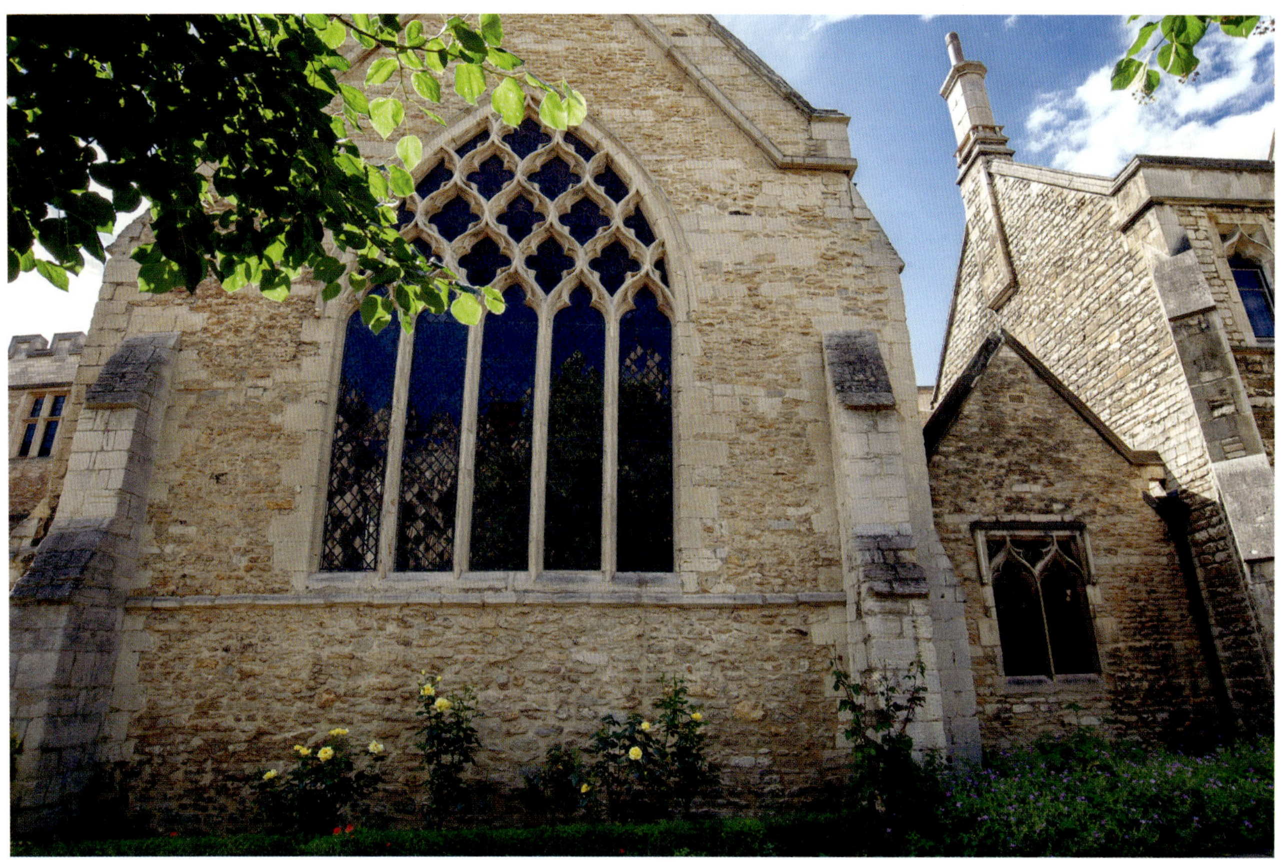

just 40 miles south-west of Peterborough. This was law by tyranny, stipulating that the right hand of certain offenders could be hacked off.[33] At this time, monarchs presumed to appoint bishops and abbots. The tension between royal and ecclesiastical authority would explode in the reign of Henry's son, John (1199–1216), when the king was excommunicated and the bishops exiled, before the reforming Fourth Lateral Council of 1215 coincided with Magna Carta and the barons' empowerment. Then in 1216 John's reign gave way to the minority of his seven-year-old son Henry III.

In the battle between Church and state, Canterbury Cathedral conjured an old story ultimately leading back to St Augustine, who had imported the authority of Rome to Canterbury in 597. This French lesson in Roman authority was specific to Canterbury[34] but its themes affected Peterborough, which stood as a monastic church in Canterbury's archdiocese, with a story almost as ancient, one avidly recorded by Hugh Candidus. It also identified strongly with Rome, and had been deeply disadvantaged by royal power. It has not been widely acknowledged that this relationship forms the template for Peterborough for the century ahead.

Peterborough borrowed certain characteristics and details from Canterbury, while maintaining well-established forms and ideas. Through such fusions an English manner emerged.[35]

Remarkably, the abbey would gain some relics of Thomas Becket through the direct involvement of an important figure, who came from Canterbury and who knew Becket closely. He was Abbot Benedict, made prior of Canterbury Cathedral in 1174, the year the cathedral burned, who was given the abbacy of Peterborough by Henry II three years later. With extensive experience of monastic management, Benedict arrived in Peterborough to witness a forest of timber scaffolding about the round arches of the nave, as far as it was built, with the preparations his predecessor had made for the western towers.

The task was greater than the new abbot imagined for this unfinished great church was in profound debt – a poisoned chalice. Yet Canterbury's vast income from pilgrimage might be replicated with the presentation of Becket's relics. He brought Thomas Becket's shirt, his surplice, and a quantity of his blood in two crystal vases, and also hauled two pavement stones from where Becket fell, with which he made altar slabs. Benedict built the Chapel of St Thomas by the abbey's gateway. The much-remodelled remaining half of this is Peterborough's only remnant of the culture of the saint's effects.

Apparently overwhelmed, Benedict retreated to Canterbury to gather resolve. When he returned, he had nursed a change of plan for completing the great church. It required the transformation of the abbey's fortunes, to pay for an extension of the nave that rejected the western towers, building further out into a western transept like Ely's. The thick walls were augmented with shafts carrying pointed arches with vigorous geometric moulding, big enough to carry twin towers (rather than Ely's echo of Peterborough's Saxon 'westwerk'). Between those towers is a broad stone vault whose ribs, composed of three basic rolls, compare in essence with those in Canterbury's new east end.

The ambition for a stone vault was carried through to the nave, where the stubs of identical diagonal ribs reach into thin air at the extreme west end. The

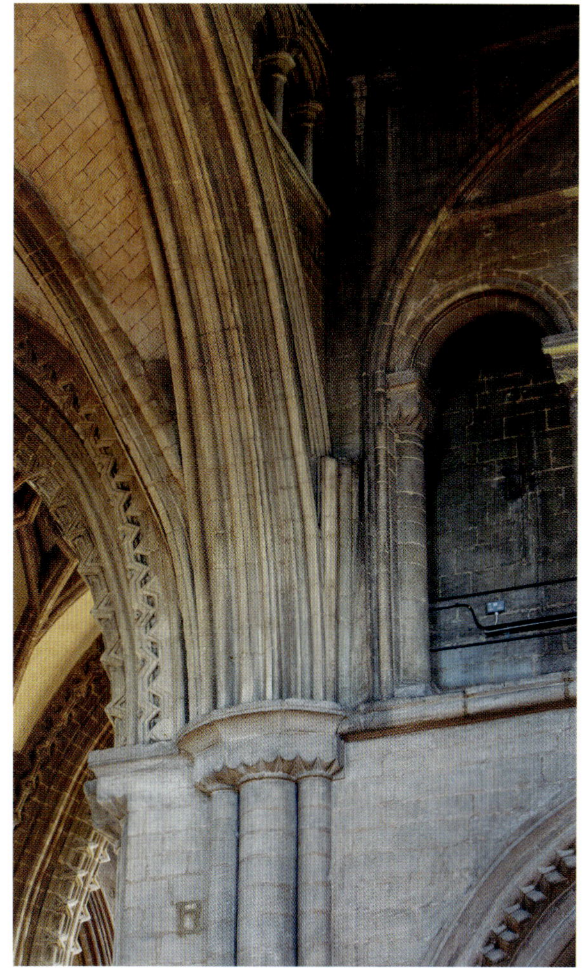

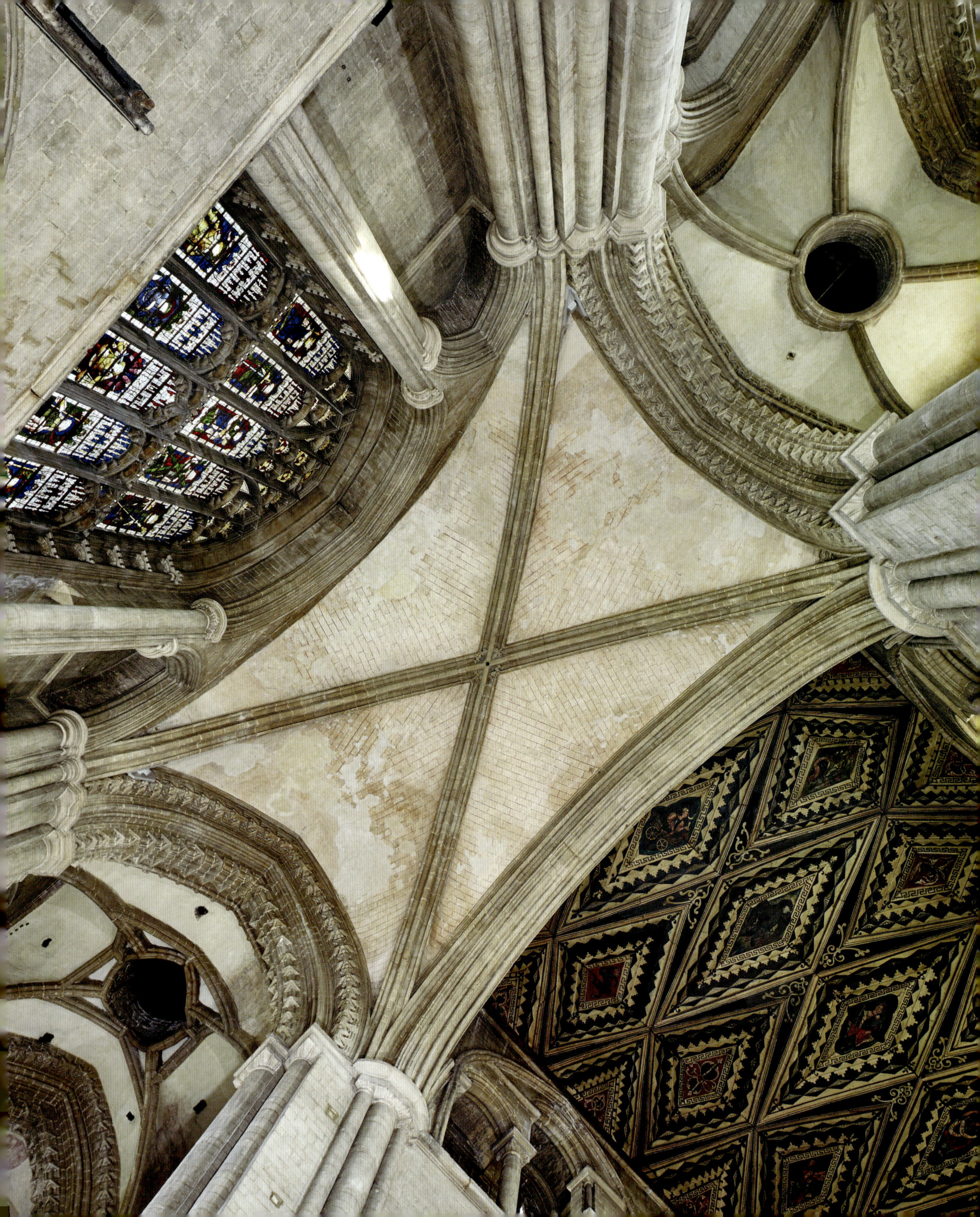

clerestory windows are surrounded by wall-ribs, the space between subsequently filled in with smooth blocks. At the east end of the clerestory, by the central tower, the vault builders cut through the round arches, betraying their work as an afterthought. All this was essential preparation for a quadripartite ('X'-plan) stone rib vault. Peterborough was by no means the only timber-ceiled Norman church to find itself with retro-fitted stone vaults, a structural burden that its engineering never anticipated. Lincoln Cathedral had also received secondary stone vaulting, added 60 years after that building was begun in 1072. It was a risk. And in 1185, the whole of Lincoln Cathedral split from end to end, collapsing in a cloud of dust but for the massive western block.

THE WEST FRONT

Around the year 1195, the builders of Peterborough Abbey embarked on an audacious scheme, one entailing both risk and expense. A talent whose name is lost to history took out his dividers and rule and began crafting a new design for a hollowed-out west front added to the western transept. The dividing line can be seen today in the masonry mouldings low on the north and south walls, which suddenly change to the templates of a new master mason.

The first concept, with stair turrets, was started and rapidly revised into a design of three great arches set out to an ingenious (if much-disputed) geometrical scheme based on squares and equilateral triangles. The abbey was, if unwittingly, about to recover some of the character of its Roman origins, for the scheme is loosely based on a triumphal arch, already adopted at Lincoln after 1072, and based on the Arch of Constantine in Rome. A reference to the same Roman arch appeared by 1159 at the opening of John of Salisbury's influential text on ethics, *Policraticus*:

> Triumphal arches add to the glory of illustrious men only
> when the writing upon them informs in whose honour they
> have been reared, and why. It is the inscription that tells
> the spectator that the triumphal arch is that of our own
> Constantine, liberator of his country and promoter of peace.

Great cranes hauled up timber scaffolding and beams, as carts rumbled into the close laden with stone for the masons' yards. The 'banker masons' worked at benches to chip away at plain blocks, the columns and zigzags of wheel windows,

ESSENTIAL GEOMETRY OF THE WEST FRONT

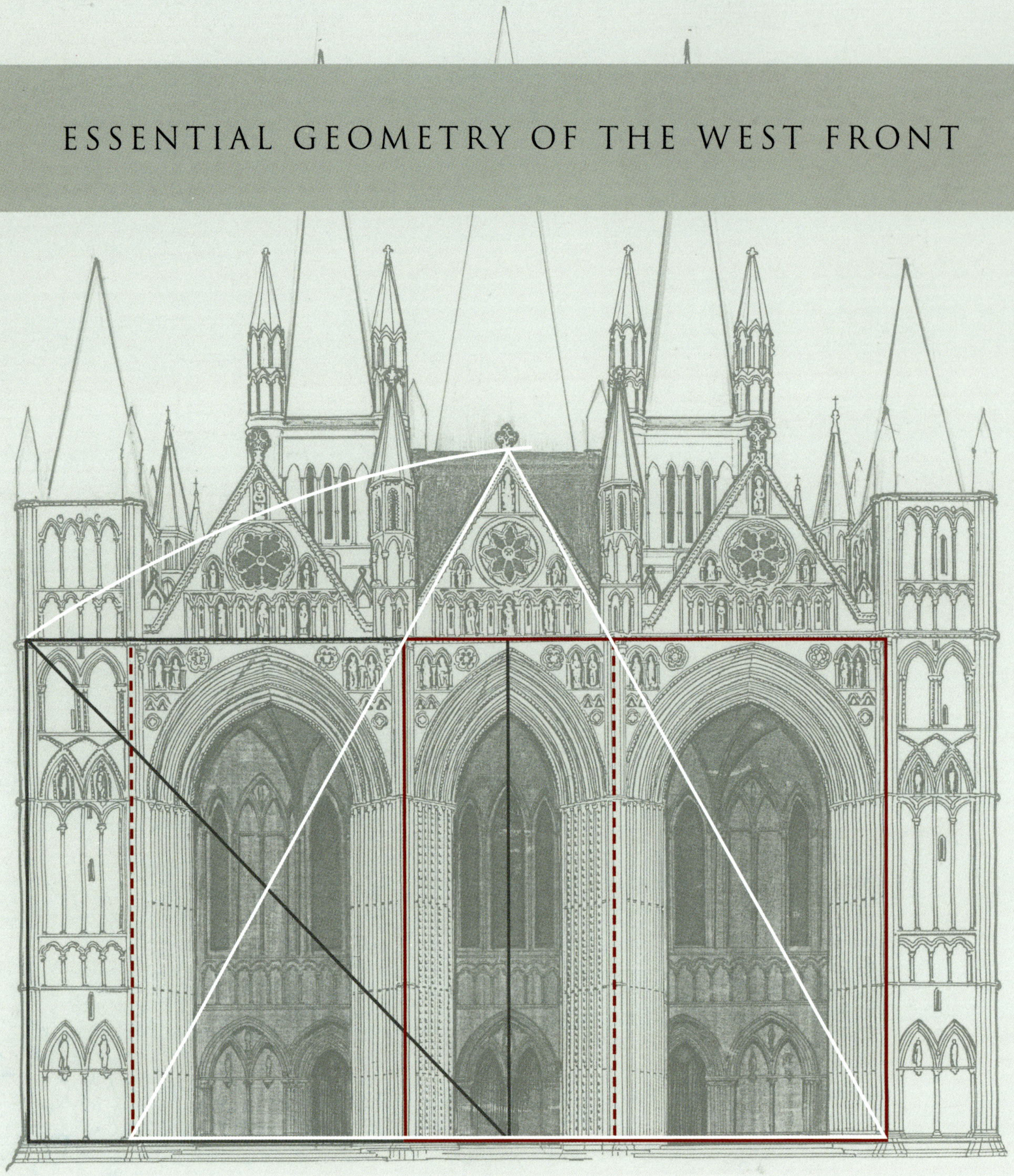

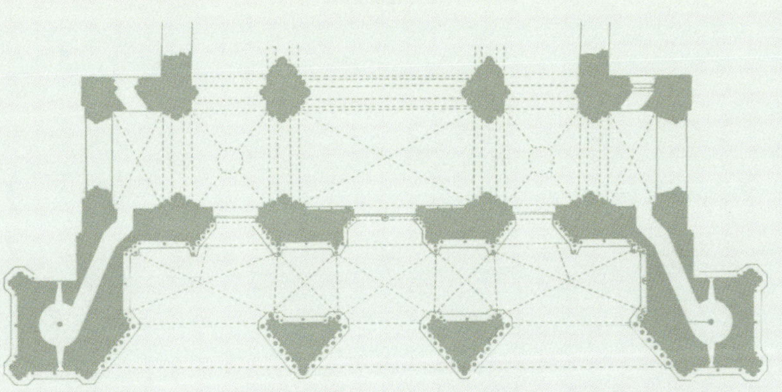

WEST FRONT GROUND PLAN

and wedge-shaped 'voussoirs' to form arches over round apertures. It appears that not all these blocks were winched up immediately, but were stockpiled during a further change of design.

The original plan mutated as the last years of the twelfth century ebbed and trouble brewed through disputes between the papacy, the English Church and the state, central to them the festering royal presumption that kings could elect bishops and abbots. Following King John's banishment of Stephen Langton as the pope's choice for archbishop of Canterbury, England was put under papal interdict, on 24 March 1208, which forbade the holding of church services. King John was excommunicated in November 1209, whereupon many of England's ecclesiasts fled abroad and their churches sat in limbo until 1213.

The hiatus in Peterborough's design belongs to these years of schism. The resulting spirit of reform influenced church architecture to become more emotive and spectacular, better grasping its audience. The focal character in Peterborough's change of approach was Hugh of Wells, who became bishop of Lincoln in 1209, probably as Peterborough's great western arches were approaching full height. Hugh was among those who went into exile, offering plenty of opportunity to revise the presentation of his churches. He returned to assume jurisdiction for Peterborough Abbey, overseeing behaviour, finances, liturgy and, to some extent, its architecture. He had come from Wells Cathedral in Somerset, which was at that time in a somewhat similar state of completion to Peterborough, though its magnificent west front had not yet been started. Remarkably, Peterborough's revision appears to be the first example of a new approach to west front design, the likely cause being the impeccable timing of Hugh's arrival as a reforming bishop. The string-course above the great arches marks the point where the change was made, already 21m off the ground.

Evidence that prepared masonry was reincorporated into a variant design is clearest in the wheel windows within the gables, which are squashed into their own string-courses for want of space. They must have been made for gables that were not so compressed, perhaps without the arcade stage just below them – the row that ends on roughly half-arches and is not integrated with the gables. The

Opposite The west front is composed of a double square, with the triangle that sets the width of the turrets generated as an elevated diagonal (value root 2) of each turret. A square set from the turrets provides the central line of the piers. This drawing also suggests the original fenestration and the possible array of intended spires.

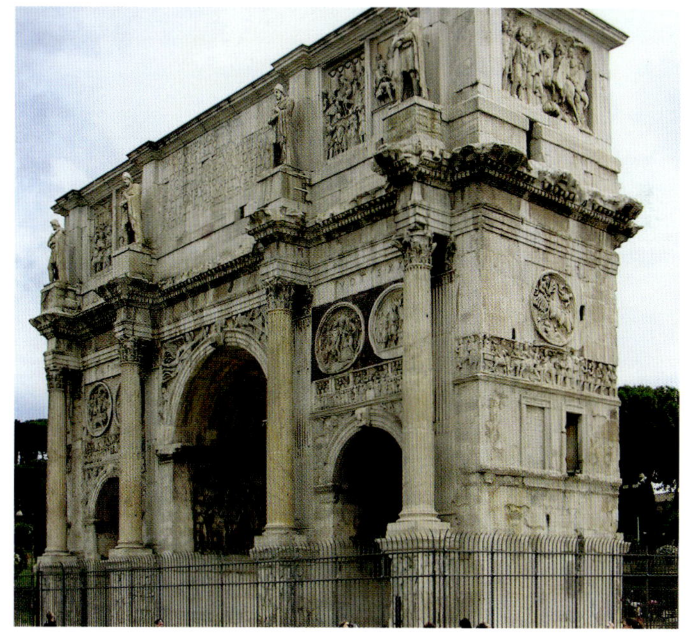

Above The Arch of Constantine, Rome; in the medieval period, this was viewed as a Christian monument, since Constantine had adopted the religion after 313.

practical purpose of this awkward adjustment is hinted at in early engravings showing the same arcade. For a century and a half, Victorian leaded windows have featured here, between the saints in their niches, but illustrators portrayed a different configuration – a vertical slot beneath a quatrefoil. The interior of this arcade presents a ledge the height of a person and so the vertical slot could offer light at midriff-level, by which a song-book could be read, and, through a quatrefoil at head-height, a voice could carry out beyond the west front. This echoes the later fronts at Wells and Salisbury, known to be for this purpose. But why would people climb the stone staircases to sing up here?

The entrance façade of any major church was considered to represent the passage into the New Jerusalem. The Frenchman William Durand (*c*.1230–96) wrote that: 'The open court signifieth Christ, by Whom an entrance is administered into the heavenly Jerusalem: this is also called porch from *porta*, a gate, or because it is *aperta*, open.'

The biblical Book of Revelation: 21 records that 'I John saw the holy city, new Jerusalem, coming down from God out of heaven, prepared as a bride adorned for her husband. And I heard a great voice out of heaven saying, Behold, the tabernacle of God is with men, and he will dwell with them.' It describes this like triumphal arches, having 'on the east three gates; on the north three gates; on the south three gates; and on the west three gates'.

As Peter was the keeper of heaven's gate, so Peterborough's triple porch, sometimes called the galilee, represents his guardianship. But it was not the only characteristic of this west front. In the early 1200s, the greatest churches in England became recast as if they were proscenium arches, decked with painted life-sized sculptures of biblical figures. Within such great stone billboards choirboys (*pueri*) were installed to chant psalms, as if the stone figures had come alive, providing orchestra and cast for a spectacular production of heaven descending to earth. This theatrical performance was staged at the climax of the Palm Sunday procession,

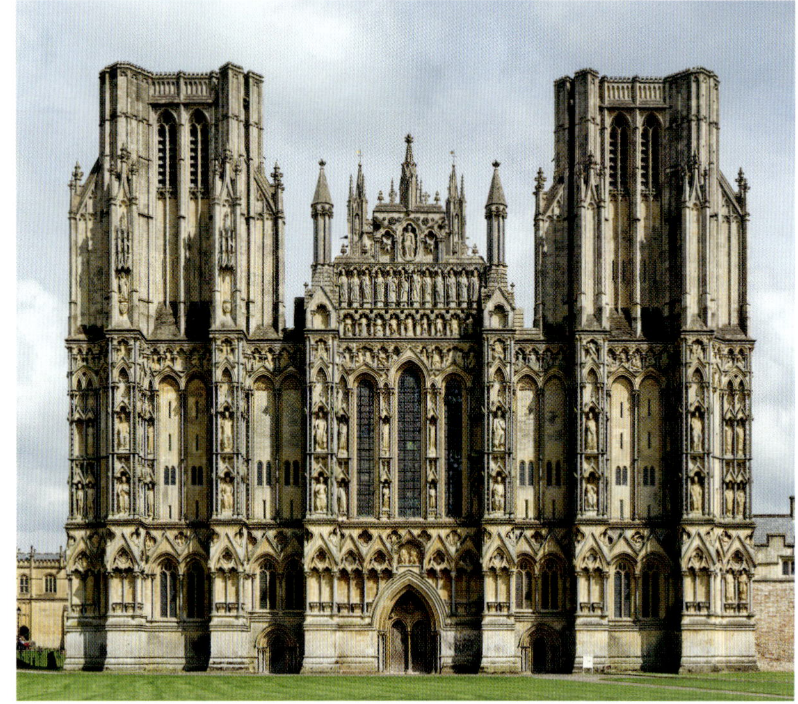

Above Wells Cathedral, Somerset; the west front here is also designed on a double-square basis, with tiers of biblical figures, behind which voice-holes transmitted the singing of concealed choir-boys.

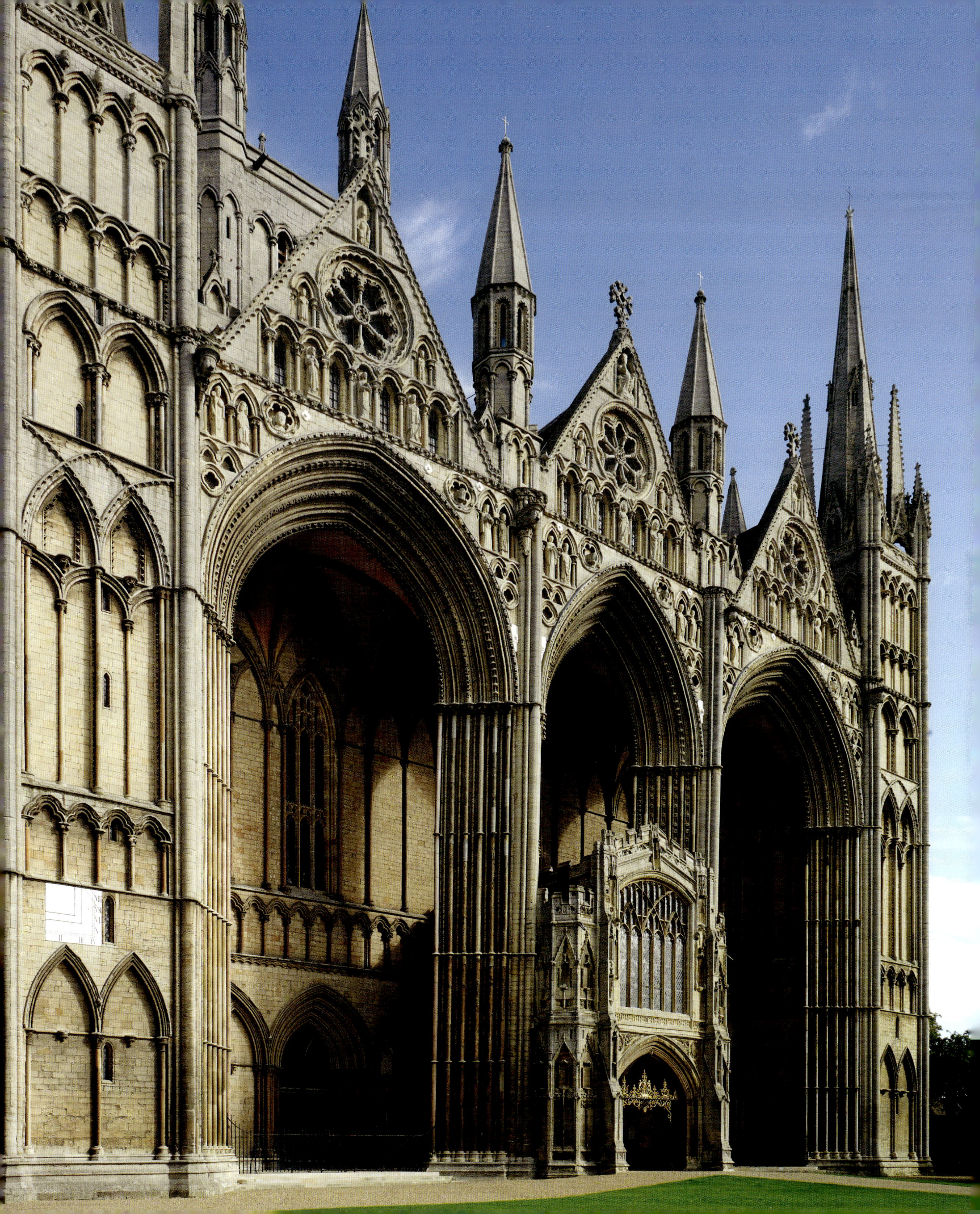

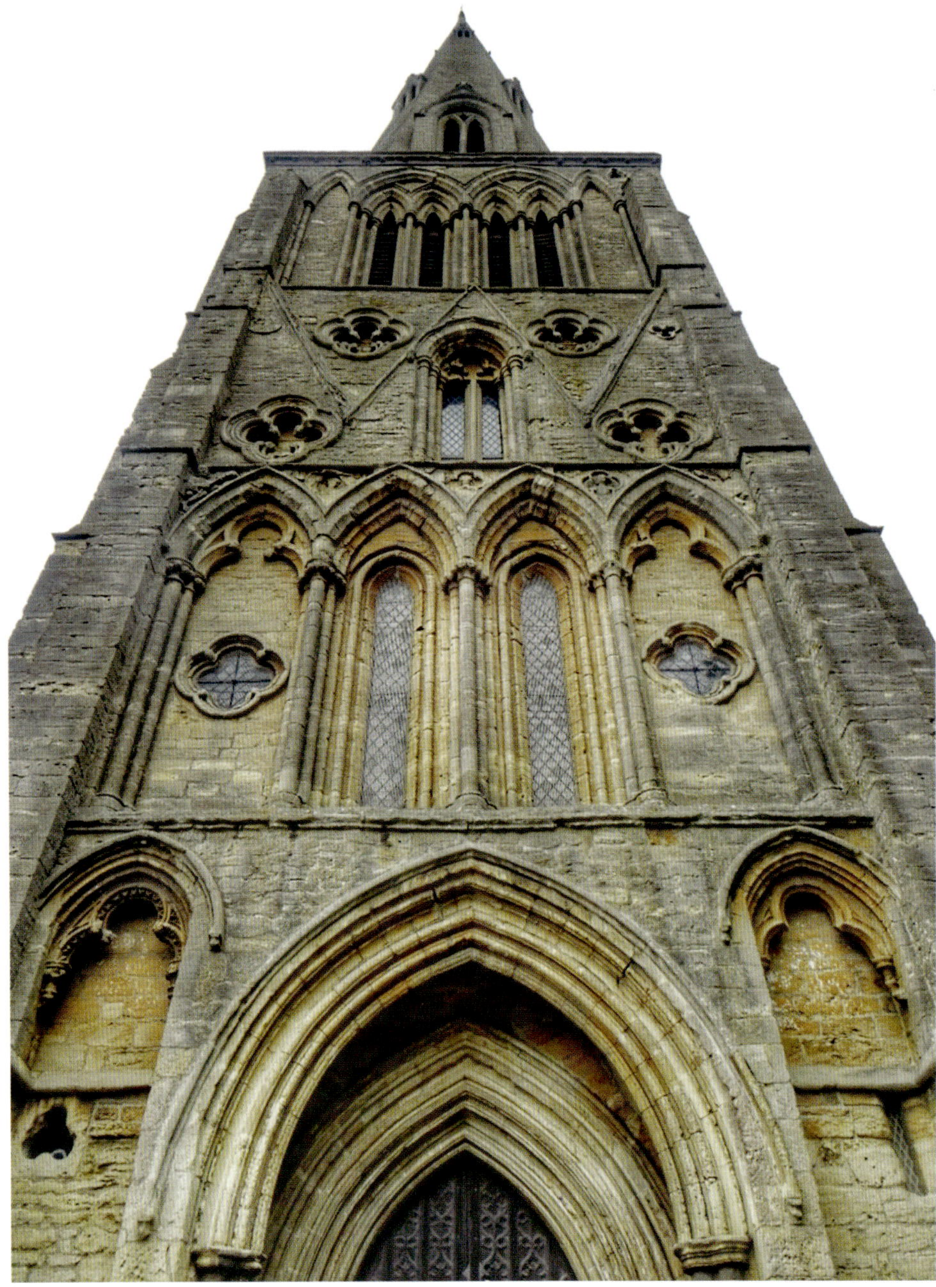

the focus of the liturgical year. The celebrants followed a route from east to west via the cloisters, stopping at stations that symbolically traced Christ's steps toward his crucifixion, the sacrifice through which the exile of Adam and Eve might be resolved by their return to Paradise. It was informed by a liturgical code from eleventh-century Old Sarum (Salisbury) called the Sarum Use, which stipulated the need for *pueri* to sing 'in a high place' at the west front of great churches. The Sarum Use met with regional interpretations; some churches had timber stages for the choir, but in other cases the singers were integrated into the architecture. The effect was the animation of the saints themselves.

Peterborough's change of direction may be due to Hugh of Wells' interpretation of the Sarum Use as the south-western liturgical code, for it seems beyond coincidence that the greatest examples of inhabited west fronts came at Wells and Salisbury cathedrals into the 1230s. Intriguing evidence for Hugh's pioneering involvement at Peterborough can be seen in the western tower of the parish church of Raunds, just over 20 miles south-west, which was built around 1220 by masons from Wells, judging by the details. The tower's rich façade includes an unusually deep-set door, like a miniature version of Peterborough's and within a triple-arched array, plus singing holes, while above are applied triangular mouldings with quatrefoils reminiscent of Peterborough's three gables. Raunds is another church dedicated to St Peter and seems to be imitating the saint's principal local sanctuary, supported by its bishop using his old connections at Wells.

Beyond this triumph of theatre at the Palm Sunday procession, which occupied only one day of the liturgical calendar, what did normal people – pilgrims, peasants or passers-by – encounter when they approached Peterborough Abbey? The key lies at the main door.

SIMON MAGUS

The essential biblical text on Peter relevant to architecture is '… thou art Peter, and upon this rock I will build my church; and the gates of hell shall not prevail against it'. If the portal is the gate of heaven, we might wonder how hell, and Peter's promise of salvation from it, was represented by Peterborough Abbey.

The unusual sculpted drum of dark, glossy Alwalton marble, called a 'socle', that props the column of the main western door is focal to the double-square geometry of the front, and demands attention. It features a unique depiction in this position of a man falling, upside-down and surrounded by demons. This surely identifies Simon Magus, a damned biblical sorcerer who harnessed magic to assume a godly status and then sought to buy St Peter's superior powers. The term 'simony' was named for him, for unethically purchasing ecclesiastical offices and privileges, a problem Peterborough had suffered acutely under Thorold.

Subsequent apocryphal texts embellishing this narrative made Simon Magus an arch-heretic, a figure of revulsion.[36] During the eleventh- and twelfth-century era of the Church Militant, characterised by the threat of hell and the violence of the first crusades, adherents of St Peter saw in Magus' headfirst descent the mirror of Peter's own fate, an upside-down crucifixion. The difference, of course, is that Peter found redemption while Magus did not, and the story of simple polarities

THE SIMON MAGUS STORY

The main source of the Simon Magus legend is the biblical Acts [of the Apostles] 8: 9–24.

9 But there was a certain man, called Simon, which beforetime in the same city used sorcery, and bewitched the people of Samaria, giving out that himself was some great one:

10 To whom they all gave heed, from the least to the greatest, saying, This man is the great power of God.

11 And to him they had regard, because that of long time he had bewitched them with sorceries.

12 But when they believed Philip preaching the things concerning the kingdom of God, and the name of Jesus Christ, they were baptized, both men and women.

13 Then Simon himself believed also: and when he was baptized, he continued with Philip, and wondered, beholding the miracles and signs which were done.

14 Now when the apostles which were at Jerusalem heard that Samaria had received the word of God, they sent unto them Peter and John:

15 Who, when they were come down, prayed for them, that they might receive the Holy Ghost:

16 (For as yet he was fallen upon none of them: only they were baptized in the name of the Lord Jesus.)

17 Then laid they *their* hands on them, and they received the Holy Ghost.

18 And when Simon saw that through laying on of the apostles' hands the Holy Ghost was given, he offered them money,

19 Saying, Give me also this power, that on whomsoever I lay hands, he may receive the Holy Ghost.

20 But Peter said unto him, Thy money perish with thee, because thou hast thought that the gift of God may be purchased with money.

21 Thou hast neither part nor lot in this matter: for thy heart is not right in the sight of God.

– good and evil, heaven and hell – had strong currency across twelfth-century Europe. Magus features far to the south, in the mosaics of Monreale Cathedral in Sicily, with the legend: 'Here in Rome, before Nero, Peter and Paul disputed with Simon Magus. Here, under the command of Peter, as Paul was praying, Simon Magus fell to the ground.'[37]

Peterborough's Magus figure could possibly pre-date the west front. But its appearance at this focal position in the mid-1190s likely had a specific political purpose, for Pope Celestine III ordered a crusade against northern European heretics in 1193, just before the west front was begun. Magus as the Petrine and Pauline heretic would have offered a most appropriate focus for an appeal to the Holy See from England's 'Second Rome', portraying a glimpse of hell upon arrival at heaven's gate.

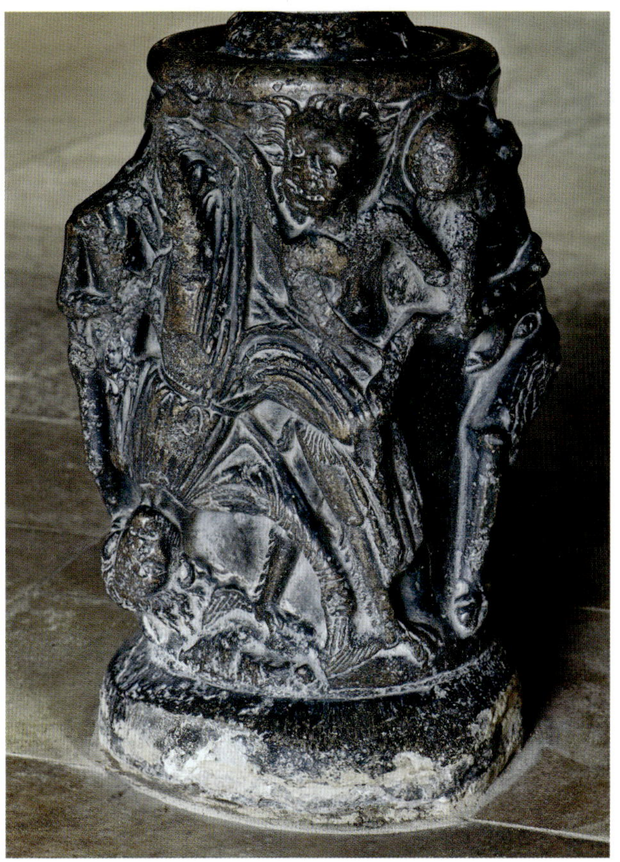

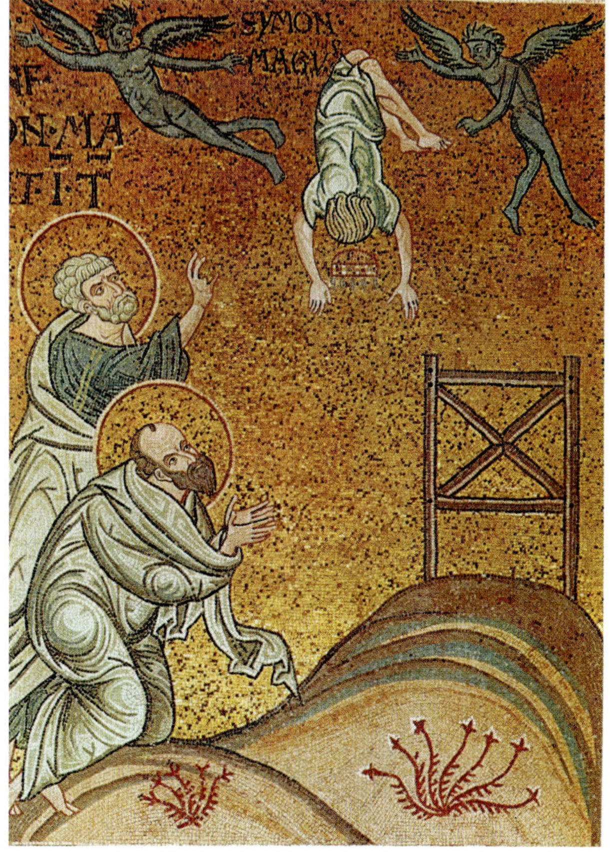

Appropriate symbolism to dress a church of St Peter would be found in a monastic library by leafing through the apocryphal texts that supplemented the biblical account of Peter's life and acts, including how he triumphed over Simon Magus. One particular text informs the architectural placement of Magus. This was the broadly circulated second-century 'Acts of Peter' (XIX), describing the Senator Marcellus' account to St Peter of how Magus was at first a guest at Marcellus' Roman house, but then expelled on Peter's behalf:

> I have for thee cleansed mine whole house from the footsteps (traces) of Simon, and wholly done away even his wicked dust. For I took water and called upon the holy name of Jesus Christ […] and sprinkled all my house and all the dining chambers and all the porticoes, even unto the outer gate, and said: I know that thou, Lord Jesu Christ, art pure and untouched of any uncleanness: so let mine enemy and adversary be driven out from before thy face.

Above left The socle of the west doors shows the sorcerer Simon Magus cast from the sky and surrounded by demons.

Above A similar vision of Simon Magus in a mosaic in the Palatine Chapel, Palermo, made for Roger II of Sicily (1095–1154). Here St Peter commands Magus' catastrophic plummet, as St Paul looks on in wonder.

Christ's face may also be linked with the original presentation of Magus at Peterborough, since the trumeau over the main west doors – since obscured by the fourteenth-century porch – was the typical position for a sculpted Christ in Majesty, looking out beyond all who arrived. If so, Magus was set beneath Christ, this indeed being at the portico, and within view of the outer gate. Beyond dispute, and long-noted, is that the sculpted saints in the gables above include a seated St Peter occupying the central apex.[38] He and Magus remain diametrically opposed in their attitudes and fate.

Guidance on this was available from *Policraticus*, the text by John of Salisbury that may already have informed the arches of the west front, for it deals with heretical magicians:

> Long ago the Christian Fathers condemned those who practised the more demoralizing forms of legerdemain, the art of magic, and astrology because they realized that all these arts, or rather artifices, derive from unholy commerce between men and demons.

It continues that the best way to show their wrongs is by contrasting vice with virtue because 'at times [...] truth must be traced by antithesis'.

When the brilliant theologian Robert Grosseteste, bishop of Lincoln and adviser to Henry III (1216–72), arrived at Peterborough to dedicate the church on 6 October 1238, work to complete the interior was already well underway. For those with eyes to behold medieval imagery, as the oak door swung open to reveal the echoing interior, Simon Magus' heresy and John of Salisbury's book of ethics would have central relevance for the reading of Peterborough's greatest work of art, the nave ceiling.

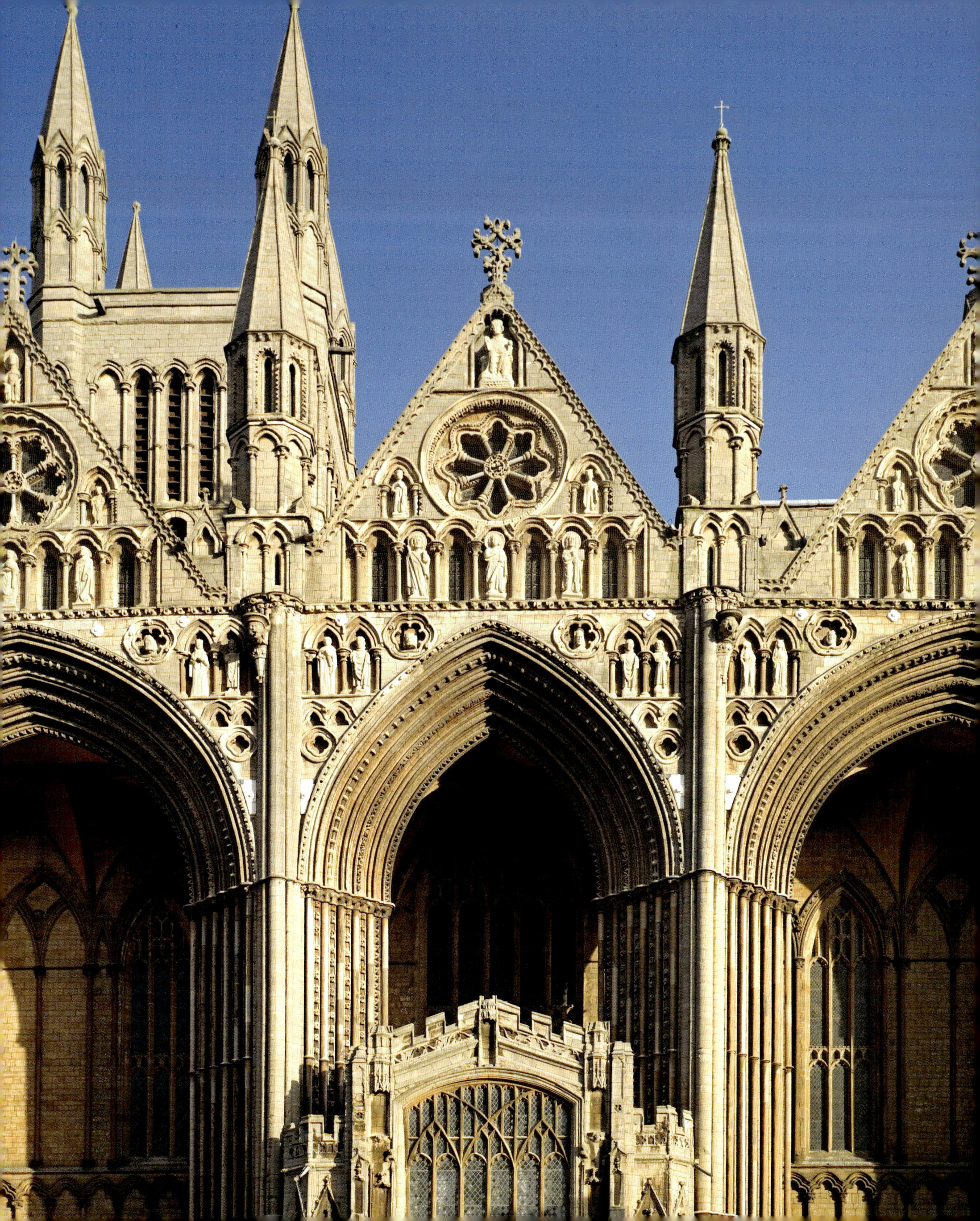

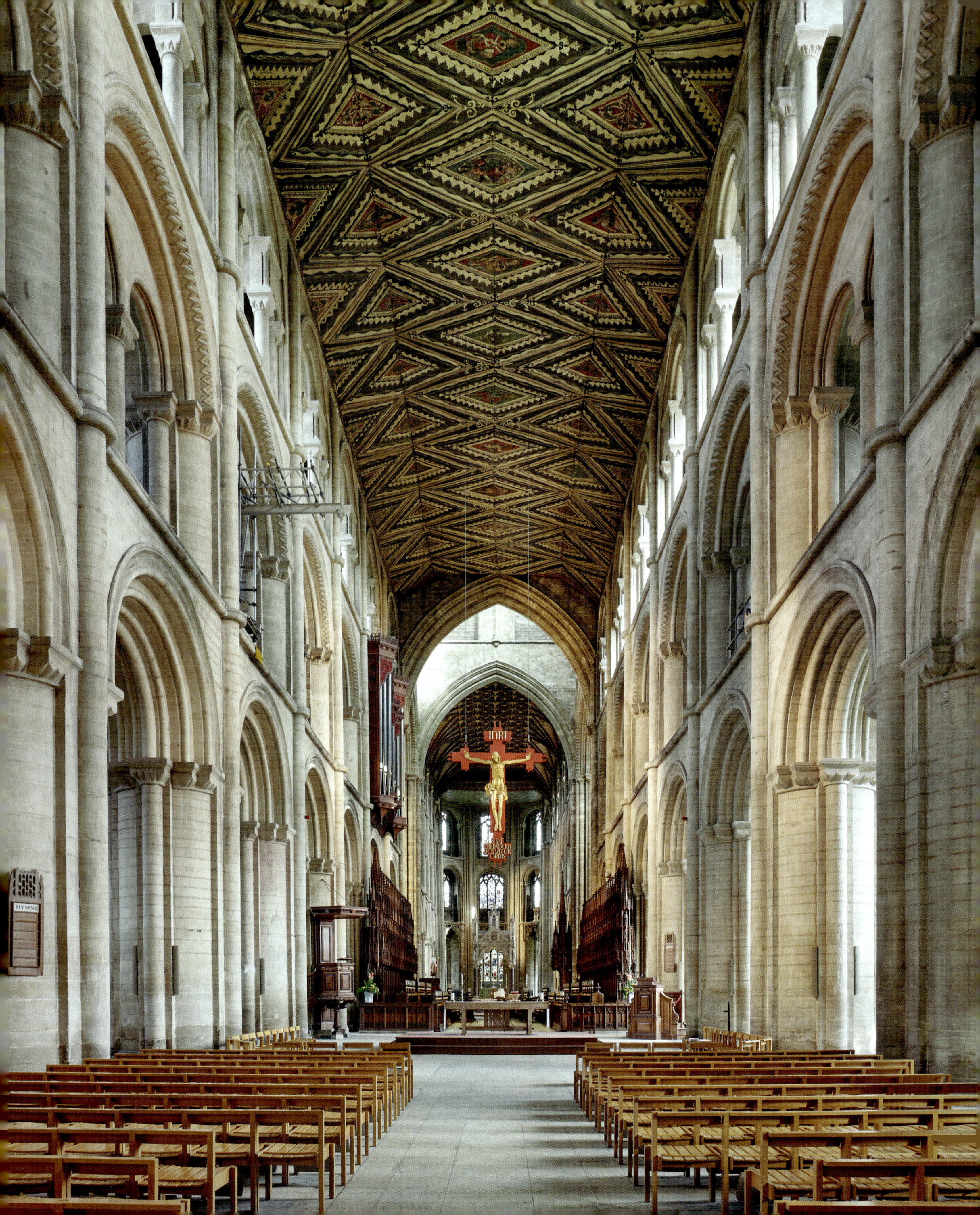

4

THE NAVE CEILING

*The fool changes as the moon but the wise
man remains steadfast as the sun*

THE FOURTH LATERAN COUNCIL in 1215 was the most important assembly in medieval Church history, a reforming moment that empowered ecclesiasts. It came in the same year that Magna Carta attempted to check royal authority in England. The charter's first principle was not the promise of parliament, law courts or public democracy, but that the Church be allowed to hold its own elections in England. That was the theory, at least. During a calamitous French invasion of England in 1216, King John created a base at Peterborough Abbey, which clearly had more work to do to throw off royal oppression. The arts of thirteenth-century Peterborough were determined by these powerful events. It was now at liberty to foster virtue through its relations with a monarchy that had for so long pillaged the abbey, and it addressed tyranny in a very public way.

The unique west front leads into the western transept, with its powerful stone rib-vaults. Recent cleaning revealed a painted shield, but there is little artwork to distract from the magnificent perspective of the nave ceiling, diagonally boarded and painted in the years after 1238. It is the largest in Europe and, as the greatest surviving polychrome work of art in the whole of medieval England, it demands the attention of any visitor.

The ceiling was not envisaged when the nave's arcades were completed by Benedict. It replaced the intended stone rib vault, whose abandoned springing arches remain forlorn high in the west end of the nave. Timber ceilings were more prone to fire than the increasingly common stone rib vaults but were nonetheless impressive, as painting required much organisation, skill and money – and achieved a more dazzling effect than stone and plaster. They also had a long pedigree. Old

Previous pages Once the intended rib vault over the nave was abandoned, possibly after Lincoln's collapse in 1185, attention turned to a painted ceiling.

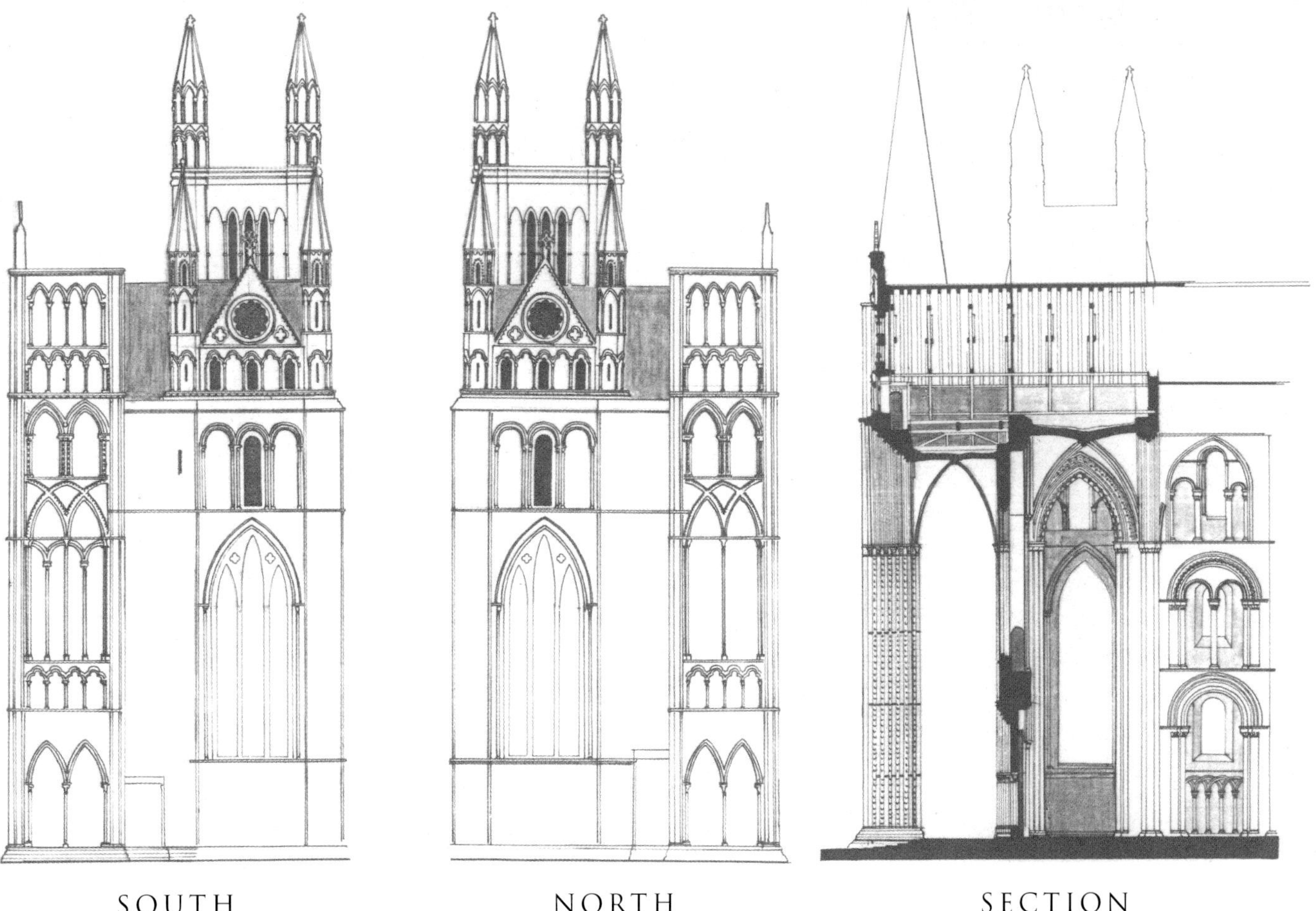

SOUTH   NORTH   SECTION

St Peter's in Rome displayed a long, deeply-coffered timber ceiling, while Abbot Benedict surely recalled the flat ceiling of Canterbury's admired painted choir – the same that Ernulf had begun, which influenced Peterborough's east end 60 years previously.[39]

The word 'ceiling' comes from the Latin '*caelum*' meaning sky or heaven, which also gives us 'celestial'. Peterborough's nave ceiling is not so much a portrayal of heaven as a compendium of big concepts, including astronomy, kings and bishops … and a monkey riding a goat backwards. As modern observers in a world of scientific certainties, we might feel strangers to a heavily symbolic and apparently random narrative, created in an age that held 'no rules for decorating large vaults and ceilings [although] there may have been common themes'.[40] So what precisely were these themes, and what did the ceiling try to communicate to its thirteenth-century audience? What follows is a new analysis of the ceiling,

Above Two elevations and a section through the western transept. The elevations offer a tentative reconstruction of the original fenestration. The section shows the position of the singing gallery behind the west front, via the door to the north turret; and also the extra height of the canted nave ceiling, compared with the vaulting level established by the western transept.

proposing that it continued the narrative of Simon Magus through the lens of John of Salisbury's book on the ethics of governance, *Policraticus*.

The canted ceiling is designed as a series of lozenges, the boards being nailed diagonally across the underside of the nave's roof trusses. It was probably conceived as 10 full-span diamonds, each containing four smaller diamonds, though the visual focus is on 20 of the smaller lozenges running in a central row at the apex. Paul Binski suggests that the assembled lozenge panels were mostly painted on the ground, before being winched up and fixed into place during the abbacy of Walter of Bury St Edmunds (1233–45), who probably inherited a nascent project. The last growth ring of the wood of the ceiling boards registers 1238, so the whole was probably finished in the mid-1240s, about the time that Henry III rebuilt Westminster Abbey.[41] This agrees with contemporary manuscript styles for the foliage painting.

The construction probably ran from east to west as customary, but we might best read the symbolism from west to east, as that was the intended route of the entrant, once past the damned figure of Simon Magus at the west door. The imagery has proved puzzling, but the following is a fresh attempt to make sense of it as a subtle and complex representation of the abbey's established concerns. A significant caveat is that the ceiling has been heavily overpainted, sometimes clumsily, in the last 250 years, and so we have to interpret others' restorations of the original imagery.

Central to the western end of the entire ceiling, in a chariot and crescent moon, is Luna, usually taken to be the moon itself. The west was always associated with the sun setting into the night, a form of death pending resurrection from the east. But this attribution is unlikely, for Simon Magus' female acquaintance was called Luna[42] and it makes more sense that this is she, clearly represented so as to continue Magus's narrative from the west door. From a passage in an apocryphal

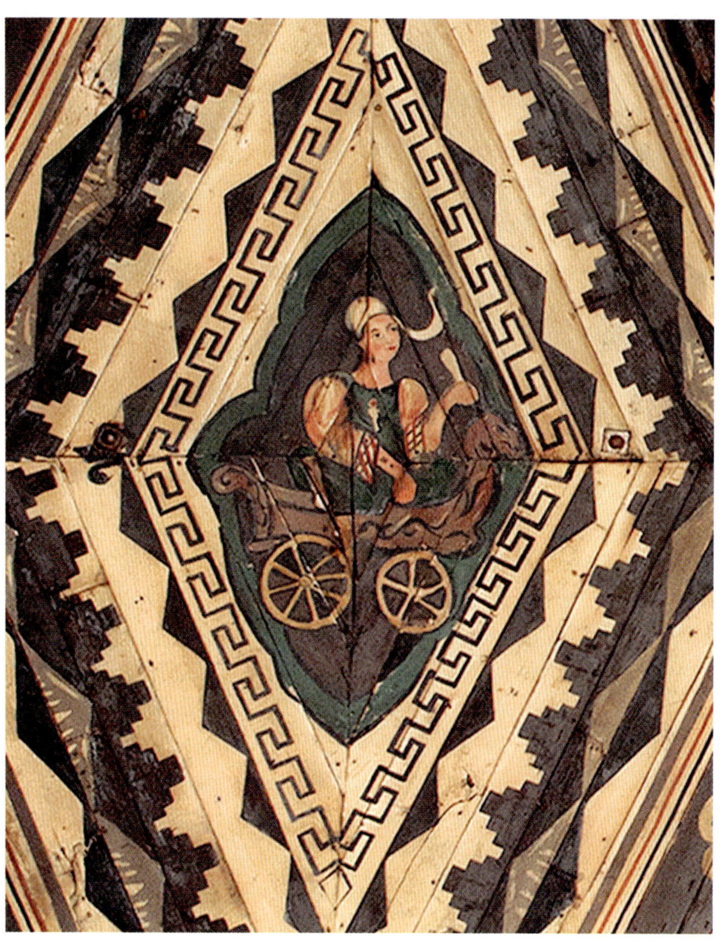

Opposite St Peter presides in the central gable of the west front, with wheel windows lined with stiff-leaf foliage, evoking the promise of spring growth. Heaven was imagined as a perennial spring of warmth and plenty; note the flowers in the cross above.

Above Luna was not merely the moon, but the companion of Simon Magus.

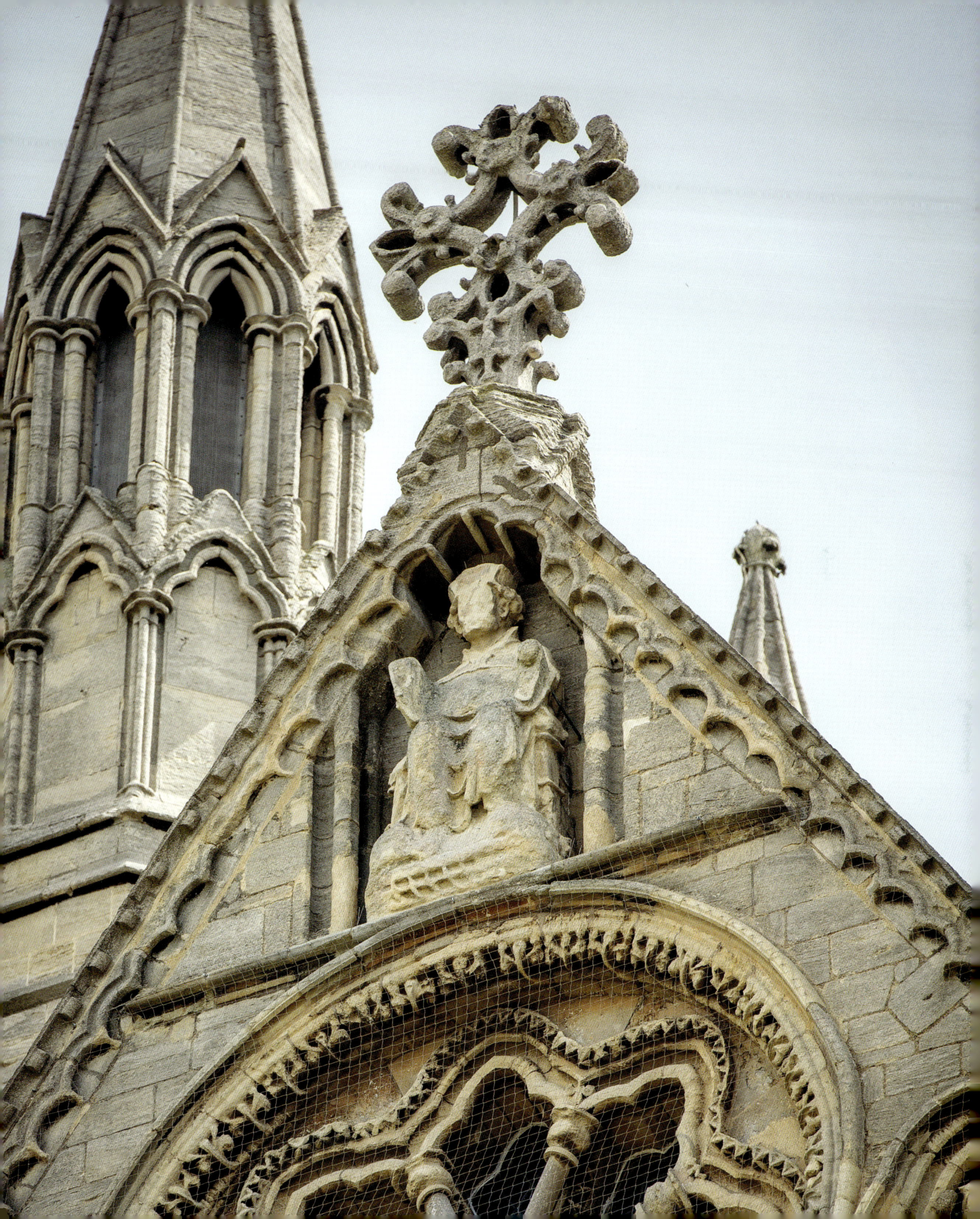

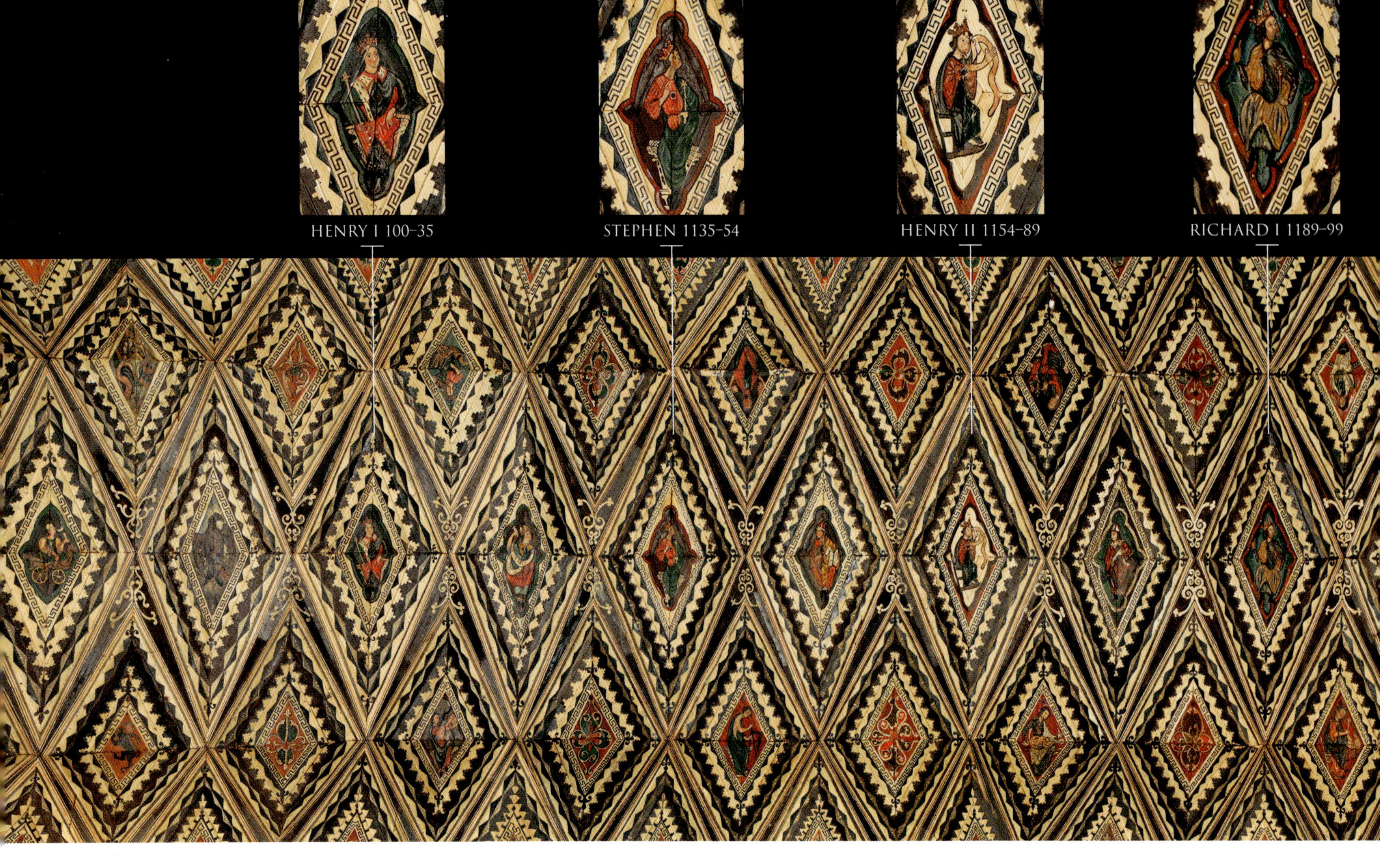

text, *Recognitions of Clement*, medieval scholars of St Peter's life learned that 'Simon took Luna to himself; and with her he still goes about, as you see, deceiving multitudes, and asserting that he himself is a certain power which is above God the Creator, while Luna, who is with him, has been brought down from the higher heavens, and that she is Wisdom, the mother of all things'.[43]

John of Salisbury equated the moon with misguidedness: 'The fool changes as the moon but the wise man remains steadfast as the sun.' If Magus and Luna symbolise ungodliness and foolishness, antitypes to Christ and the Virgin to whom all aspired, that could explain the next subject, an eagle with a crushed and bloodied object in its left talon.[44] The eagle as a symbol of St John, author of the last book of the Bible, is well known. John of Salisbury explains its role as an oracle, its wisdom allied to the sun:

> Although the eagle is surpassed by certain birds, there is none more efficient in predicting what will come to pass. He can outstrip all other birds in flight [...] and can fix his gaze upon the orb of the sun (something impossible for other living creatures).

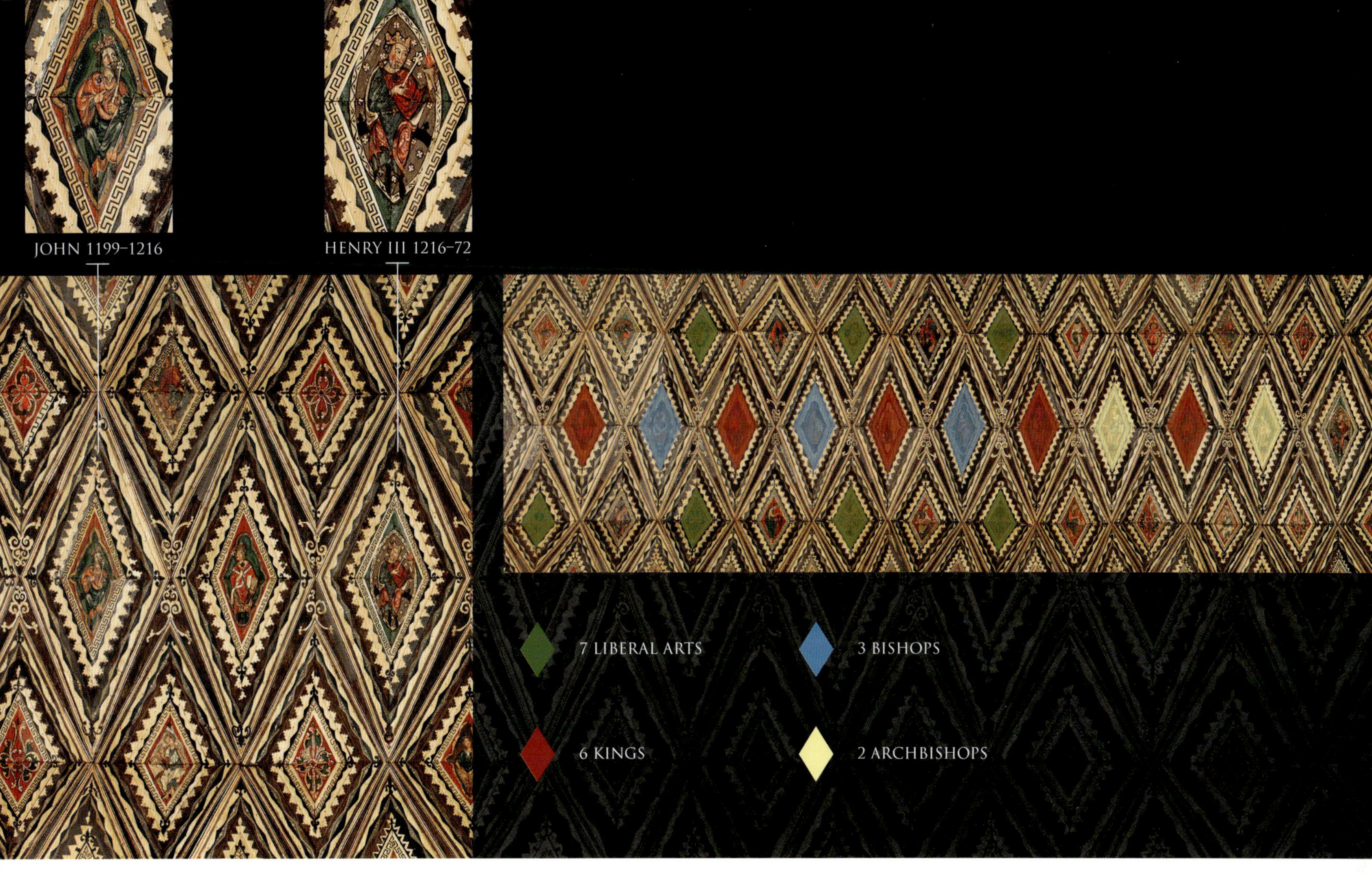

A single, rampant maned lion to the south and an unidentified figure to the north seem to reinforce the solar theme. Leo is the beast of the sun, while the Book of Revelation equated the Lion of Judah with Christ, whereby 'the just man has the boldness of the lion'.

The northern figure, as shown by Strickland,[45] is a feminine deity, possibly with the attributes of Venus, the planet with such bright reflection that it seems to emit light, but more weakly than the sun, and related both to Hesperus (evening star) and Lucifer (morning star).[46] If correct, this conflation may suggest Venus as an antitype to the sun; again, *Policraticus* offers a reference: 'Not once did Venus come before my startled vision but ill befell.'

To the east of the putative Venus we meet the sun itself, symbol of Christ and God (whose head would be shown as a sun in the later porch, see p.94). The brilliant sunlight from which all life grows comes in tandem with 'stiff-leaf', a type of stone-carving found at Peterborough as well as on this painted ceiling, and evoking the promise of perennial spring.[47] So far, then, we seem to find the sun perhaps featuring as associated with the solar themes of the virtuous eagle and lion, with the antitypes of Luna and possibly Venus.

Above **Mapping the ceiling; six English kings alternate with three bishops and two archbishops, surrounded by the Seven Liberal Arts.**

If false wisdom instead of true wisdom, and darkness displacing light, are indeed the key to Magus and Luna as heretics, then the successive central panels make clear sense. They show six kings, with three bishops and two archbishops, set alternately within cusped frames, mostly facing each other with attitudes typical of disputing scholars.[48]

The kings gesture with index fingers for emphasis, while the ecclesiastics hold open Bible texts or bear scrolls. Kings and bishops were Christian princes and exercised wisdom in the name of God-given authority. Their dialogue in this ceiling suggests either confrontation or co-operation, in an age of conflict between the powers of state and Church which had impacted Peterborough. Within the living memory of some, Hugh Candidus had yearned for the good old days when '… not only earls and rich men but also archbishops and bishops, who left their own sees, gave themselves and their belongings to God and to St Peter'. It is not difficult to imagine the desire to return to the former glories of the 'Golden City' in an age when not only abbots but a 'bishop's office required … to join Peter and be a fisher of men'.[49]

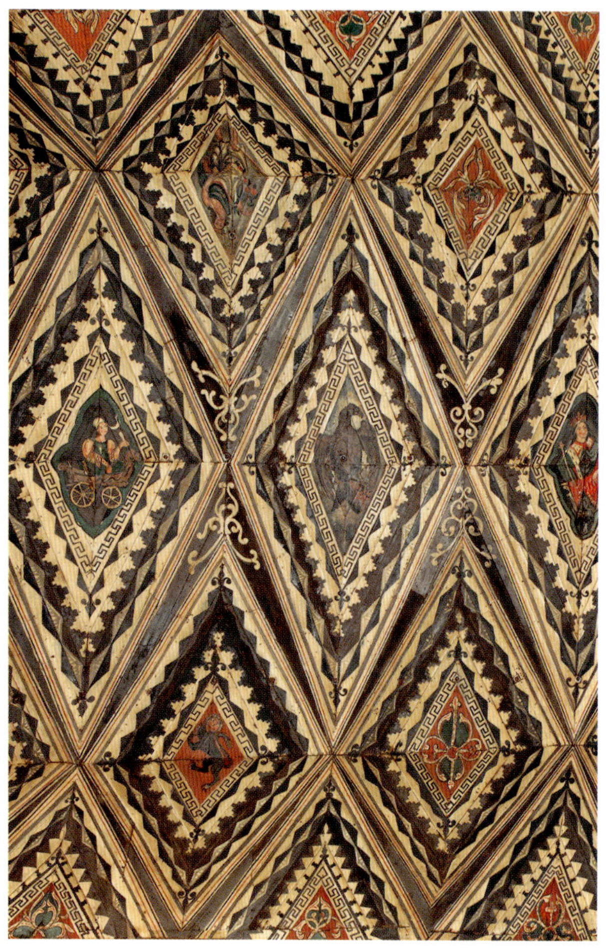

Above Luna is surrounded by the lion (Leo), the eagle and possibly Venus, as the planet with such a bright reflection that it seems to imitate the sun.

As kings and bishops were the authorities and patrons to which Peterborough Abbey ultimately appealed, it was to the abbey's advantage that *Policraticus* placed Church authority above that of kings. The ceiling shows that the Church's longstanding political problems now stood to be corrected through reform.

To either side of the disputants are characters representing the Seven Liberal Arts, a theme less common in English thirteenth-century art than in the orbit of Paris where, in imitation of antiquity, the three subjects of the *trivium* (grammar, logic and rhetoric) and the four of the *quadrivium* (geometry, music, astronomy and arithmetic) represented the standard fare of cathedral schools and universities.[50] *Policraticus* held that:

> The mind ascends the ladder of the liberal arts step by step to the throne of perfect wisdom… indeed the *ma'thesis* as taught in the schools consists entirely of these four forms and attains the perfection of worldly wisdom by these four so-called paths of philosophy.

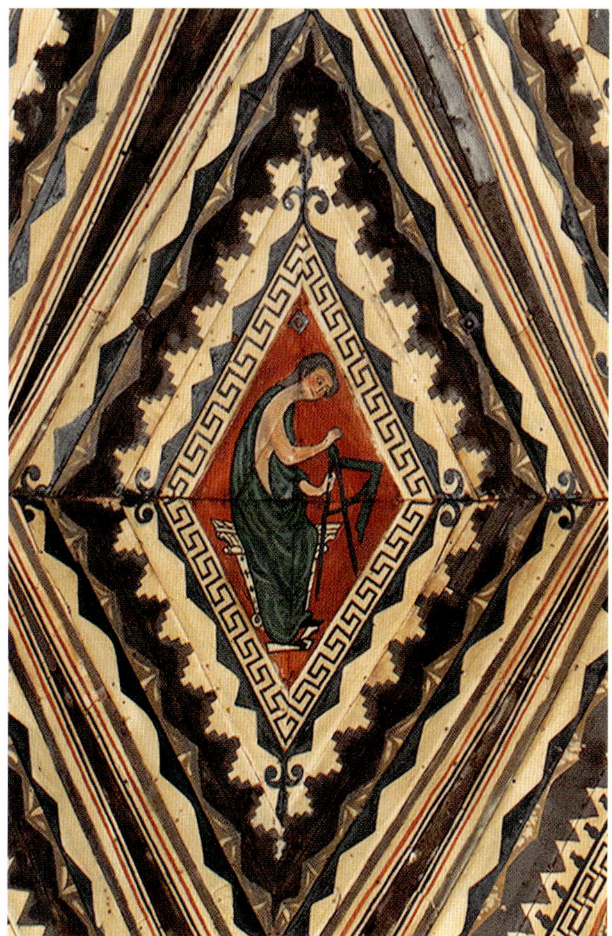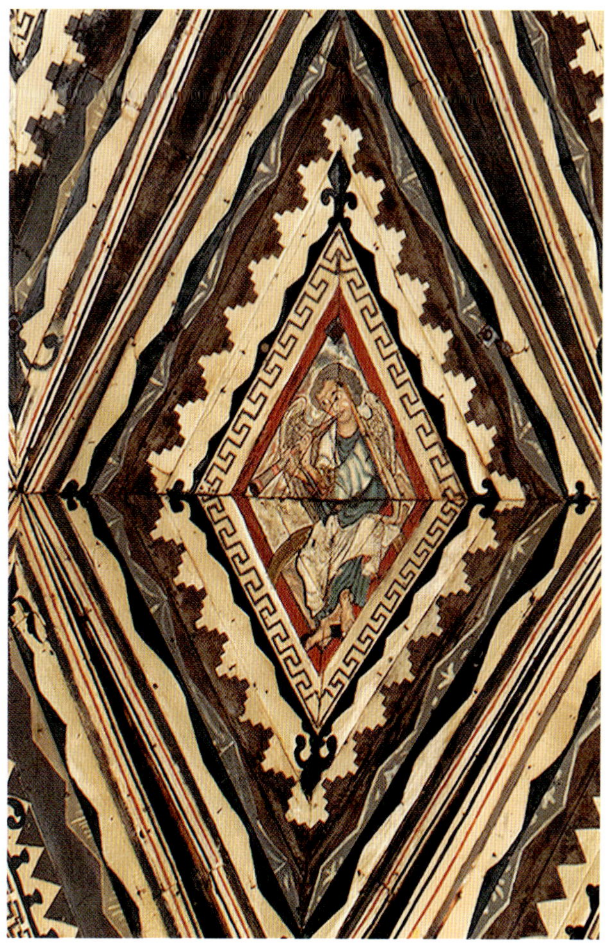

But who are these six kings? And which bishops are disputing with them? None are labelled. *Policraticus* advised against pinning blame so explicitly:

> Kings themselves have not been spared by the hand of God, which, for their wickedness, has inflicted deserved and signal punishment. We do not mention their names and the circumstances not because of lack of instances – perhaps indeed because of the difficulty of choosing amid such abundance – but in reality that we may avoid, by touching wounds still sore, causing additional pain to the smitten hearts of those still mourning. We have in fact many instances at home.

The company of six does not equate to the number of kings since the Norman Conquest, nor does it tally with ancient Saxon rulers. But it is precisely the

Above left **Geometry, one of the Seven Liberal Arts.**

Above **An angel, shown as an appropriate arbiter of music in a church.**

number of monarchs since the start of construction of the present church, raising the possibility that the figures represent the sequence of monarchs and notable bishops involved with the abbey church as it approached completion. If so, we would expect there to be a reason for two archbishops, some tell-tale symbols and a narrative that favours the ecclesiasts.

When we look closely, some visual attributes provide subtle clues. Tantalisingly, the third king from the west has a uniquely white background that draws the attention; he was no doubt once identifiable by the text on his conspicuous banner, but it is now painted blank. Among the most notorious kings was Henry II (1154–89), held responsible for the death of Becket. Subsequently a penitent, he passed an exceptionally important law to 'concede that archbishoprics, bishoprics and abbacies shall not be held in my hand for more than a year…', which Peterborough may have wished to broadcast for posterity.[51]

If that is correct, the second figure eastward (beyond Richard I, 1189–99) should be the tyrannical King John (1199–1216), and indeed this character points to his sceptre, indicating a reputation for authoritarianism, the result of which was England's submission to the pope. The easternmost king should then be John's pious son, Henry III (1216–72), who had recently been depicted on the vaults of the east end of Canterbury Cathedral.[52] He is uniquely framed, this time within a mandorla (a pointed almond shape), a form in which Christ is usually set, and against gold stars on a green ground, a decorative scheme Henry favoured in his palaces. He holds a torch and faces St Paul, who met Christ and was blinded for three days by the light.

This, then, confirms the status of a king as the earthly incarnation of Christ, a role enacted in the coronation liturgy.[53] Flattery tends toward current incumbents, so this is almost certainly the correct order for the king who, in 1245, rebuilt the English coronation church of St Peter at Westminster and reformed the coronation rites according to the direction of Bishop Grosseteste of Lincoln. Grosseteste, Peterborough's bishop from 1235 and who re-consecrated the abbey in 1238, decreed that during the coronation the Seven Gifts of the Holy Ghost were conferred upon the monarch.[54] He also held there should be no secular interference in ecclesiastical courts, whereas the king insisted on controlling abbots. King Henry was being coerced.

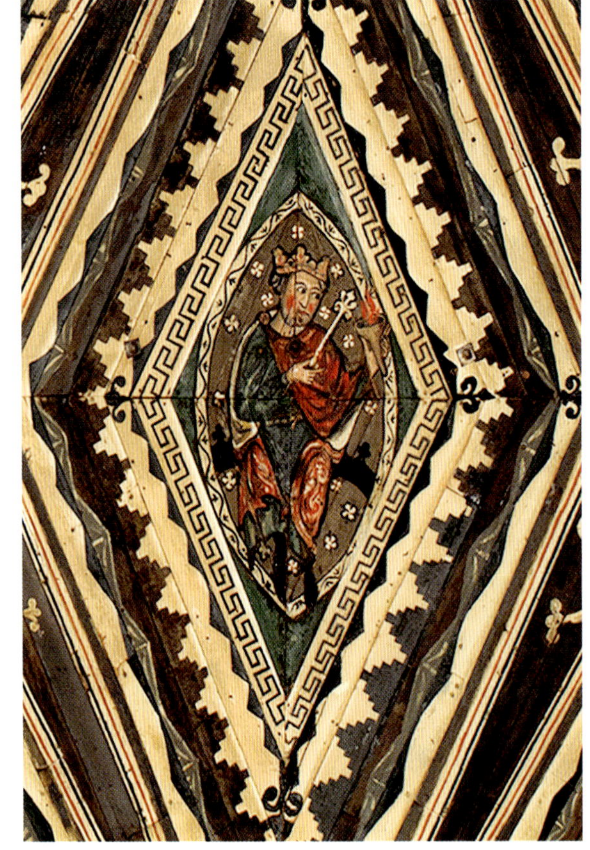

Below Henry III (1216–72), shown as a royal priest. The kingly emulation of Christ was far from new, but was now subject to promotion and refinement by Robert Grosseteste, bishop of Lincoln, who consecrated Peterborough in 1238, as the ceiling boards were being cut.

There seems to be sufficient evidence to propose this sequence:

HENRY I, 1100–35

Peterborough Abbey rebuilt anew from 1118. Refused papal legates, made ecclesiastical appointments, though this was customary.

BISHOP

Robert Bloet, bishop of Lincoln 1093–1123? Supposedly fell foul of Henry I, having served him as royal justiciar.

STEPHEN, 1135–54

The period of anarchy. Stephen confiscated bishops' properties, suspecting them of backing the rival claimant to the throne, Matilda, daughter of Henry I. Argued with the church over political primacy from 1140–52.

BISHOP

Alexander the Magnificent? Bishop of Lincoln during the Battle of Lincoln, 1141. Stephen confiscated his castles in a power struggle in 1139.

HENRY II, 1154–89

King with elaborate scroll, lost script. Came to Peterborough in 1154. John of Salisbury's *Policraticus,* a treatise on the ethics of Christian princes, was written in 1159 and dedicated to Thomas Becket, who was slain under Henry's orders in 1170. Challenged in the 'Earls' Revolt' of 1175 by knights of the soke of Peterborough, leading to his deposition of Abbot William Waterville.

BISHOP

Conceals Bible text, hence appeals to some other rationale – temporal law of Henry II? Possibly Hugh of Lincoln, who checked Henry II's will by excommunicating royal foresters and insisting on his own election to Lincoln.

RICHARD I, 1189–99

Richard the Lionheart, crusading king.

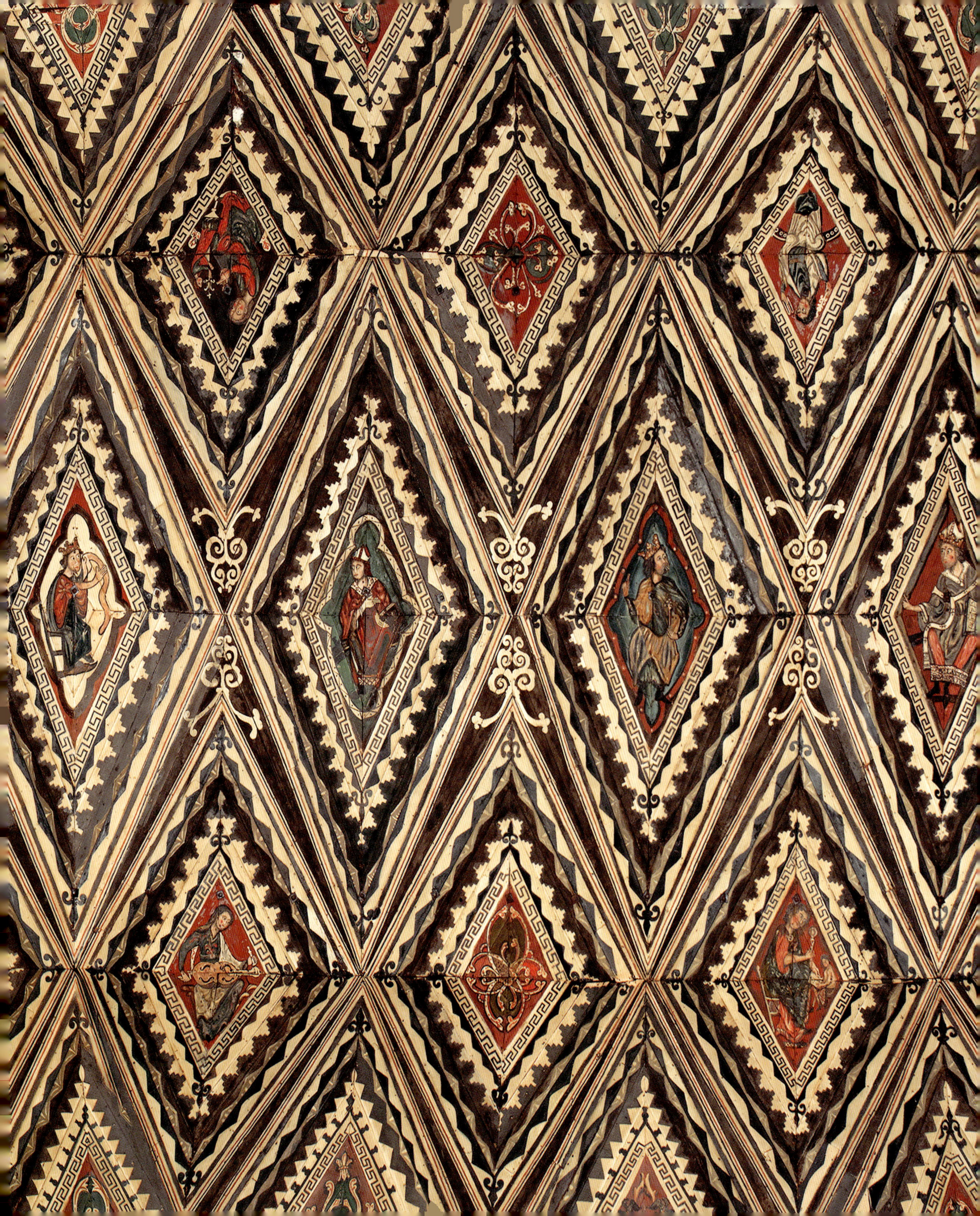

ARCHBISHOP

Hubert Walter of Canterbury, chief justiciar? Accompanied Richard I on the Third Crusade, negotiated with Saladin.

JOHN, 1199–1216

Points to sceptre, relating to his papal power struggle. Confiscated Peterborough's revenues for four years. Yielded England to papal rule in 1213. Proclaimed anyone supporting Archbishop Langton a public enemy.

ARCHBISHOP

Stephen Langton of Canterbury, archbishop during John's excommunication. Attended 4th Lateran Council in Rome, 1215, with Robert Lindsey, abbot of Peterborough. Architect of Magna Carta, divided the Bible into its present structure.

Henry III, 1216–72

Christ-like mandorla; holding the light of truth to St Paul. Granted the abbey a market at Kettering and annual Lent fair in 1227. Nave ceiling completed in his reign, early 1240s.

[Grosseteste of Lincoln may not have wished to be portrayed in a scene of current personal politics with Henry III. Instead the theme turns to St Paul to flatter and encourage the king]

Next in sequence from this parade of modern Christian princes who steered Peterborough's recent past is the contrasting tomfoolery of an ape holding an owl while riding a goat backwards. This theme, which has ancient origins, involves three unclean animals. The monkey represents the avatar for uncivilised mankind, disputing with the owl, a nocturnal bird that fouls its nest and shuns the light, while riding a goat to its fate, the transport of medieval criminals. In the flanking panels, we start to see bad musicians, such as an ass braying while impossibly plucking a harp with its hooves, throwing into contrast the sober purpose and discipline of the monk's choir below. Once again the theme is found in *Policraticus*, which explains that:

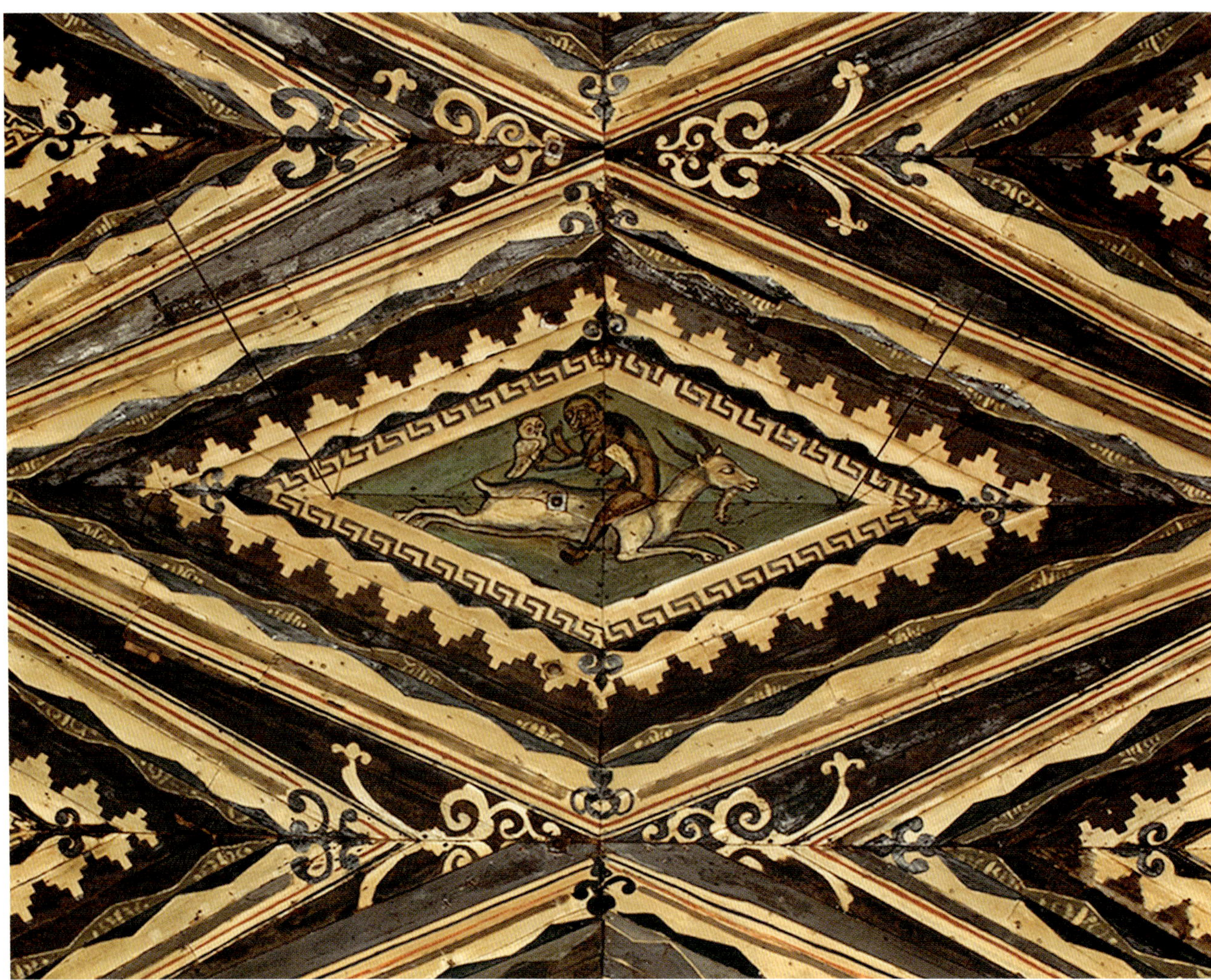

Above **Three unclean beasts: a monkey imparts its idiocy to an owl while riding backwards on a charging goat whose direction it cannot gauge.**

The very service of the Church is defiled, in that before the face of the Lord, in the very sanctuary of sanctuaries, they, showing off as it were, strive with the effeminate dalliance of wanton tones and musical phrasing…when this type of music is carried to the extreme it is more likely to stir lascivious sensations in the loins than devotion in the heart.

To continue the central row, St Peter stands at St Paul's other side to this nonsense, holding aloft his keys while addressing us face-on, to remind all that only good behaviour begets a mansion in heaven. Eastward again is the model for emulation, the *agnus dei*, Christ portrayed as the pure white 'lamb of God' whose blood was sacrificed for mankind's salvation as the price of Paradise. Saints Peter and Paul

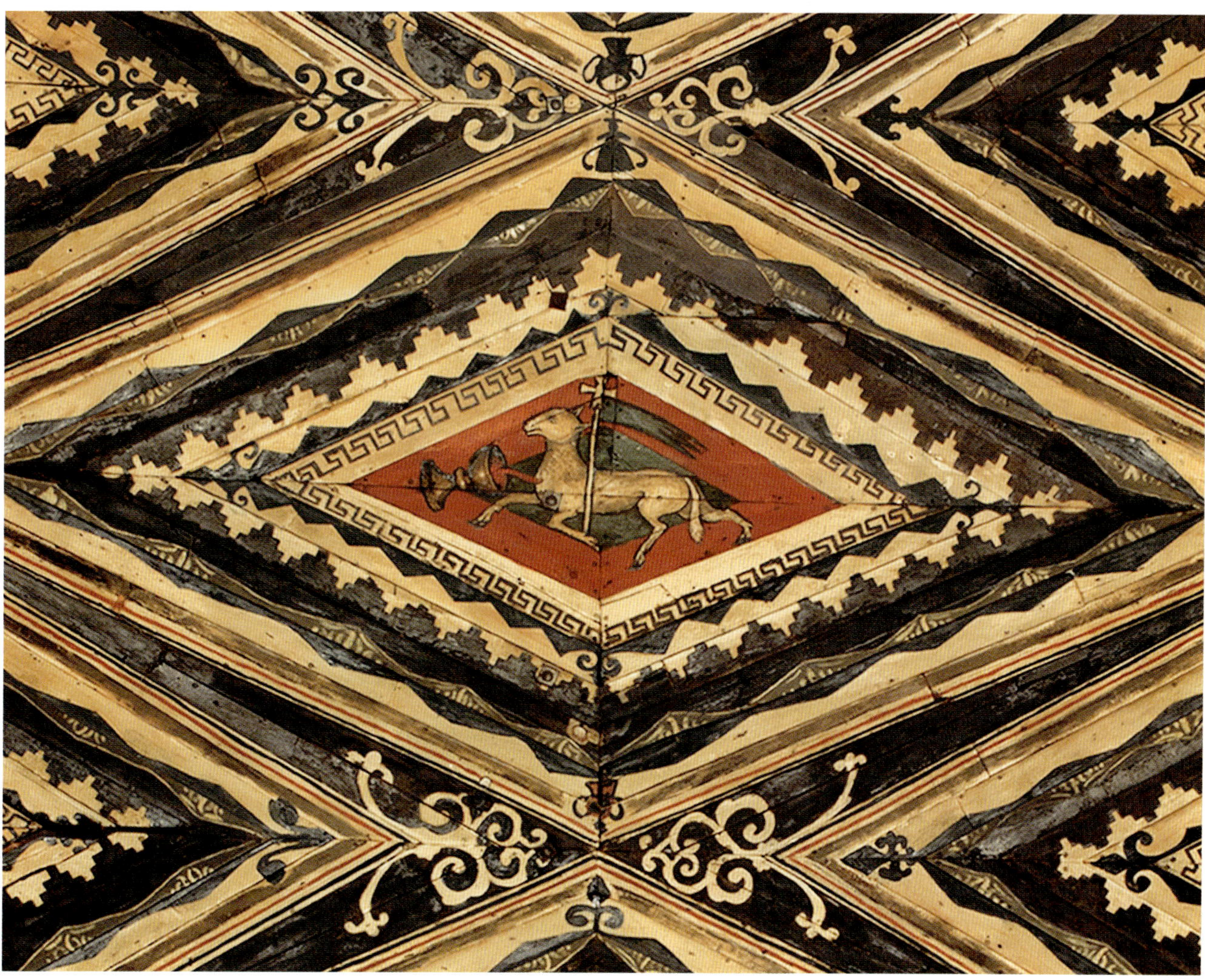

were recognised as the defenders of the lamb. The lamb's blood is shown being let into a chalice as communion wine, the dogma of transubstantiation having recently been accepted through the Fourth Lateran Council in 1215.[55]

By yet further apt contrast, we are reminded that trouble remains in paradise; the garden of Eden was, after all, the realm of the serpent.[56] Right on cue in the next lozenge east is the devil, the foil to Christ's charity, the wolf to the lamb and, as St Peter declared in the apocrypha, the true culprit in the Magus story, being the sorcerer's possessor. His vulpine bloodthirst is magnified by terrifying flanking characters of a typically blood-sucking wolf-headed dragon (north), and an anthropophagus feasting on limbs (south).

This stark cautionary representation of heaven versus hell is further articulated by the next subject in turn, what is often taken to be a Janus head, looking simultaneously in two opposing directions. It is as likely to be Judas Iscariot, about whom *Policraticus* is curt: 'Influenced by repentance indeed, he hanged himself. He therefore ended his life by a death richly deserved.'

His fate forces a choice, because as well as gazing on the hopeless eternal hell of the devil – the fate of Simon Magus – Janus/Judas also looks to the final lozenge, comprising a fish surrounded by four beasts, usually taken to be lions. Now, at face value, this concluding imagery makes little sense. The beasts are curiously maneless, as would be four lionesses.[57] There is another possibility, if we can admit to confusing quadrupeds, for restorers did make mistakes.[58] It seems likelier that these were originally dogs, being closely comparable to those chasing rabbits in a manuscript owned by Peterborough Abbey after *c*.1220. Their significance on this concluding panel is that several hounds and a single fish were accessories to St Peter's triumph in the tales of Simon Magus. The sorcerer set ravenous dogs on Peter, who made them disappear, while as evidence of God's superior power, he made a cured fish return to life.[59] This brings a suitably coherent conclusion to Peterborough's narrative, which is surely the nation's greatest single political work of art of the thirteenth century.[60]

The ceiling was just the most major part of Abbot Walter of Bury's furnishing of the church. Beneath its eastern bays, the choir also swelled by 30 souls, who were accommodated in new oak choir stalls. To judge from the surviving fragments, incorporated into a later seat now within the north transept, they featured tall shafts terminating in stiff-leaf carving, much like the architecture of the recently completed west front, and particularly the wooden capital on its original door. The backs of the stalls featured images of biblical types and antitypes complementing the contrasting themes in the nave ceiling above.

For all this, Peterborough's remarkable west front and ceiling seem not to have been influential. The nave ceiling came at the end of a tradition, as stone vaults took over (or timber imitations of stone ribs), while the west front met with no known imitators, not least because most great churches were completed by the time it was finished, around 1230, or already had existing west towers as a basis for added screen facades.[61]

English thirteenth-century great churches had another clear priority. From the late 1100s, the popularity of the Virgin Mary had been on the ascendant. Although little information on Christ's mother was offered in the Bible, her identity had been forged in the late Antique world by adapting the mould of Aphrodite/Venus, while apocryphal texts filled in the gaps, explaining her bodily assumption into heaven in lieu of a shrine around any mortal remains.

In the early twelfth century the reforming Cistercian abbot St Bernard of Clairvaux (1091–1153) underlined Mary's identification with the colours red and

PETERBOROUGH'S MARBLE EFFIGIES

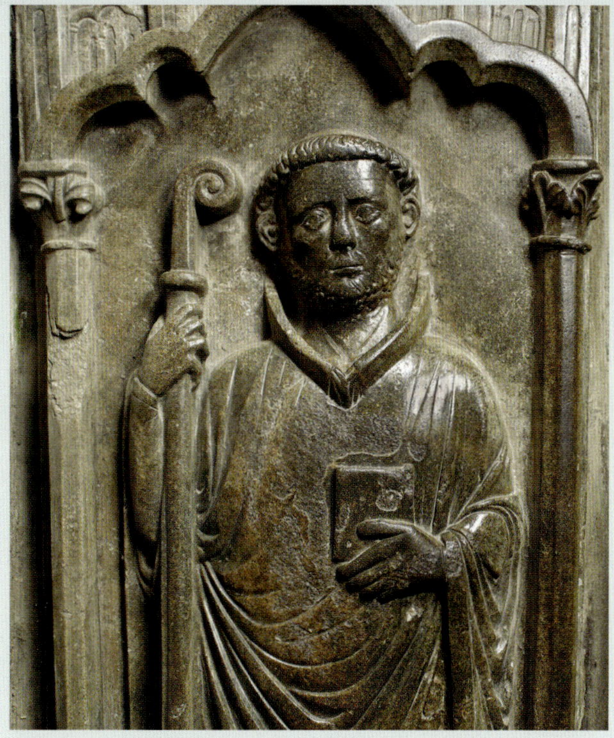

Alwalton 'marble' is a Jurassic stone composed of oyster shells. Difficult to carve, it is resilient and accepts a glossy finish. It was used for the shafts of the west front after 1195 and for the early thirteenth-century font bowl at the west end of the nave. Peterborough retains five funerary effigies of its Benedictine abbots from this era, carved in Alwalton marble, the finest collection in one church. None are in their original positions, for they were smashed, defaced or displaced in the Civil War.

Above and above right The identity of the five figures is disputed. Architectural historian Dr Ron Baxter suggests that while all five date to after *c*.1200, these, with higher relief, are likely to belong to the years *c*.1220–30. This is too late for Abbot Benedict's death, but they may be part of a suite cut in retrospect to improve tomb monuments.

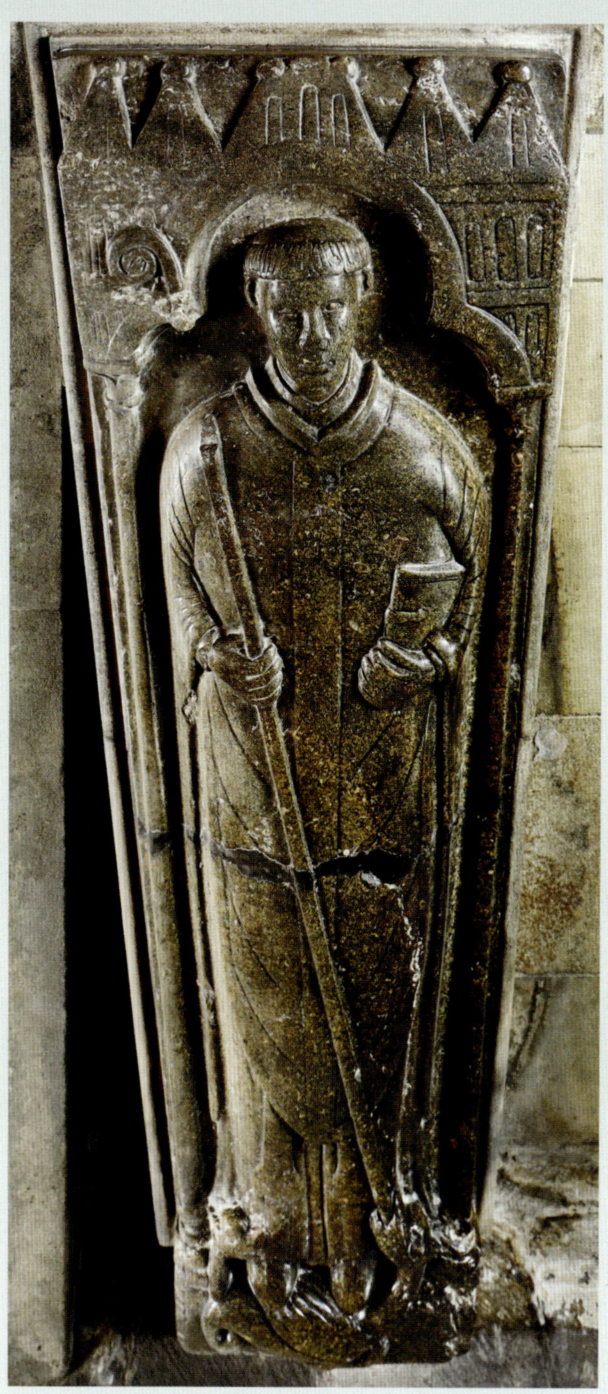

white: red for her charity in the blood her sacrificed son spilled for mankind; white for her virginal chastity. He also dedicated all the highly influential Cistercian abbeys to her. Mary was seen as promising the end of the road travelled by medieval Catholics: the figure whose sorrows eclipsed and absorbed their own and who would welcome them to a garden symbolising her own impregnability. Peterborough was on the route to Walsingham Abbey 60 miles east, Mary's principal shrine in England, which had developed over the scene of an eleventh-century miracle.

As Queen of Heaven, she was shown by artists and sculptors draped with white and red roses, in scenes of an eternally fertile and warm spring. Many such images were presented in Lady Chapels, England's distinctive architectural response to Marianism, which usually projected east from great churches. Peterborough's

Below The site of the Lady Chapel; there was also a smaller chapel between the Lady Chapel and the north aisle of the quire.

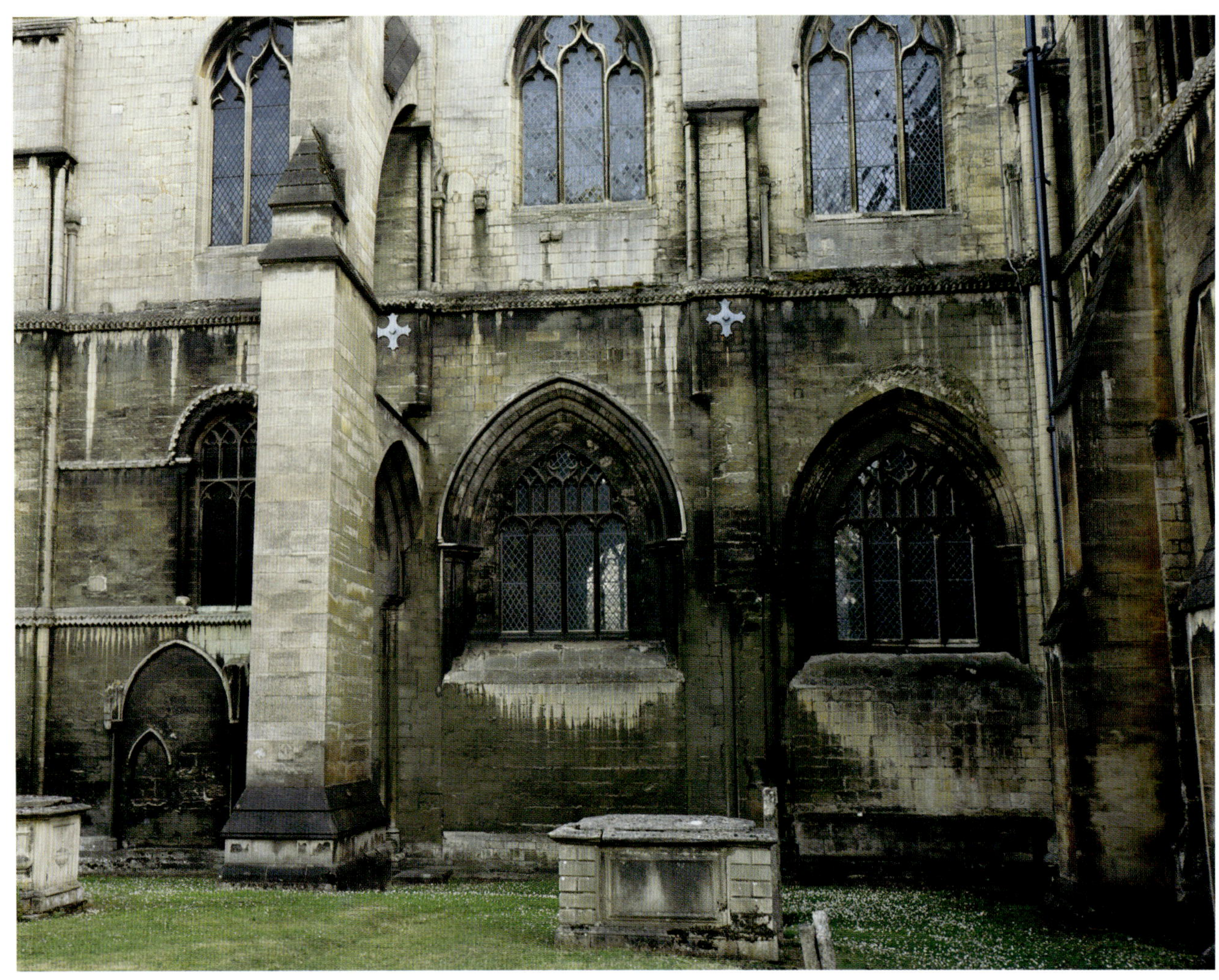

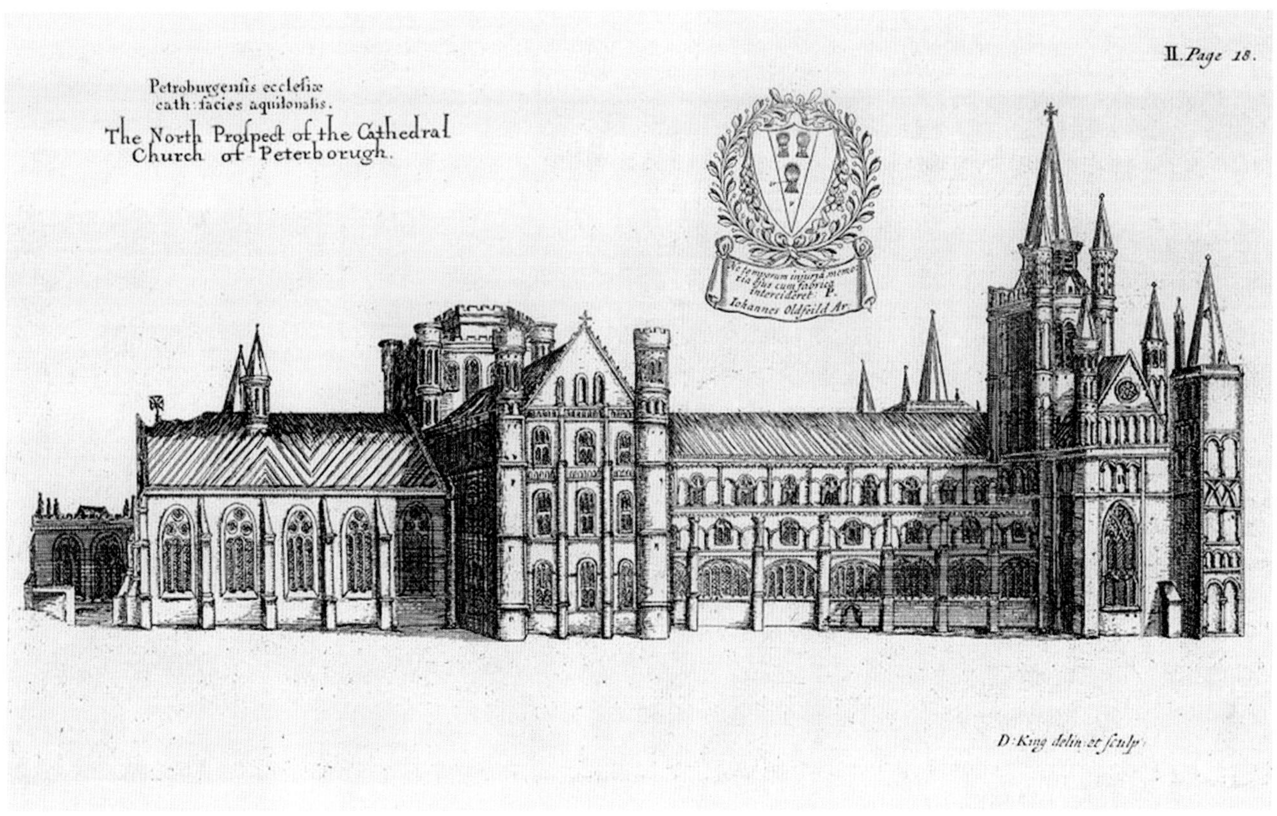

rectangular Lady Chapel was set north of the presbytery and was reached through the north transept. This has been compared to Ramsey Abbey, but it also followed the pattern of a chapel that stood parallel to the influential Angel Quire of 1256–80 at St Mary's Cathedral, Lincoln.[62] Peterborough's Lady Chapel had bar-tracery like Lincoln's Angel Quire, and a leaded roof. As the chapel was pulled down in the seventeenth century, we are left to imagine how the interior was sculpted, painted and furnished, but it certainly had a gilded ceiling and fine stained glass (as a metaphorical reference to Mary, since glass is penetrated – by light – and yet remains uncorrupted). While it existed, it influenced the position and shape of the greatest Lady Chapel in the land, at Ely Cathedral.

Peterborough had broadcast its political anxiety through applied arts with good reason. In 1262 Robert Sutton acceded to the abbacy and allied himself with the barons to occupy Northampton in defiance of Henry III. When the king regained power, the abbey was fined in payments to the royal family and subjected to a pledge of allegiance; when the barons took the upper hand they in turn fined the abbey for disloyalty – in all £4324 18s 3d was disbursed.

Above Daniel King's engraving, made after the Civil War, shows the Lady Chapel positioned inaccurately, being too far south: the line of the gable remains impressed on the east face of the north transept (see image on p.45)

THE FOURTEENTH CENTURY

Warm summers had brought plentiful harvests during the two centuries up to 1300. That proved to be a significant year for adherents of St Peter. Impressed by the growth of pilgrimage crowds, Pope Boniface VIII called a Jubilee, offering absolution to all who would travel to the saint's remains in Rome. Forgiveness and plenty must have seemed a panacea – until Pope Boniface overreached in his own presumptions of supreme authority in 1303 and the papacy was forcibly removed to Avignon.[63]

During these years Edward I, conqueror of Wales, visited the abbey, while the Thorpe family, its stewards and land agents, built a handsome new tower at their manor house in Longthorpe, decorated by an exceptional suite of wall-paintings. At about the same time, wall-paintings of heraldry and seated figures were added to Peterborough's choir, probably under the wealthy and energetic abbot Godfrey of Croyland (1299–1321), an enthusiast of excess who was charged with adultery, the death of his chamberlain and sharing his monks' confessions.[64]

In July 1307 Edward I bequeathed the throne to his 23-year old son Edward II. That year the abbey began work on the first bridge over the Nene, bringing trade and traffic to the abbey gate, which was being crenellated, as was the Knight's Chamber entrance to the abbot's palace. The nobles' alarm at the prominence afforded to Edward's favourite, Piers Gaveston of Gascony, found focus in the East Midlands, headed by Henry Earl of Lincoln on behalf of the local barons, whose grievances were addressed in the Statutes of Stamford in 1309.

Within two years, in 1311, Edward was forced to accept a series of Ordinances limiting royal power and Gaveston was thrown into exile. His beheading in 1312 allowed for compromise with the barons, and Edward II chose to show his strength by taking on the rebellious Scots. He came to Peterborough in 1314 on his way to Bannockburn, near Stirling, where he assembled around 20,000 English troops, only to be bogged down and defeated by Robert the Bruce, in a travesty of his father's successes in Wales. Amid such turmoil, the age of militant confidence and high spending was waning. The following year, Edward passed through Peterborough again, a king in retreat.

After a spate of cold winters, the rains began in May 1315 and did not let up until September. The deluge laid waste to crops across northern Europe and grain production fell 30% below the previous decade, producing a crop which failed to feed the burgeoning population. Peterborough fell into debt, which was blamed on the hospitality budget, wars and exactions by the profligate king. The abbey's reliance on the tithes from agricultural income was jeopardised; although

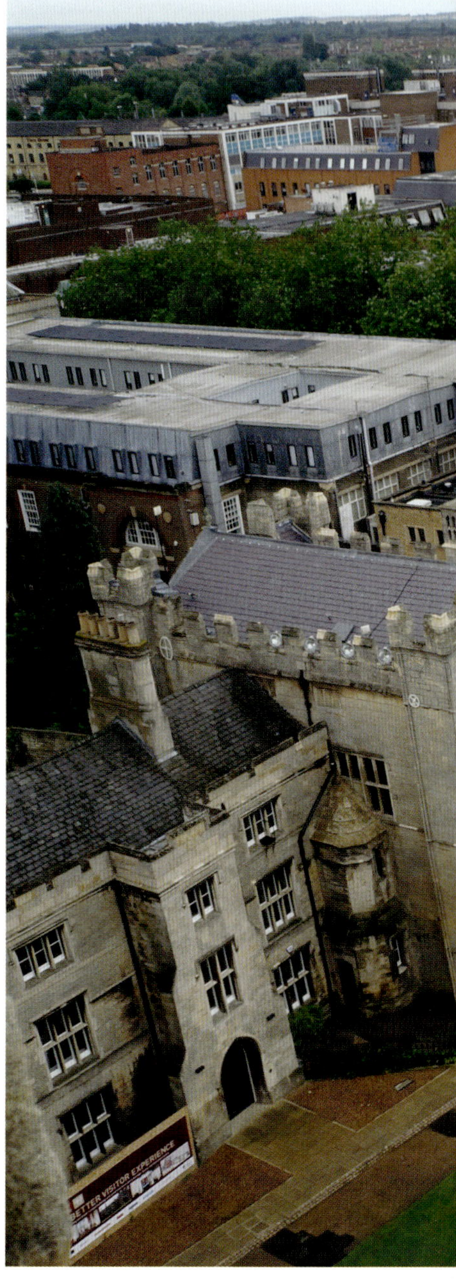

Above The close, showing the late thirteenth-century Knight's Chamber with intact statuary, the twelfth-century entrance gate, remodeled in the early fourteenth century, and the late twelfth-century Becket Chapel, rebuilt with a large new east window during Edward III's early reign.

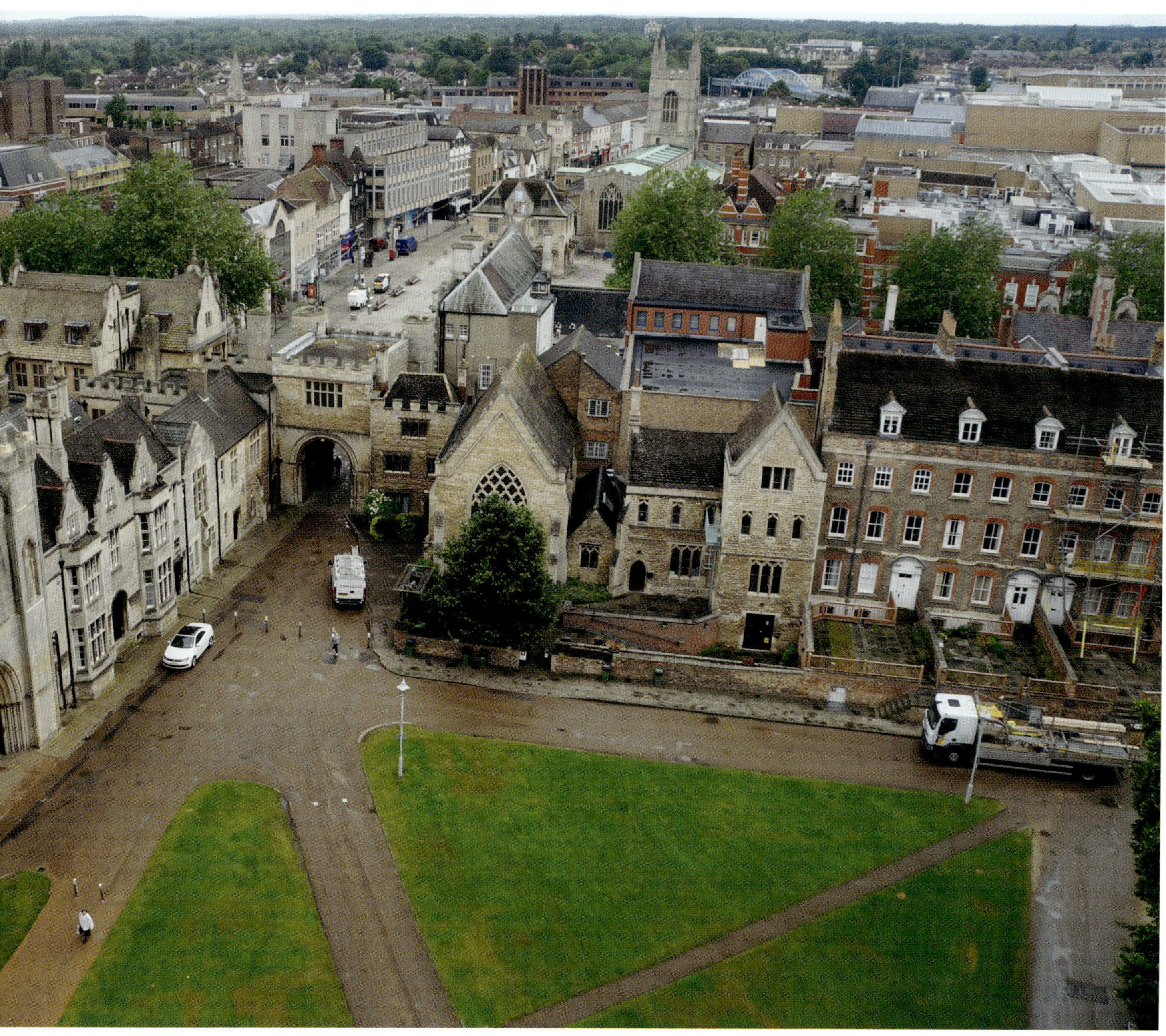

grain was suddenly six times as expensive, there was much less of it. Many were forced to the decision to eat seed crops, when a bushel of wheat was needed to grow the next year's harvest. By such grim economies, the famine lasted seven years. Coincident comets and earthquakes created popular fear that apocalyptic pestilence would follow. It surely did, though the Black Death would take three decades to arrive.

THE PETERBOROUGH PSALTER

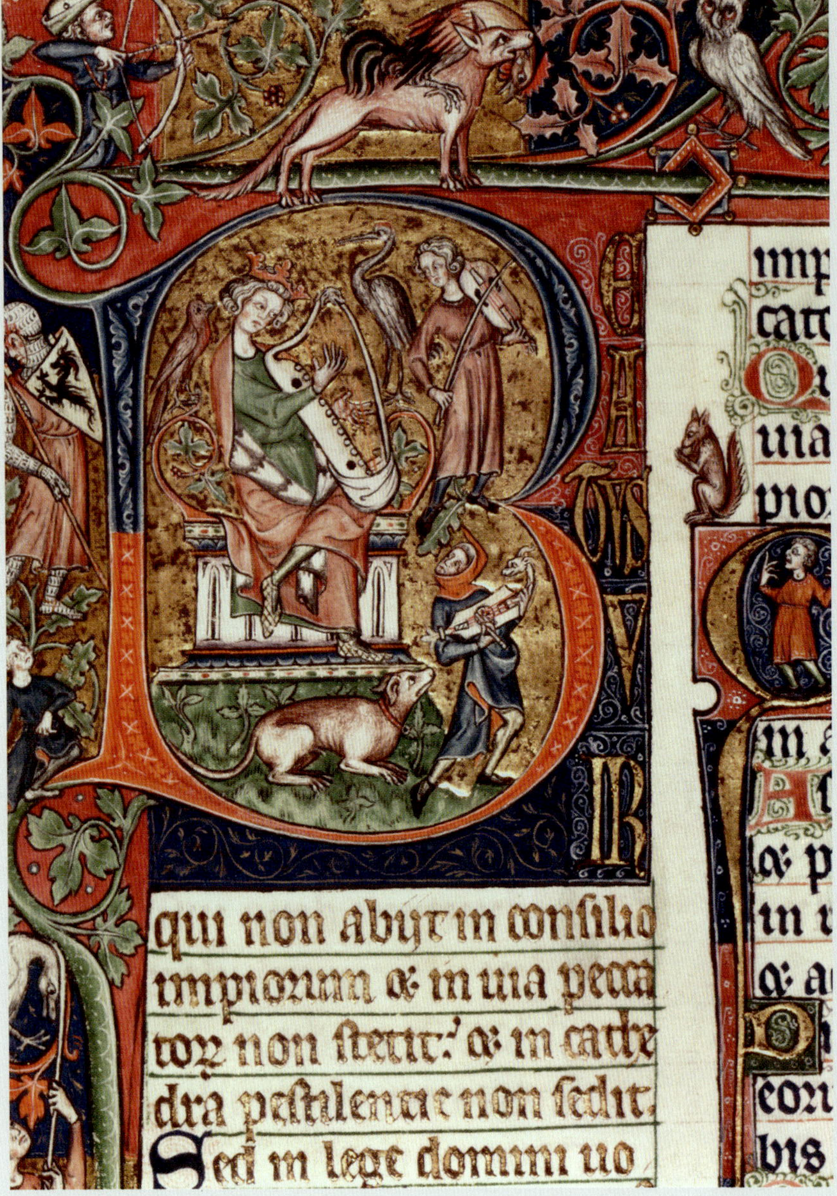

Sometime before 1318, the abbey scriptorium was charged with the production of a richly-illustrated psalter, for Abbot Godfrey of Croyland. Psalters illustrated the psalms, and this volume features biblical 'types' probably gleaned from the paintings on the backs of Peterborough's thirteenth-century choirstalls, which in turn were derived from the windows of Canterbury Cathedral.

The psalter's ownership is no less remarkable, since it passed from Godfrey to Pope John XXII (1316–34) in Avignon. We are left to speculate about the connection between Godfrey; Isabella, the young French Queen of Edward II, who came to the abbey in 1314; and Peterborough's gift to the French pope. Thereafter, the psalter passed to Clémence of Hungary, Queen of France; Philip VI of Valois; the Louvre Library; Philip the Good of Burgundy; and eventually to the Bibliothèque Royale de Belgique in Brussels.

Above **The Peterborough Psalter, gorgeously limned. Among the rich imagery, the central meaning lies in the queenly figure facing a squirrel eating a nut; the ingested seed symbolises pregnancy. The words 'BEATVS VIR[GINE]' leave us in no doubt that this portends Christ.**

Abbot Adam de Boothby (1321–30) was a sub-cellarer, presumably elevated from his humble station as a relief from Godfrey of Croyland's outrageous *modus vivendi*. Boothby had to dig deep to fund a spate of royal visits by Edward III, starting in 1327, then annually between 1332 (when he brought his mother, sisters and three bishops for 10 days at Easter) and 1336. The 1332 visit cost almost the entire annual revenue from the abbey's manors across six counties. Still, funds were found to remodel the chancel of the Becket Chapel. It is tempting to think of the timing of this investment in Becket's presence as an extension of the royal politics of the nave ceiling.

This was just part of Peterborough's facelift. At the other end of the abbey, windows were inserted to illuminate the apse. Each is different, contributing further to the effect of variety in the twelfth-century piers. The interior of these windows features canopies of flying ribs in the style of Bristol Priory (now Cathedral). Builders set up scaffolding on the west front and reached for the skies to build the south-western spire, in an exceptionally accomplished design. But the community at Peterborough was watching even greater industry across the fens at Ely, where the central tower collapsed in 1321, to be rebuilt as a spectacular octagon with a timber lantern of eight beams, each weighing 10 tons. Its opening matched the height and width of the oculus of the Pantheon in Rome, by then a church dedicated to St Mary.[65] The following year, Ely also started work on its vast Lady Chapel, with its finely-carved detail setting new standards of intricate workmanship in the region through to its completion in 1348–49.

Peterborough Abbey set about a scheme for its own central tower, whose mass was too great for the slender crossing piers below, risking Ely's fate. To judge

Above The fourteenth-century timber quire ceiling. Blue commonly evoked heaven; against it, the network of gilded bosses seems to form an ordered constellation. It was repainted under Dean Saunders (1853–78), having been 'at one time painted all over yellow and white', according to the Rev. W.D. Sweeting.

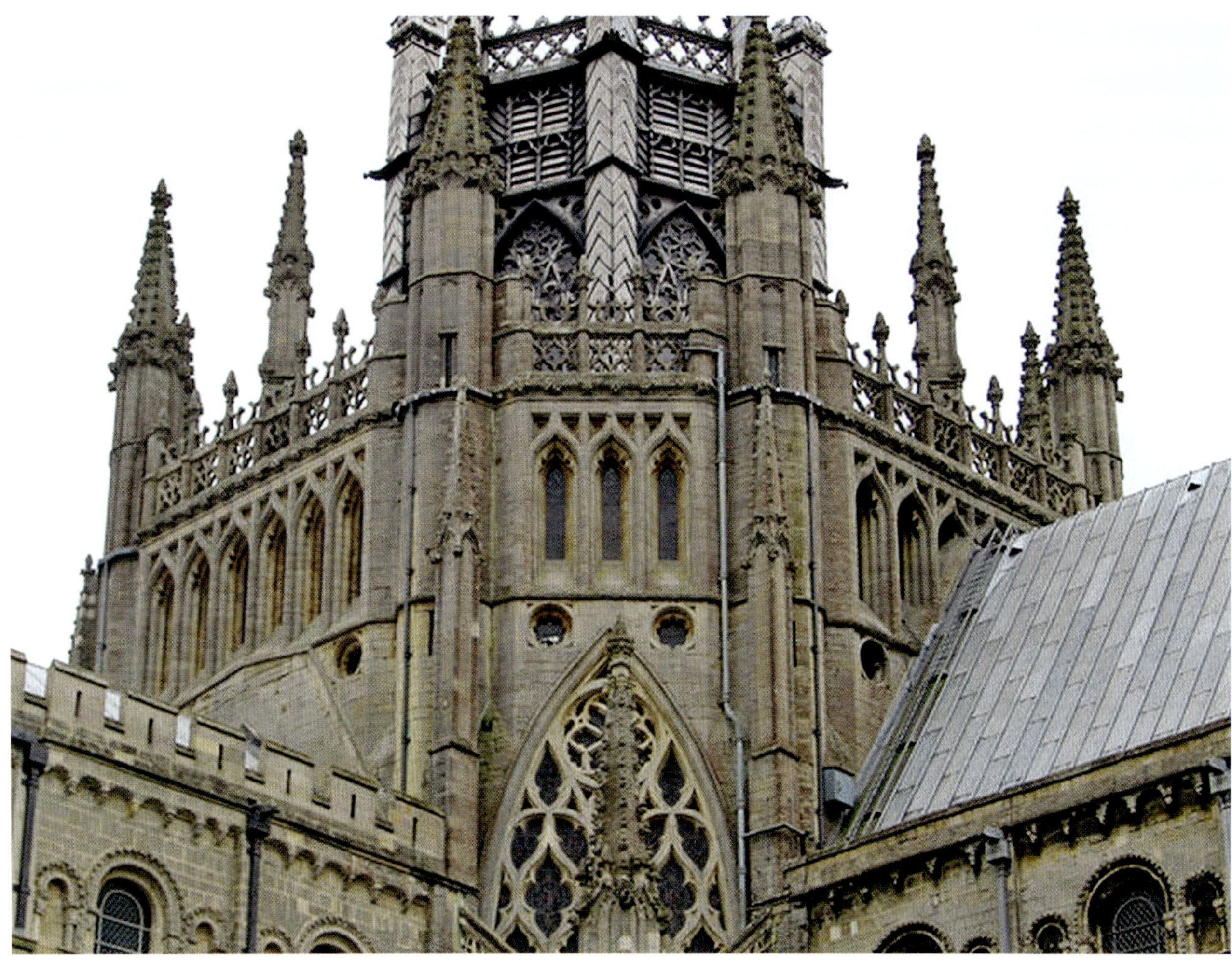

from the tracery of the lantern stage, this work started around the 1340s. Without replacing the crossing piers, Peterborough could not imitate Ely's broad octagon, but large windows lightened the load while illuminating the choir below. The masonry shell of the tower was probably in progress when disaster struck.

The Black Death came in June 1348, a scythe sweeping the land from the south. That God seemed to have deserted the people was a lament marked elsewhere in graffiti; it is unrecorded what the monks of Peterborough felt as half their number, 32 out of 64 brothers, was suddenly consigned to the earth. After five years of death and fear, discipline was impoverished among those who remained. Hugh de Spalding broke the abbey's locks and gates and took to hunting and fishing, then in 1360 the monks violently attacked secular clerks. War resumed when Edward III and his son Edward (later called the Black Prince) set off for France in 1356, as the fundamental shift of social order led to the Peasants' Revolt in 1381:

… at Burgh (Peterborough) the neighbours and tenants of the abbot rose against him and proposed to kill him – which they would have done without redress had God not laid his restraining hand upon them at the last moment. For help came in the shape of Lord Henry Despenser, bishop of Norwich, who, through the agency of divine mercy, arrived with a strong force.

Several were killed, but violence was not the only issue. The rise of Lollardy brought worship in vernacular English, which threatened the millennium-old Catholic Latin tradition that Peterborough stood for.

Amid this turbulence, work on Peterborough's central tower lumbered on. It was eventually provided with an octagonal drum, which survived into the nineteenth century. Over it, a timber spire was probably envisaged and possibly completed. Without a superstructure to support, the octagon was pointless; the timber vault inserted beneath, dating to the 1370s, never had a central opening to transmit light.

Below *Peterborough Cathedral from the North-East*, by J.C. Buckler, *c.*1812, showing Peterborough's fourteenth-century octagonal spire base. This poses questions as to precisely what form of spire it supported, and what happened to it.

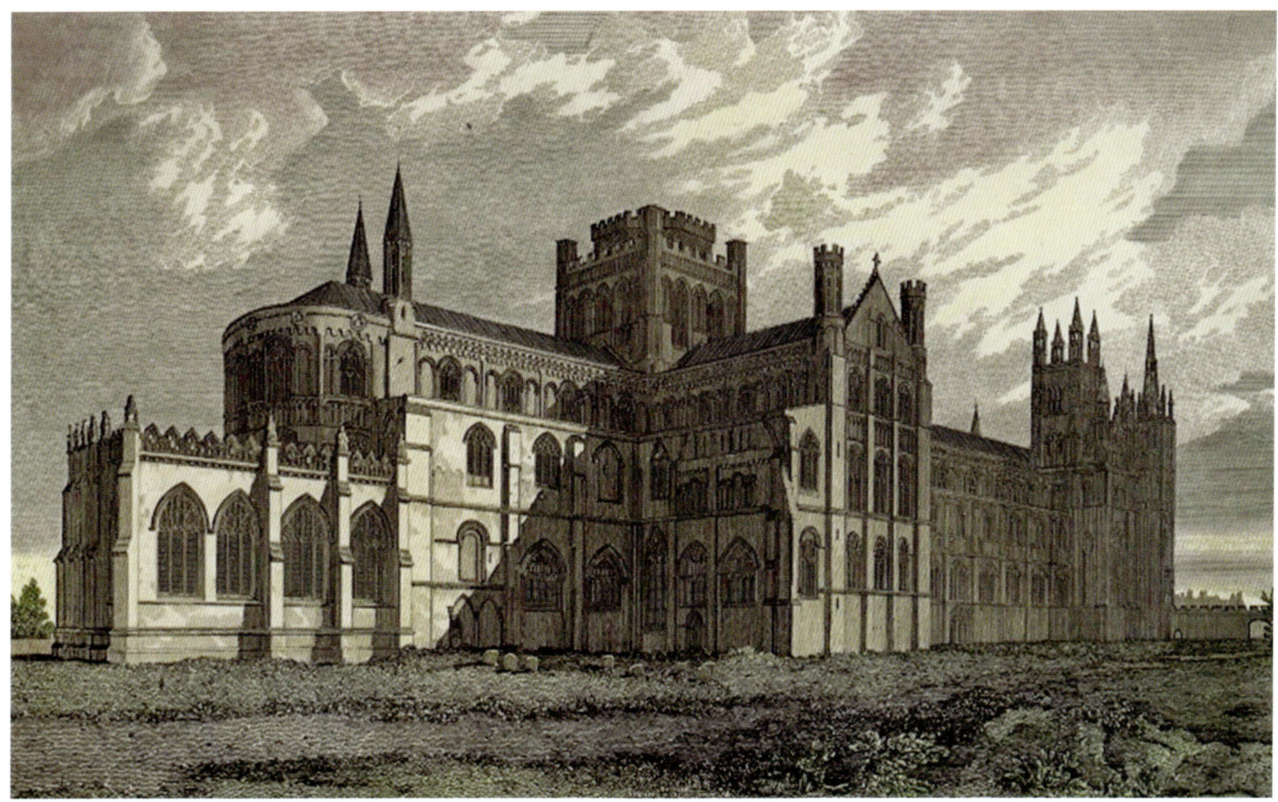

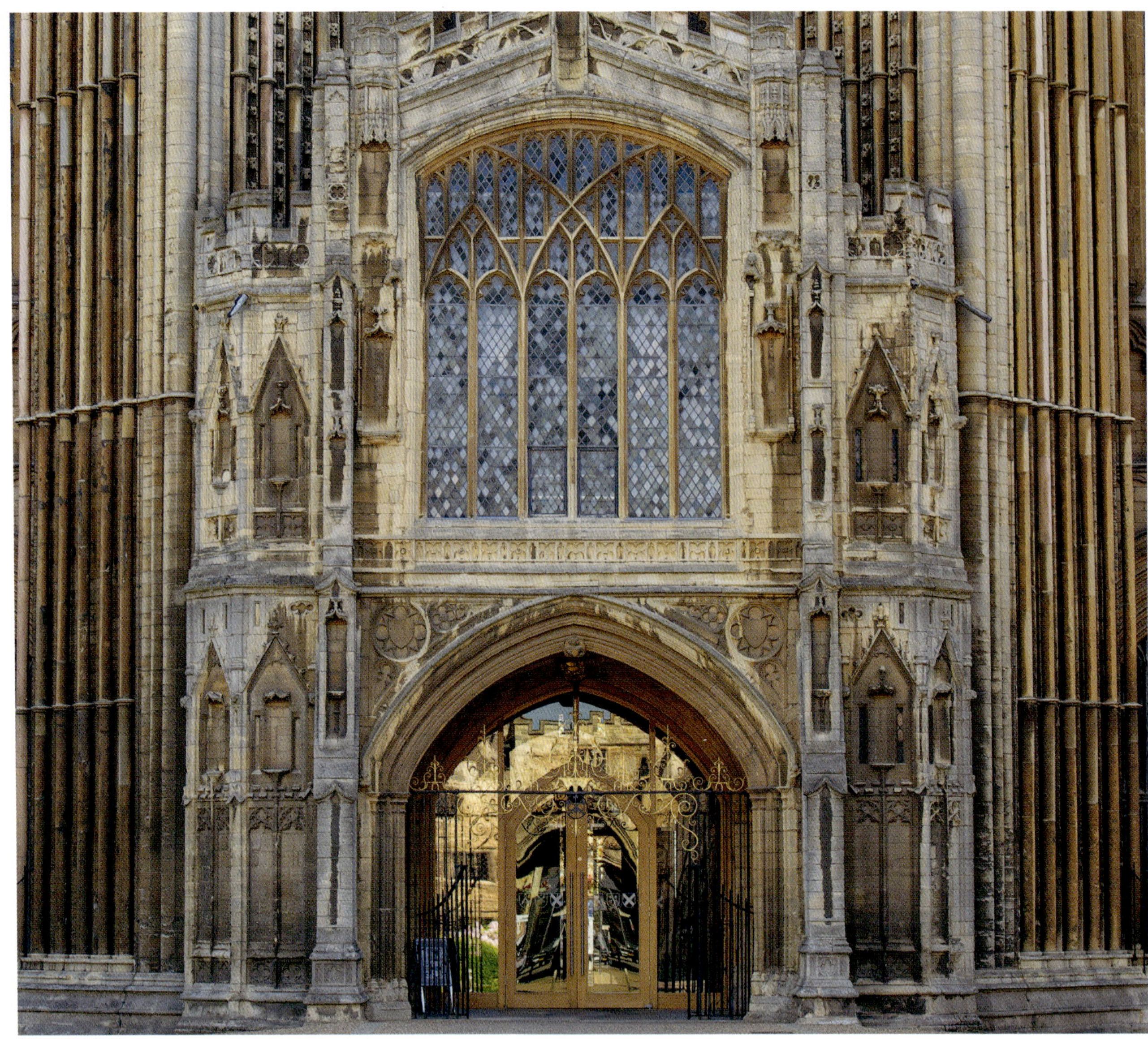

As the carpenters worked on the tower vault, masons assembled at the west front to fill the lower half of the central arch with a new porch, a room reached by a stair vice above a stone vaulted passage. The bosses on the porch ceiling carry the important symbolism. Closest to the main door we find the Trinity, God shown with his head as the sun, the giver of life on earth and the perennial spring of the garden of paradise. Mary appears to the left. Westward, a pelican pecks its breast to feed blood to its young, a symbol of Christ's blood sacrifice. Next we find the Assumption of the Virgin at the centre of the western bay, where she is bodily carried aloft by angels to assume her role as queen of heaven. As evidence of an

Above The mid fourteenth-century porch, with an early essay in what came to be called 'Perpendicular' window tracery illuminating its upper storey. The gabled tabernacles likely evoked the mansions of heaven that housed the saints, while its crenellations form a fortress defending the celestial realm against hell.

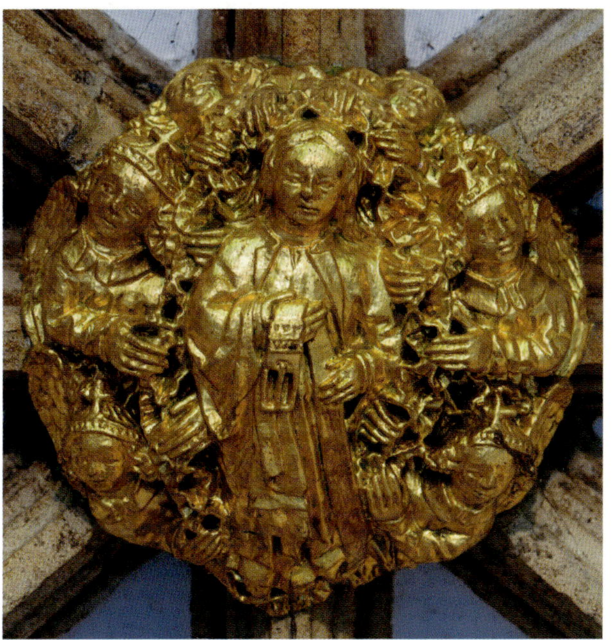 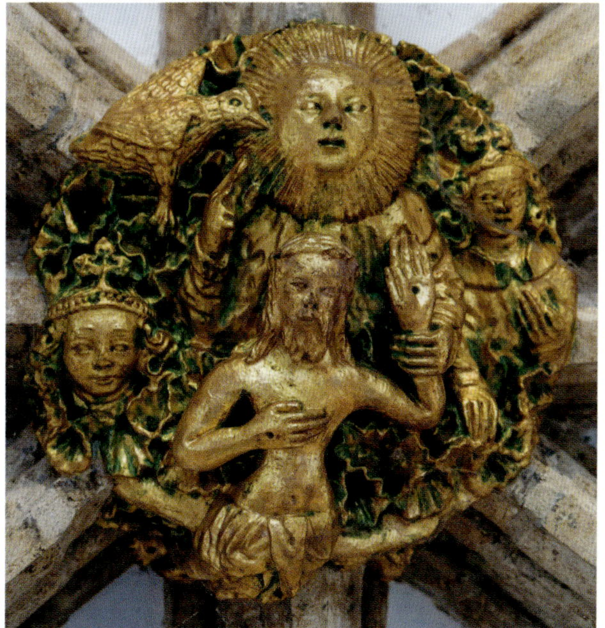

event not described in the Bible, she drops her girdle, claimed to be the principal relic of Prato Cathedral in Tuscany.[66] Marian roses frame the main arch, the five red petals symbolising the wounds of Christ, next to painted shields. The porch thus gives visitors an insight into the price paid for their promise of heaven; it was won by the sacrifice of Christ's blood, given by God and the Virgin as their son.

Strictly the nave reached through this porch was a public space, but Peterborough had its own parish church. In 1402 Abbot William Genge became the abbey's first mitred abbot, acquiring the powers of a bishop. He was the rector of the old church of St John the Baptist (to the east of the abbey) and made an agreement with the citizens who were 'sorrowfully complaining that in wintertime, when the rains overflow, they are not able […] to go to their parish church'. The solution was to build the present church by the well-trodden market place, with salvaged materials from both the old church and the protruding nave of St Thomas, the Becket Chapel, by the abbey gate.[67] The latter must either have been little used or in serious need of repair by then, perhaps both, and the lone chancel of the Becket Chapel remains today inside the gatehouse. It says much about the small size of Peterborough that St John's was its only medieval parish church.

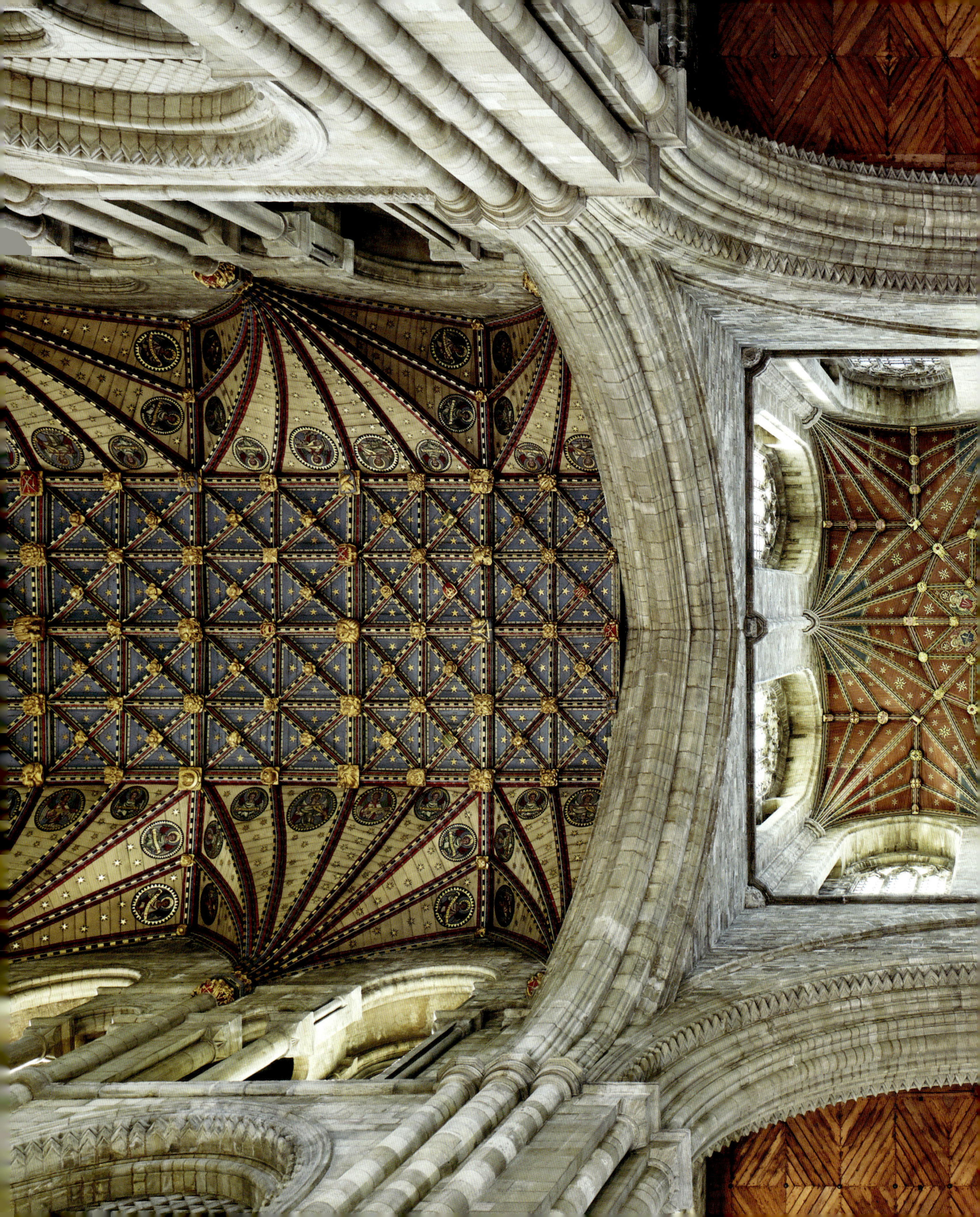

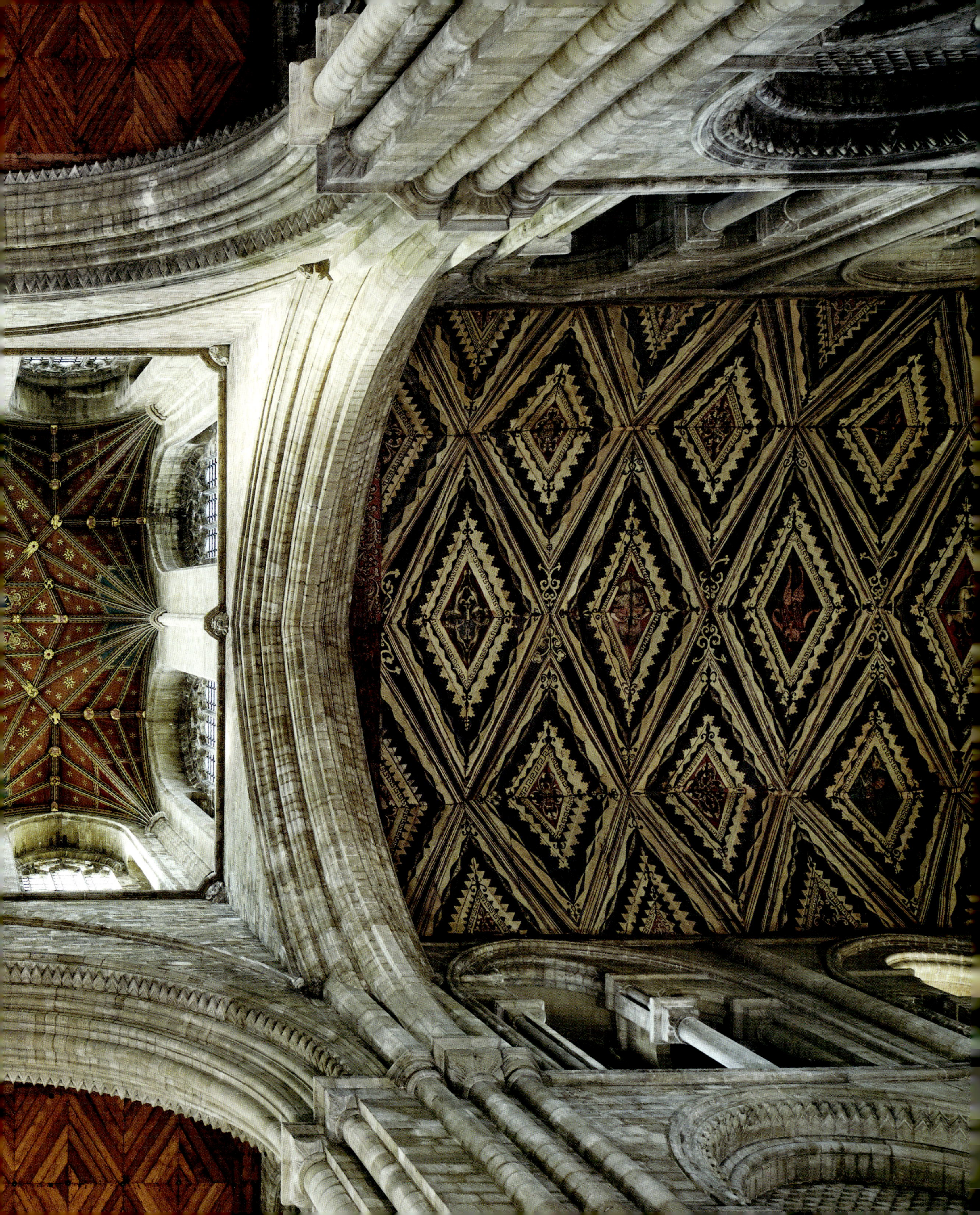

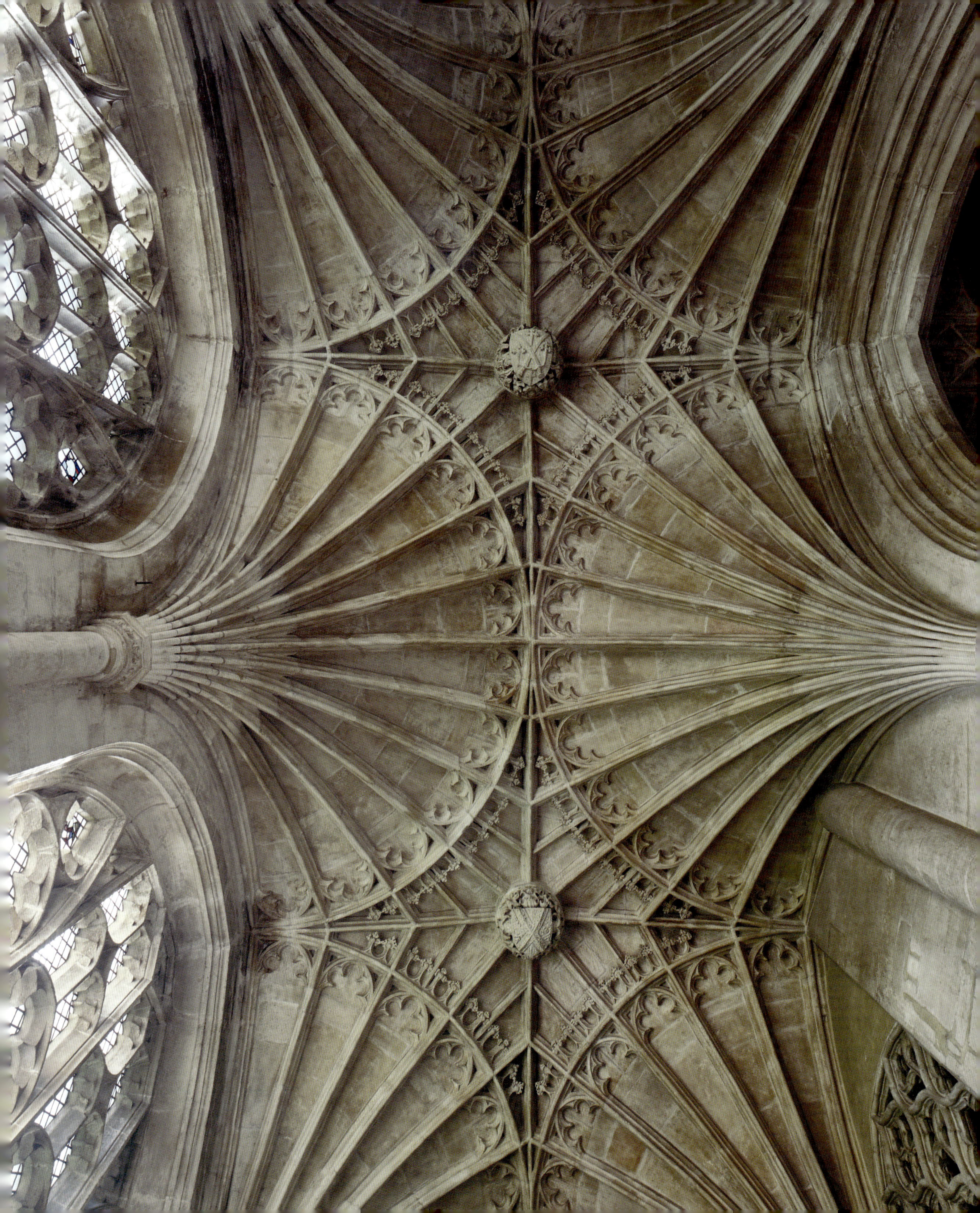

5

THE END OF AN ERA

*Royal art became distinctly continental,
embroiled with organic vegetation
and richly symbolic*

The early Tudor period saw a final flourishing of architectural ambition in the technically and aesthetically outstanding form of Abbot Kirkton's New Building. Great patron as he was, however, Kirkton was also part of the problem, neglecting his duties and his monks. Dissolution of Peterborough's monastery came only 20 years later – followed by the immediate reinvention of the church as a cathedral.

FIFTEENTH-CENTURY FASHION demanded large openings of tracery in stone and timber. The old windows of the transepts were replaced with new stone tracery, while a screen was set across the nave to match the pattern of windows in the aisles; this can now be found reconfigured to serve as the parclose screens of the north transept. The brass eagle lectern symbolic of St John, the assumed author of the Book of Revelation in which heaven was promised, was delivered in 1471–96, by Abbot William of Ramsey.

When Robert Kirkton was installed as abbot of Peterborough on 13 March 1497, Henry VII had reigned for over a decade, in what would become one of the most famous and disputed periods of English history. Some received ideas remain misunderstandings. What we call the Tudor age was not recognised as such then, for the king did not hang his royal identity on his Welsh family name but on his descent from Edward III, through the Lancastrian line.[68] Nor was the double rose a 'Tudor rose' representing the uniting of the York and Lancaster dynasties, but a device coined before the Tudors even got to the throne, as an emblem combining the white and red roses of the Virgin Mary.[69] Henry's court was not insular and mean, but cosmopolitan and rich. He had spent his youth abroad, and royal art during his rule became distinctively continental, embroiled with organic vegetation and richly symbolic. The identity of the Tudors was coined from the outset and rigorously maintained; they were to be seen as saviours who returned the land to a state of paradise after civil war, a political message that was first introduced to

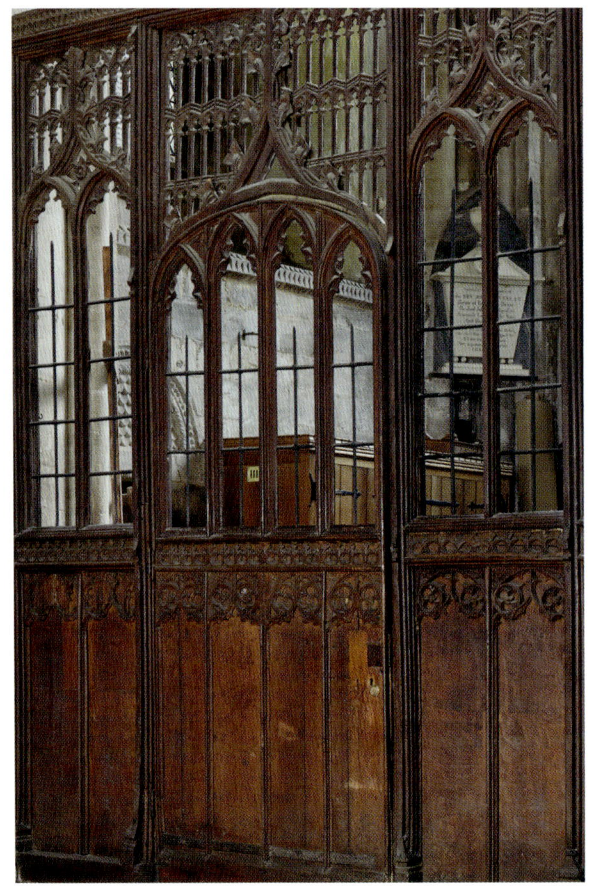

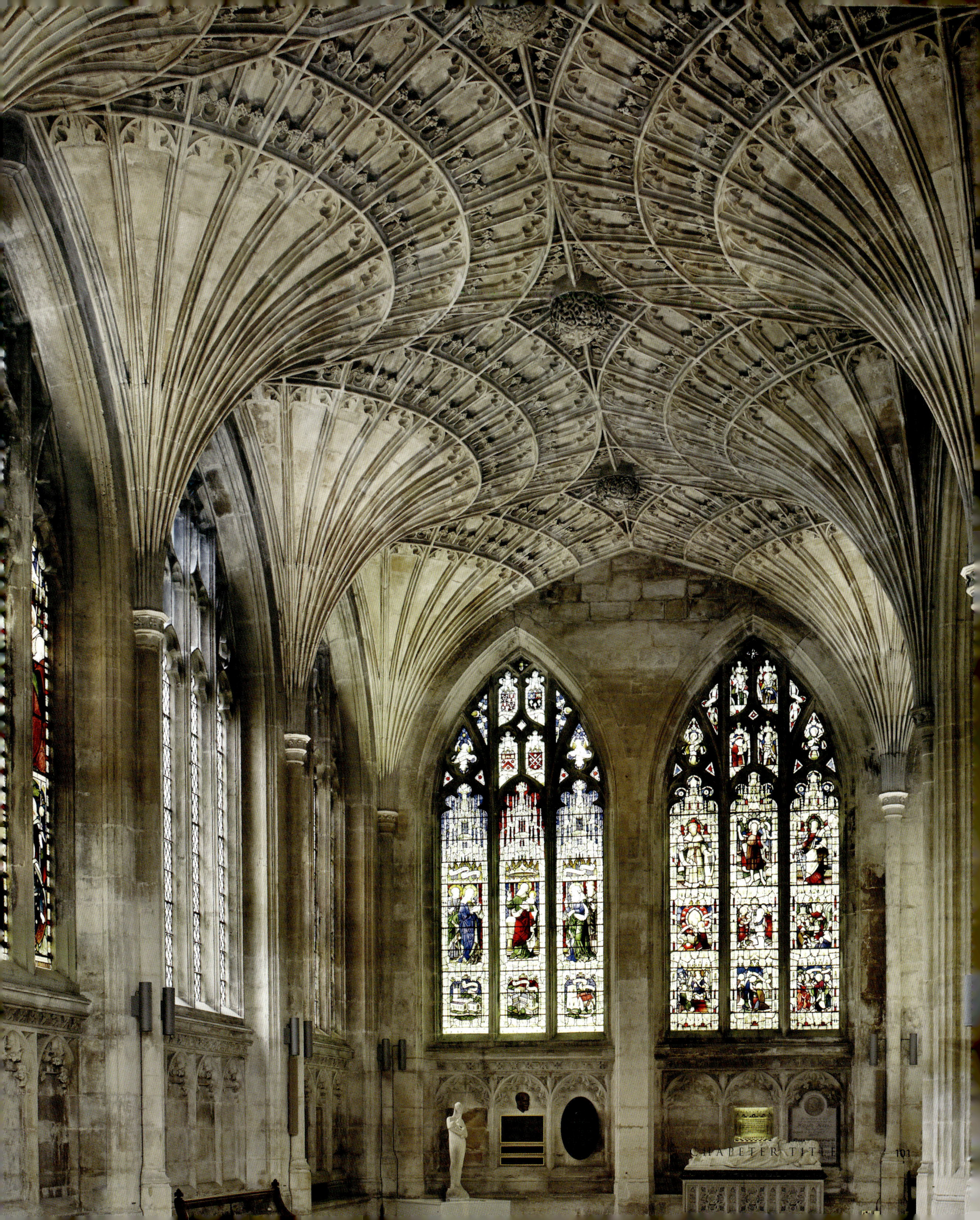
CHAPETER TITLE

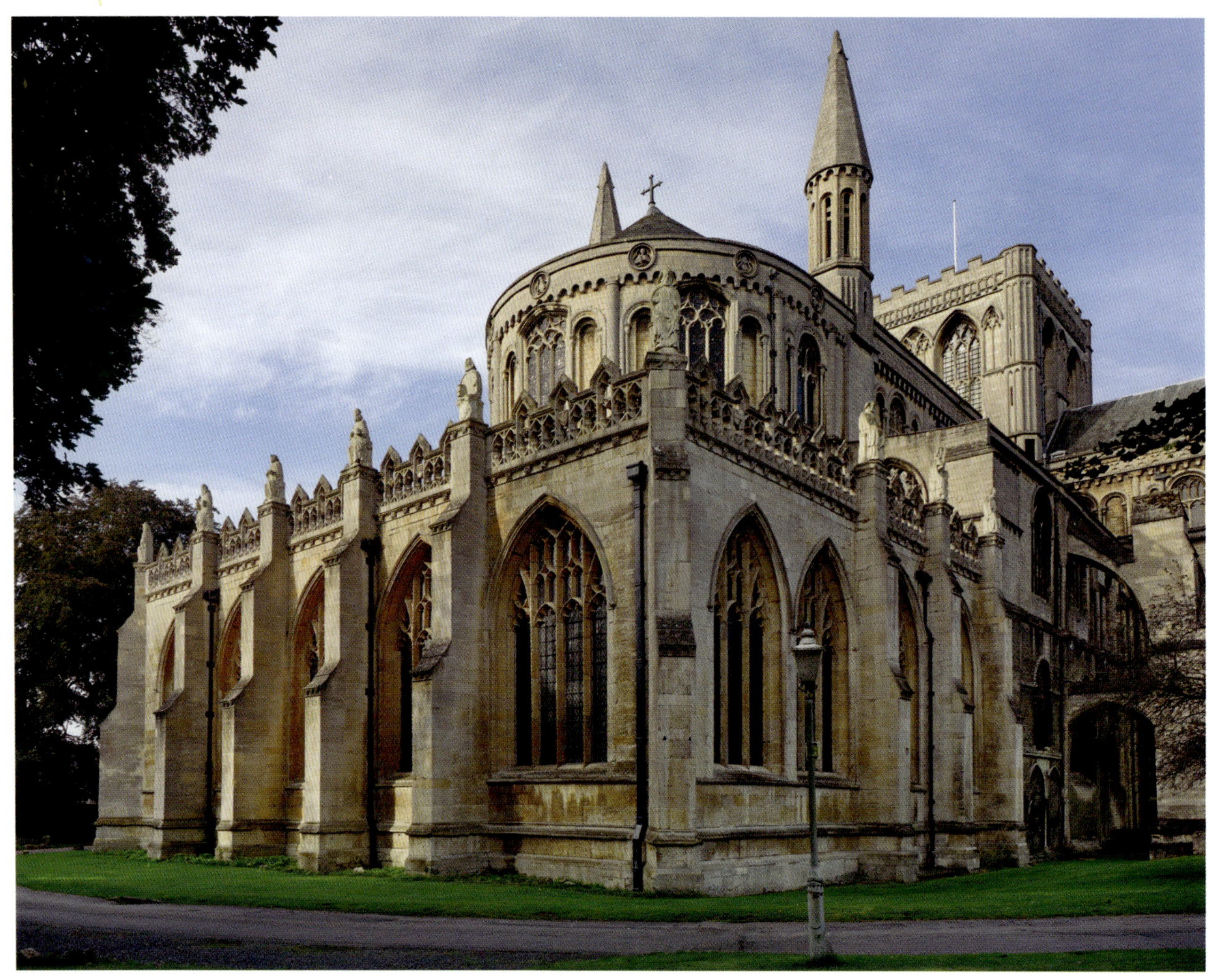

Peterborough only two weeks after the marriage of Henry Tudor and Elizabeth of York, in a visit during March 1486.

Robert Kirkton brought this architecture and cosmopolitan court sculpture to Peterborough in the New Building, an eastern extension or retroquire that, finally, broke through the eastern apses and won space for altars. There is no dispute about its patronage, for Kirkton branded his building with his rebus, a pictorial puzzle where symbols are combined to sound out names. In his case, he shows a robin (medieval 'robert') a church ('kirk') and a barrel ('tun').

The architect of Kirkton's New Building was apparently John Wastell (1460–1518), a native of Bury St Edmunds who had recently built Canterbury Cathedral's central tower with a similar fan vault beneath, its piers braced by perforated strainer arches much like those bridging the New Building with the

Above The 500-year-old New Building, an extraordinarily accomplished work of court masonry typical of the royal circle in the later years of Henry VII and early reign of Henry VIII. Twelve figures, presumably apostles, preside from the parapets.

old apse. Wastell would go on to build the vaults of King's College Chapel, Cambridge, after 1509. While Peterborough's retroquire is so visually similar to that of the King's chapel as to be from Wastell's drawing table, its construction technique is closer to William and Robert Vertue's Lady Chapel, Henry VII's Chapel, at Westminster Abbey, of 1503–12. Kirkton travelled to see the king and also took counsel from Margaret Beaufort, the king's mother, who held estates locally.[70]

If Westminster's masons helped to construct the New Building, this may explain its details, immersed in the style of Henry VII's court, not least his marriage bed. This style finds its focus in Westminster's Painted Chamber, where bishops assembled before Parliament. One boss of the arms of the bishop of Durham includes a cross fleurie, a symbol of Christ that appeared in precisely this form on the marriage bed.[71] That bed's pierced carving emulated the cosmopolitan Germanic style of organic vegetation that swept Europe's court arts in the 1480s, and Kirkton's perforated bosses are similarly composed. One example shows the arms of St Peter over a rose bush. This can be understood not as the 'Tudor' rose, but as the combined heavenly Marian rose adopted by the Tudors, first seen here in single form in the western porch. Other bosses include St Andrew's cross and St Paul's swords with crosses.

The New Building was accompanied by a new presbytery ceiling of flat timber ribs and bosses of stylised roses and eagles with scrolls, apparently a reference to the Book of Revelation. The flat ceiling of the apse may have been painted with Christ and the vine, though it was so completely overpainted in the nineteenth century for this to be questionable. It is safe to say that everywhere were allusions to heaven, portraying an age more at peace with itself than it had been for decades.

Both projects were in progress when Henry VII arranged the marriage of his son Prince Arthur, his presumed heir, to Katherine of Aragon. She was born the last of the five children of Ferdinand and Isabella of Spain, on 16 December 1485, and was betrothed

Above Rebus of Abbot Robert Kirkton, a pictorial symbol of his name.

Below The vault of King's College Chapel, Cambridge, a mature work by John Wastell after *c*.1510.

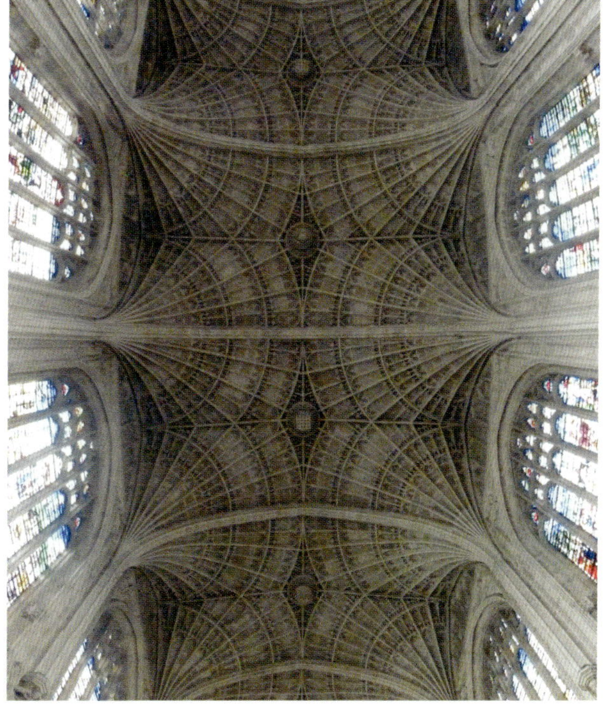

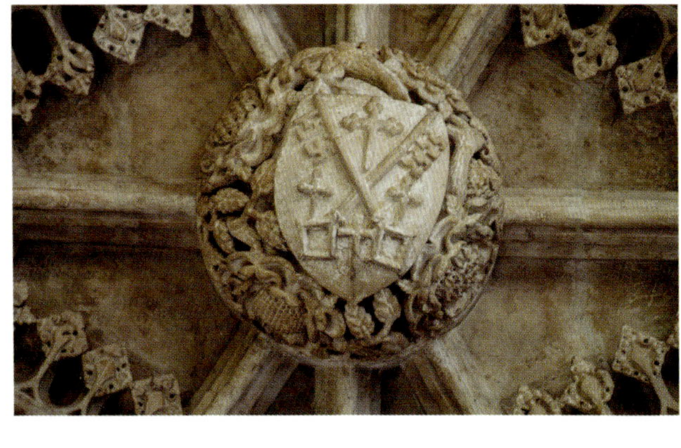
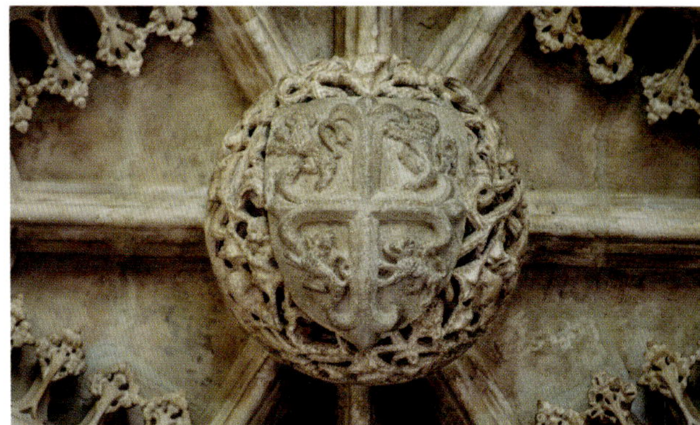
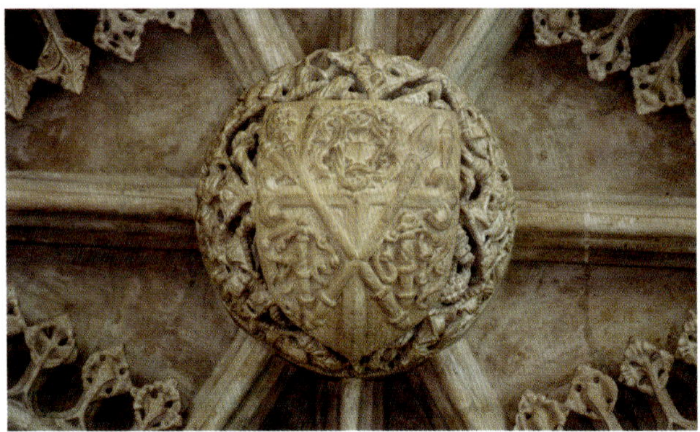
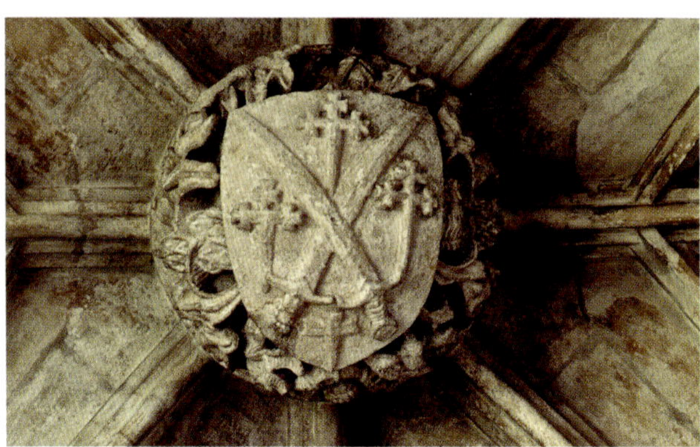

to Arthur at the age of three to bolster Spain's alliances against France. When she left her homeland with a household of 60 souls on 21 May 1501, she took with her her chosen symbol of the '*granada*', the pomegranate, emblem of Granada. Its seeds evoked fecundity; as they also resemble pellets, they gave their name to the explosive grenade. The conflation would prove ironic.

On 14 November 1501, a congregation at St Paul's Cathedral witnessed the Spanish bride escorted by Arthur's brother, Henry, Duke of York. Upon Arthur's death the following spring, Katherine avoided marrying his father, a recently-widowed 45-year-old. Her dowry having been partly paid to English coffers, she was destined to marry Prince Henry on 11 June 1509, a fortnight before his accession as Henry VIII.

The bishop of Lincoln's visitation of the abbey in 1518 found much that was wanting. The beer was thin and the food inadequate, while the sacrist was charged with prising jewels from St Oswald's shrine as gifts for local women. Kirkton held the title of master of works, which explains two other new buildings in Peterborough. His gatehouse building to a new deer park, north of the cathedral's west front, is draped with royal arms and Marian roses, while Heaven's Gate in the abbot's palace is a Petrine reference within earshot of the west front's heavenly

Above Four bosses from the vaults of the New Building, showing (clockwise from top left) St Peter's keys; the arms of the diocese of Durham; St Paul's swords; and the instruments of the passion.

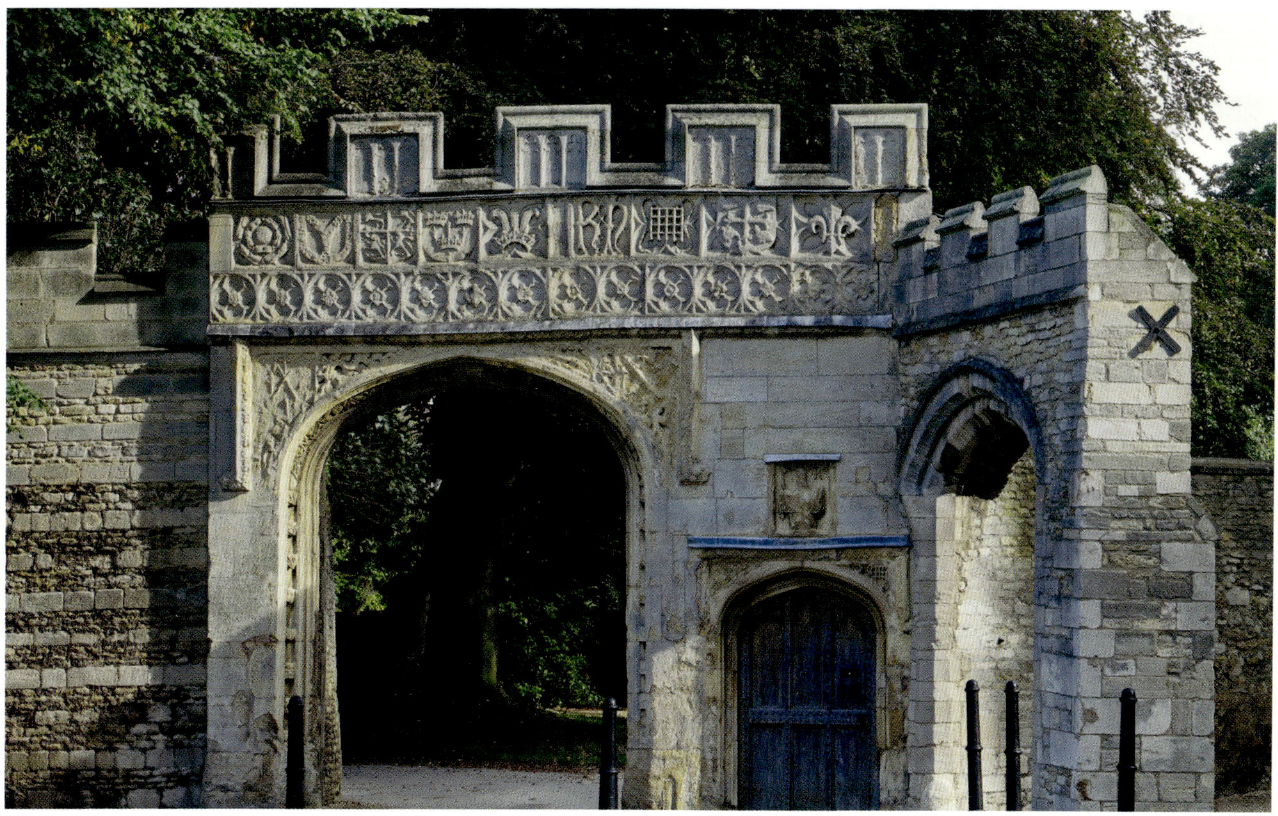

Above Prior's Gate, constructed by Abbot Kirkton; the court heraldry of the Prince of Wales' feathers, Edward the Confessor's cross, St Edmund's arms and the fleur-de-lys all feature alongside the Marian rose in the decoration. This was abbot as statesman and courtier.

portals. Kirkton's indulgence was accompanied by his neglect of the education of monks, who took to drinking, singing and dancing after dark.

Peterborough Abbey's shortcomings were redressed by Abbot John Chambers (1528–39), elected by Cardinal Wolsey's assent. Wolsey would call on Chambers' hospitality at Peterborough *en route* to York in 1530, accompanied by his retinue and 12 carts. The cardinal stayed from Palm Sunday to the following Thursday to escape the black cloud of Henry VIII's marital crisis, and held the Maundy service with Chambers. It was perhaps for that visit that Chambers had the suite of oak panels carved, which are now in the south transept. One design features an obtuse rebus of Chambers' name ('A' [bbas] eagle = John; a deer or chers for 'Ch[amb] ers'); while another is a fortification, roses tumbling from its impregnable walls, as a metaphor for Mary's womb.

Peterborough would yet be transformed by the king and queen, who separated in 1531, five years after Henry met Anne Boleyn. In May 1534 a defiant Katherine moved to Kimbolton Castle, 25 miles south of Peterborough. She was admired for her courage, and needed it. In the following months, others who denied Henry's rejection of papal supremacy and self-declared status as head of the English Church

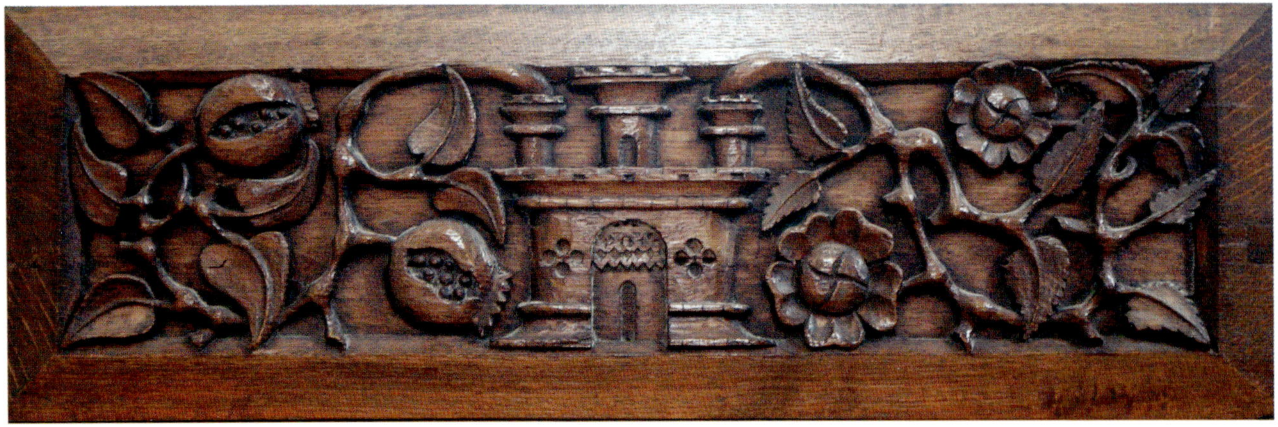

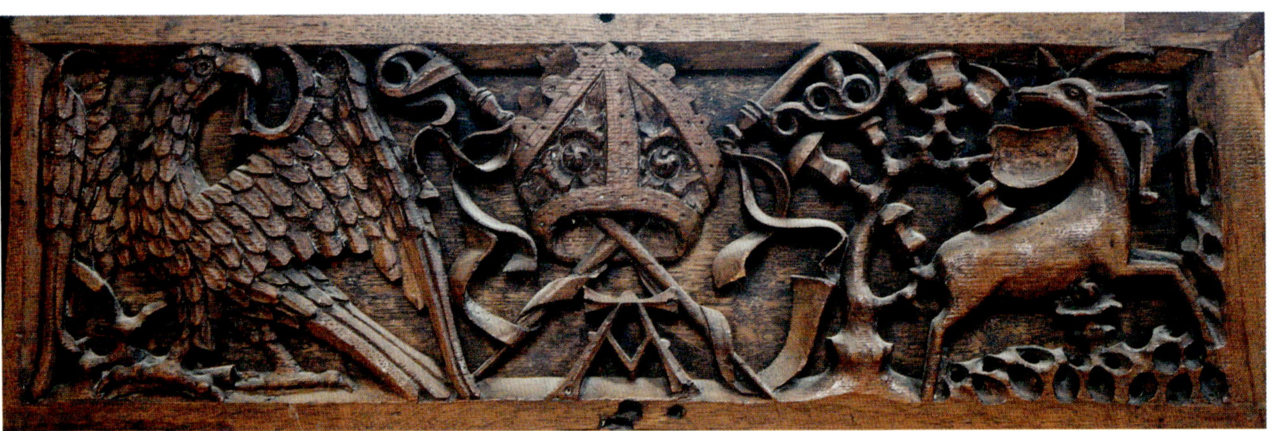

were condemned to execution. Her own death was near, conceivably aggravated by unfolding events, and Henry decreed that she be buried at Peterborough as his brother's dowager. The funeral at Peterborough on 29 January 1536 was attended by her daughter, Princess Mary, who would become queen in 1553.

Katherine's tomb was a grey marble plinth, perhaps with an altar. It was destroyed in 1643, but she still lies in the north arcade of the choir, beneath a simple slab. Her motto was *'Humble et loyale'*, qualities scarce in Henry, whose rejection of his Spanish queen brought the opprobrium of Europe, not least of her nephew, Charles V, the Holy Roman Emperor. As 1535 wore on, the king knew he had become the enemy of France, Spain and the Germanic states, and had to fortify the English coast against the fleets of Europe. Valuations confirmed he could pay for political isolation from Europe by dissolving the nation's monasteries, stripping the jewels from their shrines and the lead from their roofs, and granting estate lands to favourites. Peterborough Abbey faced utter ruination.

Top Detail of a fort and roses, from the suite of oak panels installed by Abbot John Chambers and now in the south transept.

Above Abbot John Chambers' rebus, from the oak panels he installed.

This great monastery escaped the first wave of dissolutions of smaller houses in 1536. Abbot Chambers was concerned to prevent the townsfolk from joining the Lincolnshire rebellion just as Peterborough's high bailiff, John Lord Hussey of Sleaford, was accused of being a ringleader of this flagrant denial of royal authority. Any dissent within the abbey could have led to its surrender and demolition, and instead Peterborough played the political game of granting Thomas Cromwell, Henry VIII's prime mover in the dissolution, a pension, which 43 other religious houses also did.

Ultimately, at the second Act of Suppression, the abbot surrendered to Henry's men on better terms, on 29 November 1539. The wreckers' business lay in dismantling the shrines and monastic buildings, leaving many of the monks to withdraw to a pensioned retirement, a life for which they were unprepared after their sheltered monastic existence. That Peterborough's church was spared and chosen to be the seat of one of six new bishoprics, amongst 'new foundations', was no small miracle, certainly not one borne of deference to Katherine of Aragon's remains.[72] John Chambers was made warden of the abbey, before becoming Peterborough's first bishop in 1541, his territory carved from the vast diocese of Lincoln.

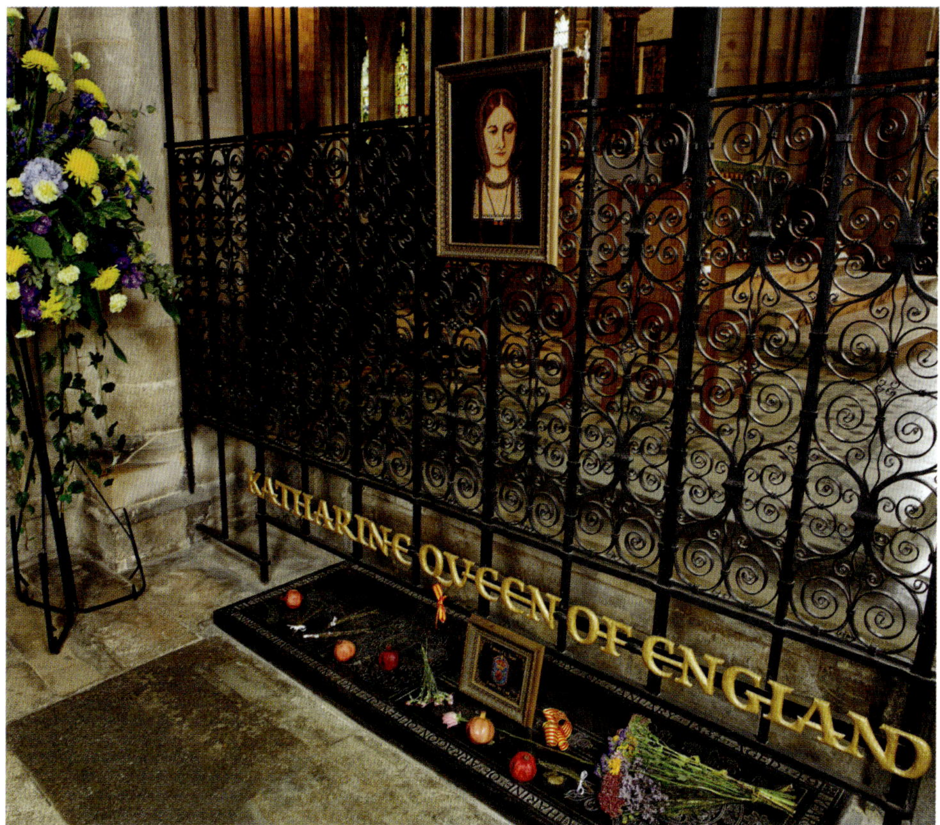

Left The resting place of Katherine of Aragon. Ironically, her plain dark slab closely matches that of Henry VIII at Windsor, for whom no monument was completed.

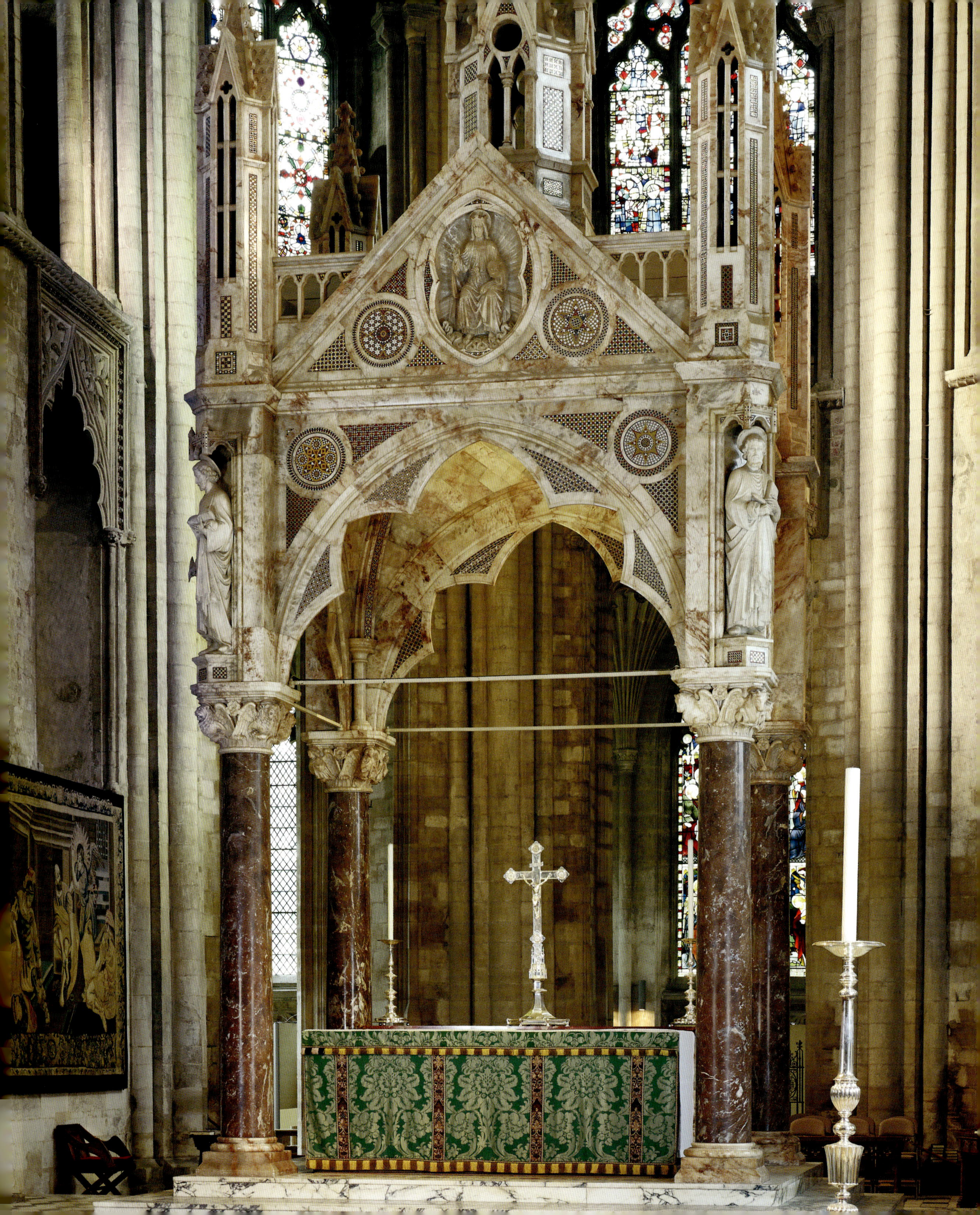

6

SURVIVAL AND RENEWAL

*He did most miserably deface the
Cathedral Church, break down the
Organs, and destroy the glass windows*

The final act of royal purloining was the division of the former abbey's lands between magnates supportive of the Tudor regime. Lord Burghley established a new park on the limestone land toward Stamford, while the Orme family would build a mansion called Neville Place in Priestgate. Thus stripped of assets, this was not a wealthy cathedral, its revenues of £414 19s 11d making it 19th out of 23 cathedrals in 1575. Still, it was important. Mary, Queen of Scots, who had died at Fotheringhay, was buried here in 1587, witnessed by the sexton, Robert Scarlett, then 91 years old, whose portrayal and rhyme can be found above the west door.

T HE REMAINS of the monastic buildings lay all around, some being repurposed for houses, though the Lady Chapel survived this round of damage. Enough of the wrecked cloister remained that its traceried arches were salvaged to fill the windows of the north aisle of the choir. Although the shrines had gone, the nave's screen stood, set before the thirteenth-century choirstalls. Past them could be seen the three spires of the early fourteenth-century presbytery screen. That was, until:

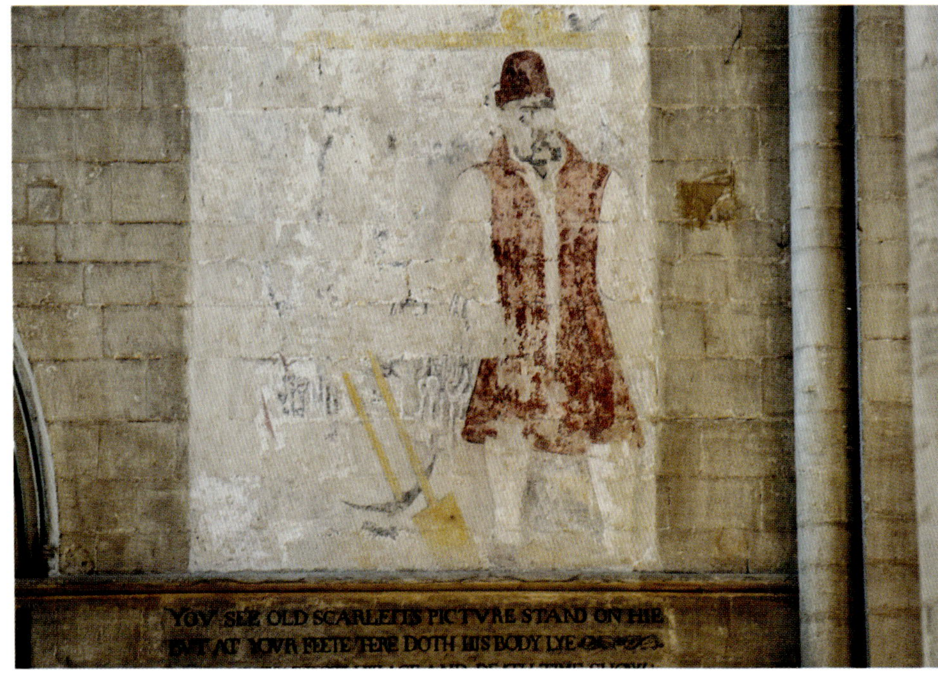

In the year 1643 it was beaten down to the lowest base of plain work, and so stood as a deformed spectacle some eight years, and then 1651, a private person disliking it because there was not a thorough reformation, it was ordered that the remainder, with the whole mound whereon it was erected, should be levelled with the pavement of the Quire.

The Civil War found Peterborough Cathedral in the home territory of Oliver Cromwell, who was born in Huntingdon in 1599. His parliamentarian troops used great churches for stables and barracks and were not overly concerned with religious imagery, but considered funerary monuments as signposts to gold rings, staffs and chalices. They came to Peterborough in the spring of 1643, and the Royalist publication *Mercurius Aulicus* declaimed that:

Above One of the windows from the cloister, reset in the north aisle of the presbytery after the adjacent Lady Chapel was destroyed.

Colonel Cromwell had bestowed a visit on that little City, and put them to the charge of his entertainment, plundering a great part thereof to discharge the reckoning, and further that in pursuance of the thorough Reformation, he did most miserably deface the Cathedral Church, break down the Organs, and destroy the glass windows, committing many other outrages on the house of God which were not acted by the Goths in the sack of Rome, and are most commonly forborne by the Turks when they possess themselves by force of a Christian city.

Few of Peterborough's charters and books were spared by soldiers who, unable to decipher the Latin text, mistakenly assumed that they were destroying papal bulls.[73] One notable escapee was the Swaffham cartulary, hidden behind the choirstalls at the outbreak of war by the precentor Humphrey Austin, only for it soon to be revealed when the wainscot was destroyed by Cromwell's wreckers. Austin bought its safety for ten shillings, a deal recorded in the book:

I pray let this scripture book alone for he hath paid me for it; therefore I would desire you to let it alone, by me Henry Topclyffe, souldyer under Capt. Cromwell, Coll. Cromwell's sonn; therefore I pray let it alone.

By me Henry Topclyffe

Francis Standish, an eyewitness, recorded that 'thus was a fair and stately building, in the course of about a fortnight, quite stript of its ornamental beauty, and made a ruthful spectacle; a very chaos of desolation and confusion; nothing scarcely remaining but bare walls, broken seats, and shattered windows.'

On 18 February 1651, the great church of Peterborough faced its ultimate fate when a parliamentary committee recommended that 'all Cathedral Churches, where there are other Churches or Chapels sufficient for the People to meet for the Worship of God, be surveyed, pulled down, and sold, and be employed for a Stock for the Use of the Poor'. That it was saved was due to the intervention of Oliver St John, Lord Chief Justice, who in August 1651 gave over the cathedral to public worship. It was recast as a centre of preaching and a workhouse. Soon after the Lady Chapel, being 'ready to fall', was pulled down by the citizens of Peterborough as a desperate measure to pay for the repair of the damaged cathedral roofs. Renewed civic pride extended to the Guildhall, funded by public subscription

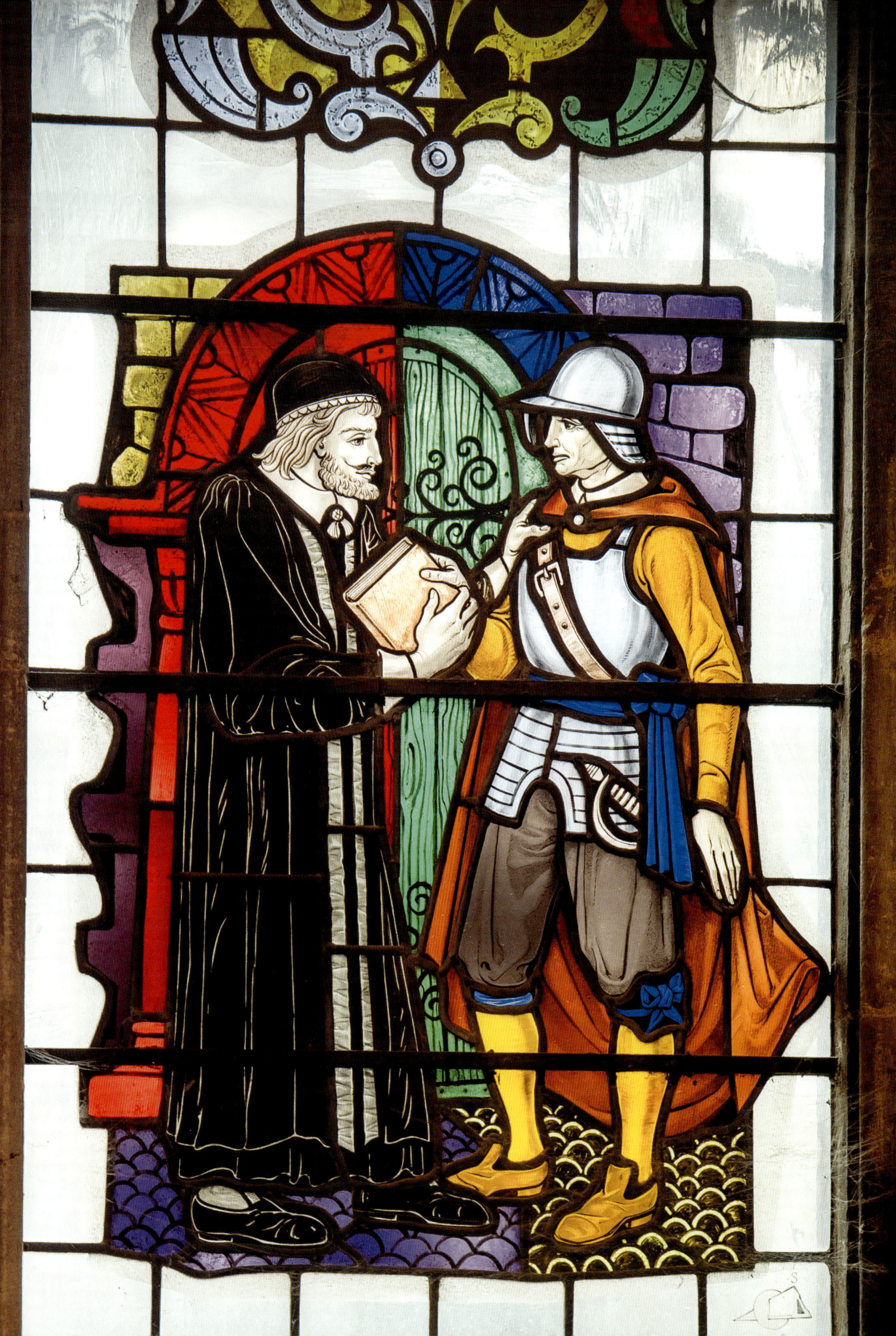

at the restoration of Charles II in 1660. Completed by 1671 over a functional sheltered marketplace, it was designed by John Lovin who also repaired the ransacked Bishop's Palace.

Remarkably, not all the war damage was irreparable, for a quite recently rediscovered book illustrates Peterborough's glass and tombs with a record of monumental inscriptions. It was composed in 1640, two years before the Civil War broke out, by the early antiquarian William Dugdale and illustrated by William Sedgwick. Having been privately owned by the Earl of Macclesfield until 1994, it is now in the British Library and something of a salve to M.R. James' lament that: 'The Englishman returning from a visit to Amiens, Chartres, or Troyes, is apt to feel very keenly the poverty of his own country in such matters as painted glass, statues and bas-reliefs, ancient vestments and plate.'

As the Industrial Revolution ushered in a curiosity for a world left behind, the cathedral represented a grand building seeking renewed relevance. Simon Gunton (1609–76), a prebend of Peterborough, was also a notably early historian of cathedrals, who even as a boy transcribed the same monuments that Dugdale and Sedgwick had recorded. Gunton's documentary research was compiled into his *The History of the Church of Peterburgh (etc)* in 1686. This was an outstanding contribution in the pattern of Dugdale's *Monasticon Anglicanum*, which collated as much as he could find on the dispersed collections of medieval monasteries, of course including Peterborough.

It speaks of the evocative quality of the local monuments that the Spalding Gentlemen's Society was founded in 1710, attracting the membership of William Stukeley of Stamford, the greatest antiquary of the mid-eighteenth century. Peterborough lay between the two towns and Stukeley visited on 17 August 1747 to witness work in progress beneath the warm lead of the high roofs:

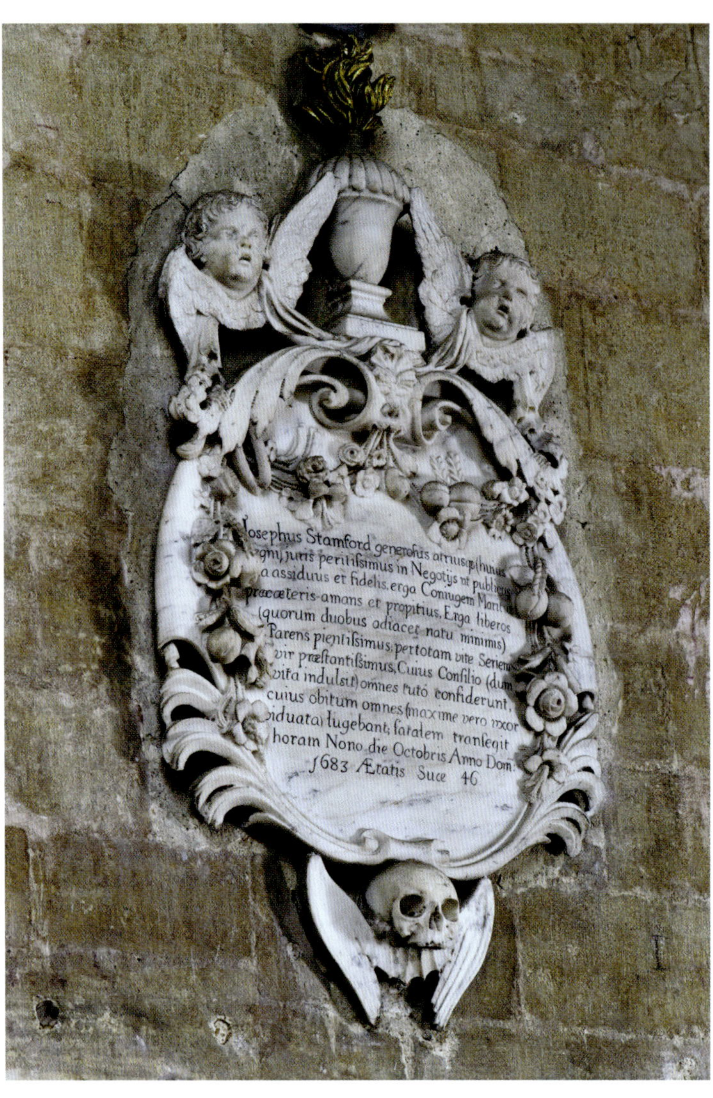

Above **The fine marble plaque of Joseph Stamford, d.1683, for whom *fatalem transegit horam*, 'the fatal hour has passed'.**

I went to Peterborough. They are new whitewashing, or rather dawbing the cathedral, and new painting the roof in ridiculous filigree work, partly-coloured, that has no meaning in it; and above all they have, for greater ornament, as they fancy, painted the ceiling over the high altar in imitation of marble.

Between the repainting of the cathedral's faded nave ceiling in the 1740s and 1830s (well-meant if not always accurate), Dean Tarrant (1764–91) gathered the fragments of smashed glass that remained, and formed a mosaic for the two central east windows. Georgian-era improvements included the proud installation of new funerary monuments in Latin texts, so recently despised by Cromwell's troops.[74] The grandest is that of the wool merchant and former high sheriff of Northamptonshire, Thomas Deacon (d.1720; and his wife Mary d.1730), who established a charity school to educate and financially support 20 boys. His name and purpose still resound in the Thomas Deacon Academy.

Even as the noisy city mutated into brick fields, goods yards and strands of terraced houses after the railway came in 1850, a renewed esteem for the stone church in its ancient enclosure saw the west front represented on the frieze of the Royal Albert Hall as a noble ancestor of the greatest Victorian engineering triumphs. Archaeological standards improved throughout the nineteenth century, which in turn enhanced scholarship and empathy for the cathedral.

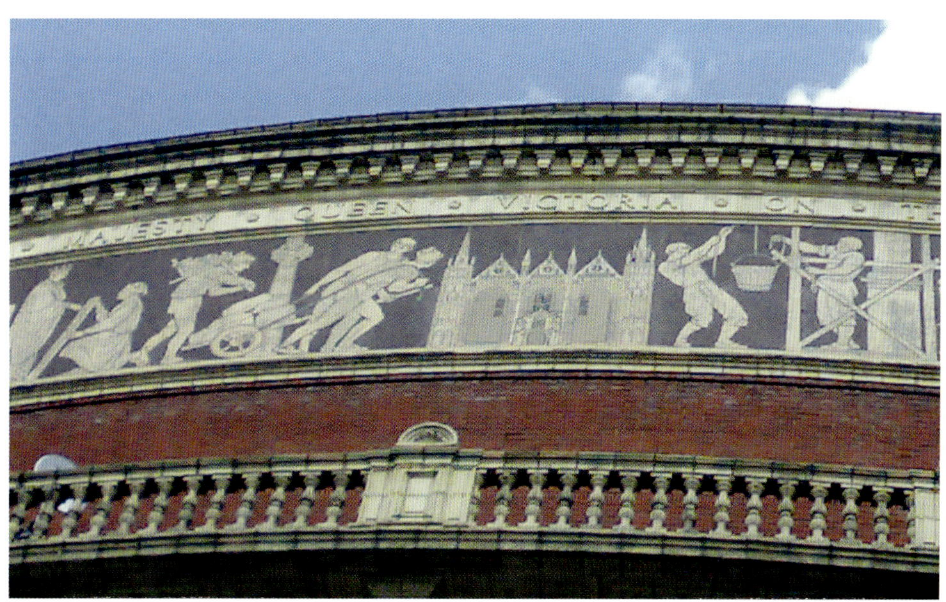

Left Peterborough Cathedral's west front on the north-western side of the Royal Albert Hall's 800 ft-long terracotta mosaic frieze, which celebrates the triumphs of arts and culture. The west front is part of *Workers in Stone; Workers in Wood and Brick; Architecture*, designed by W.F. Yeames and executed *c.*1871.

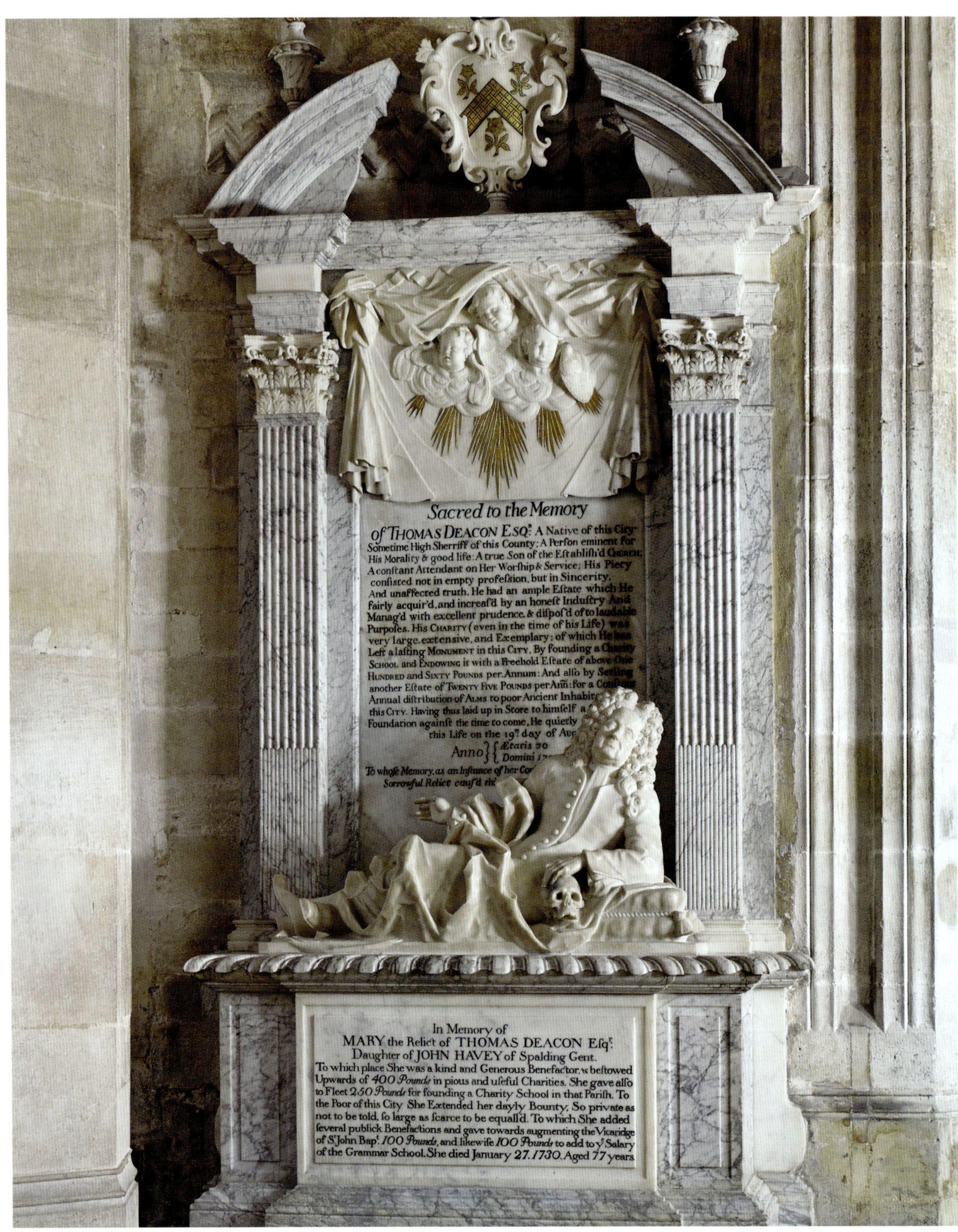

Sacred to the Memory
of THOMAS DEACON ESQ: A Native of this City
Sometime High Sherriff of this County; A Person eminent for
His Morality & good life: A true Son of the Establish'd Church;
A constant Attendant on Her Worship & Service: His Piety
consisted not in empty profession, but in Sincerity,
And unaffected truth. He had an ample Estate which He
fairly acquir'd, and increas'd by an honest Industry And
Manag'd with excellent prudence, & dispos'd of to laudable
Purposes. His CHARITY (even in the time of his Life) was
very large, extensive, and Exemplary; of which He has
Left a lasting MONUMENT in this CITY, By founding a Charity
School, and ENDOWING it with a Freehold Estate of above One
HUNDRED and SIXTY POUNDS per Annum: And also by Setling
another Estate of TWENTY FIVE POUNDS per Ann: for a Constant
Annual distribution of ALMS to poor Ancient Inhabitants
this CITY. Having thus laid up in Store to himself a
Foundation against the time to come, He quietly
this Life on the 19.? day of Aug
Anno { Ætatis 70
      { Domini 17
To whose Memory, as an Instance of her Con
Sorrowful Relict caus'd thi

In Memory of
MARY the Relict of THOMAS DEACON Esq:
Daughter of JOHN HAVEY of Spalding Gent.
To which place She was a kind and Generous Benefactor, s bestowed
Upwards of 400 Pounds in pious and useful Charities. She gave also
to Fleet 250 Pounds for founding a Charity School in that Parish. To
the Poor of this City She Extended her dayly Bounty, So private as
not to be told, so large as scarce to be equall'd. To which She added
several publick Benefactions and gave towards augmenting the Vicaridge
of St John Bapt. 100 Pounds, and likewise 100 Pounds to add to yt Salary
of the Grammar School. She died January 27. 1730. Aged 77 years.

In the 1880s the central tower cracked and threatened to collapse. Under the direction of the architect J.L. Pearson, workmen rebuilt it stronger than before, and beneath it carpenters reinstated choirstalls with bristling oak canopies, a six-year long task. Pearson's remarkable alabaster baldacchino echoed the ancient pinnacles of the screen with a nod to St Peter. The cathedral was also fortunate to secure the services of the surveyor J.T. Irvine (1826–1900) who lived in Cromwell Road and assiduously recorded discoveries even as he conjured engineering solutions. As the west front's three gables stood precarious in the 1890s, Victorian engineers under Irvine's direction pinned and repaired them. But not everyone was impressed by Peterborough's architectural direction and taste in ornament and materials.

Opposite **Thomas Deacon's splendid baroque monument at the southern entrance to the New Building.**

Below **These sponsored stalls were carved and erected in 1890–93, replicating the position of the Benedictine choir. For the previous few centuries, box seating had been set in the three westernmost bays of the presbytery.**

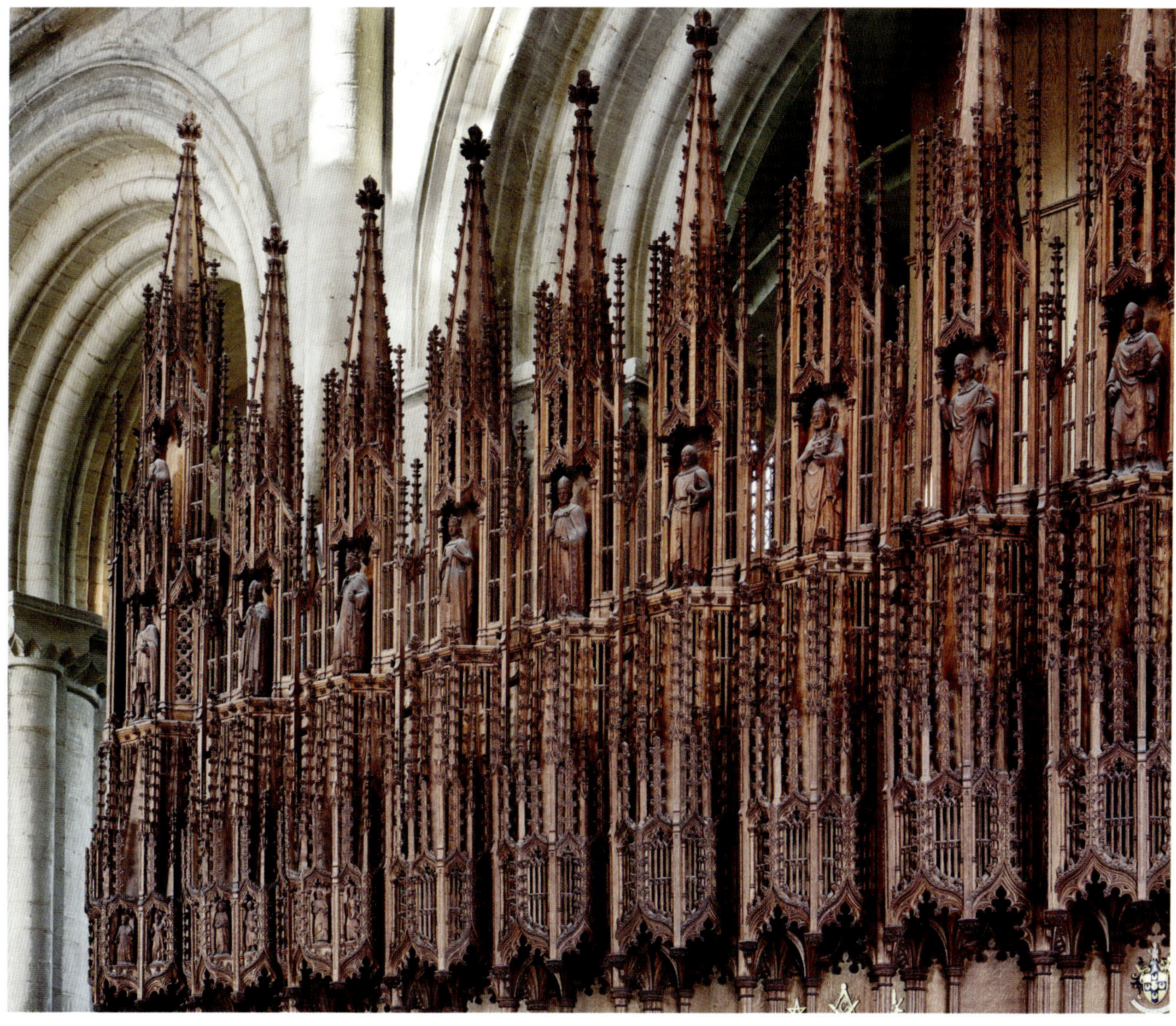

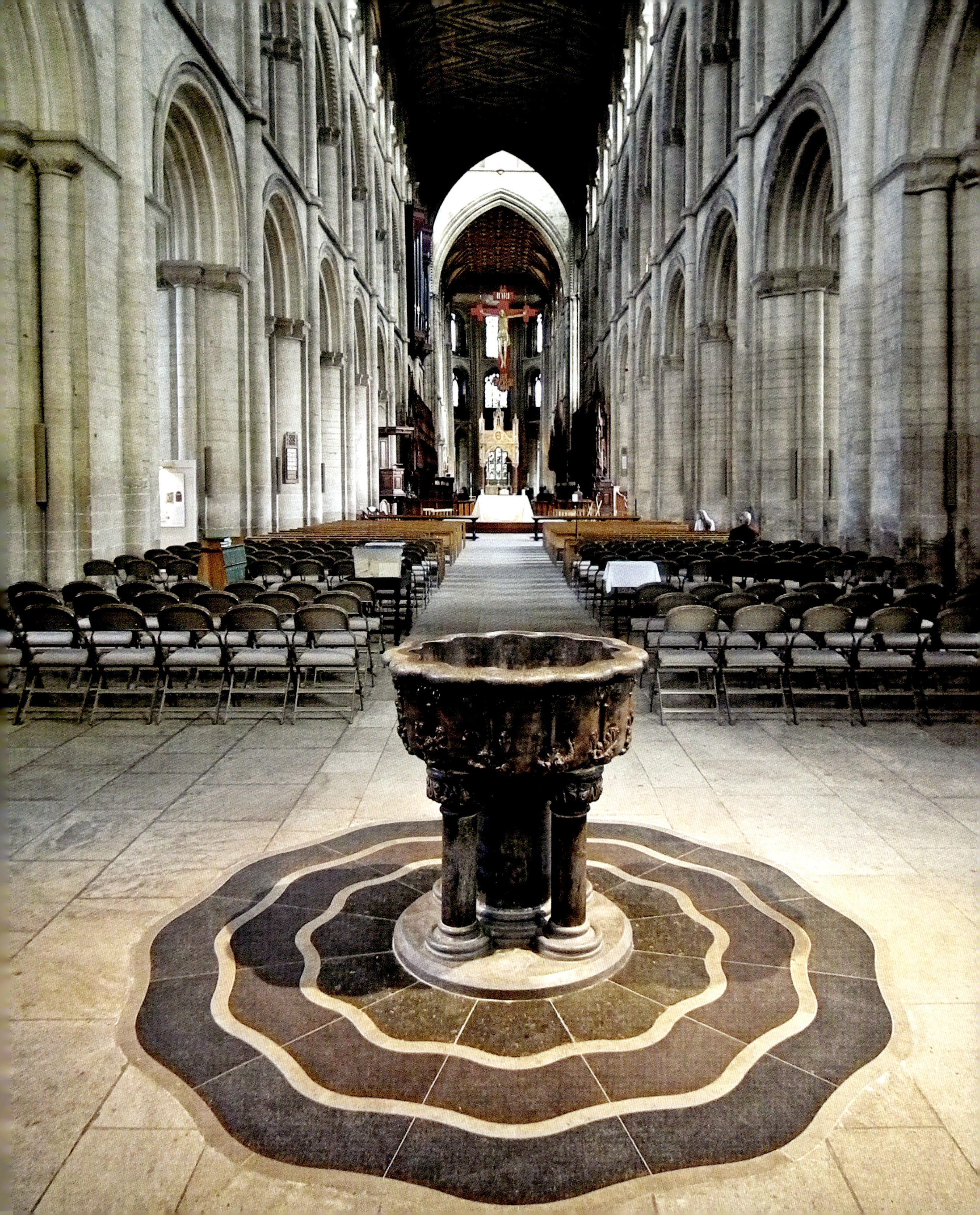

WILLIAM MORRIS

William Morris (1834–96), the founder of the Society for the Protection of Ancient Buildings (SPAB), knew Peterborough Cathedral as a boy and composed a poem on it. Later in life, he composed letters to protest at schemes to replace parts of the cathedral with new designs intended to achieve stylistic conformity.[75]

On the central tower, rebuilt with its original fourteenth-century stones rather than anew in Norman style (*Pall Mall Gazette*, 10 September 1889):

It is 'highly creditable to the good sense of the Chapter that they refused to allow the church to be disfigured with an experimental modern Norman tower, especially as much pressure was put upon them in favour of that absurdity. Let us hope that they will understand their responsibilities in the future as well as they did on that occasion.'

On the internal refurbishment (*Daily Chronicle*, 13 December 1895):

'…so much mischief has been caused in many places by rich men shaking bags of money at "restoration" committees, and their not being able to resist the temptation of doing something splendid at the expense of losing almost all the interest of the building in their charge.'

On the west front, following storm damage and settlement, encouraging the consolidation rather than rebuilding of the three gables as Pearson suggested (*Daily Chronicle*, 1 April 1895):

'There are two ways in which it may be dealt with by its responsible guardians; the first would be the successful, the second the unsuccessful way. If treated successfully, it will come out of this trial with its beauty intact, its external appearance unchanged from what we have known and admired in our lifetimes. Unsuccessfully treated, it will bear the appearance of a modern piece of work founded on an ancient design; and in that case it will have lost the greater part of its interest in the eyes of the historical student and the wide-minded artist; in short it will have been "restored," and its genuine existence will have come to an end.'

In hindsight, the conservation movement was surely right to retain, not replace, medieval material wherever possible. The unlikely survival of this extraordinary place can never be taken for granted, for its continuing function as a place of worship and community has depended on many generations taking firm and conscientious action, and Peterborough Cathedral's story of care and commitment is ongoing. When a stack of plastic chairs was set ablaze in the north aisle of the nave in November 2001, quick action prevented the damage turning to calamity: the thick smoke that engulfed the masonry and painted ceiling was carefully cleaned. Moreover, potential disaster provided an opportunity to better understand this exceptional historic resource. A vessel set on the margins of land and water, one of earthly riches and heavenly aspirations, Peterborough Cathedral retains its ancient capacity to surprise and inspire, and its story is far from over.

Opposite Peterborough's exceptionally fine early-thirteenth-century font, with fish motif recalling the fisherman St Peter, recently resituated on the axis of the nave on an inset modern pavement of wavy, shell-rich marble.

Right The apse ceiling:
repainted in the nineteenth
century under George Gilbert
Scott, it may reflect evidence
for the scheme from *c.*1500,
when vines were among the
most prevalent of church
imagery.

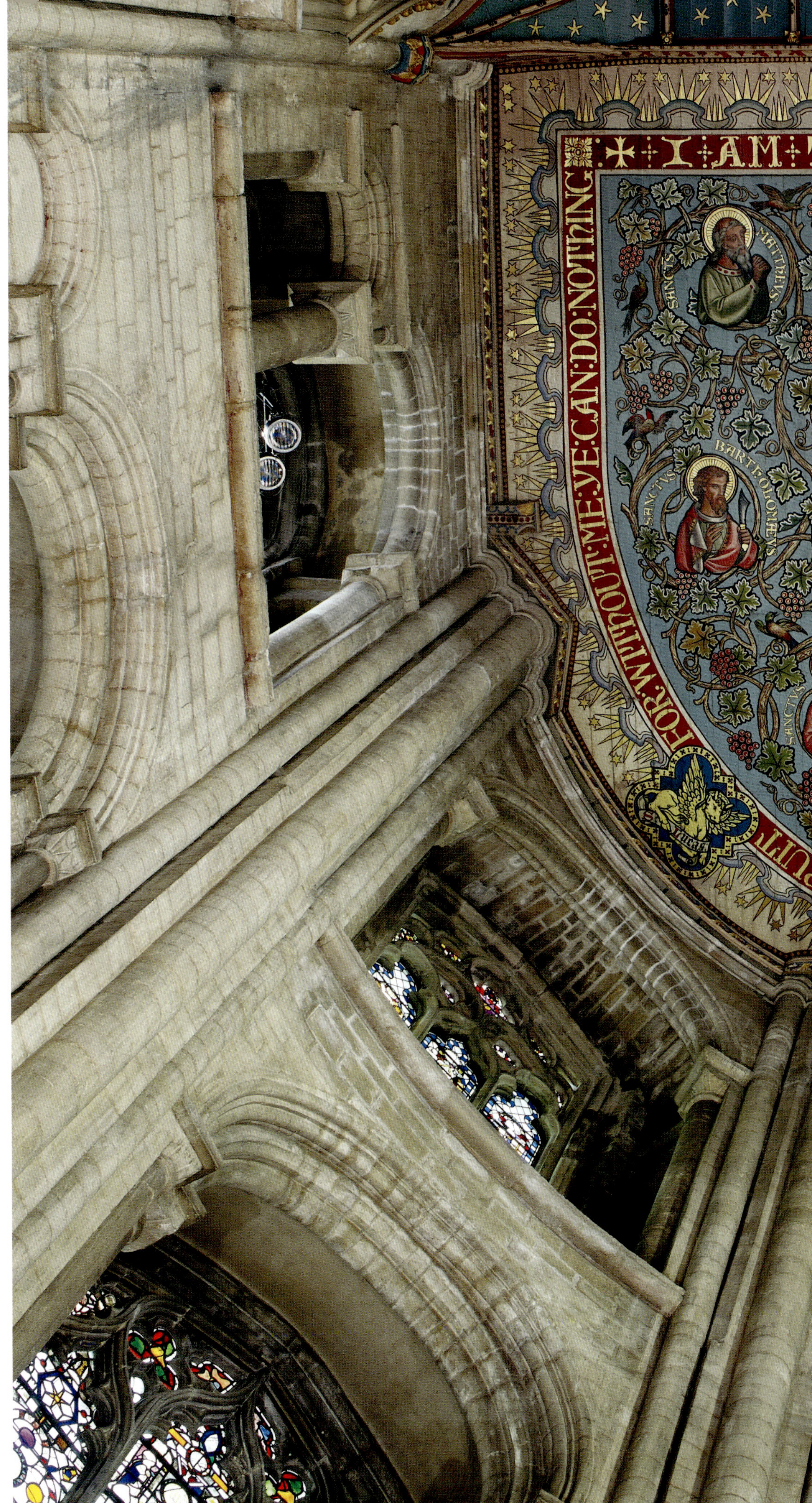

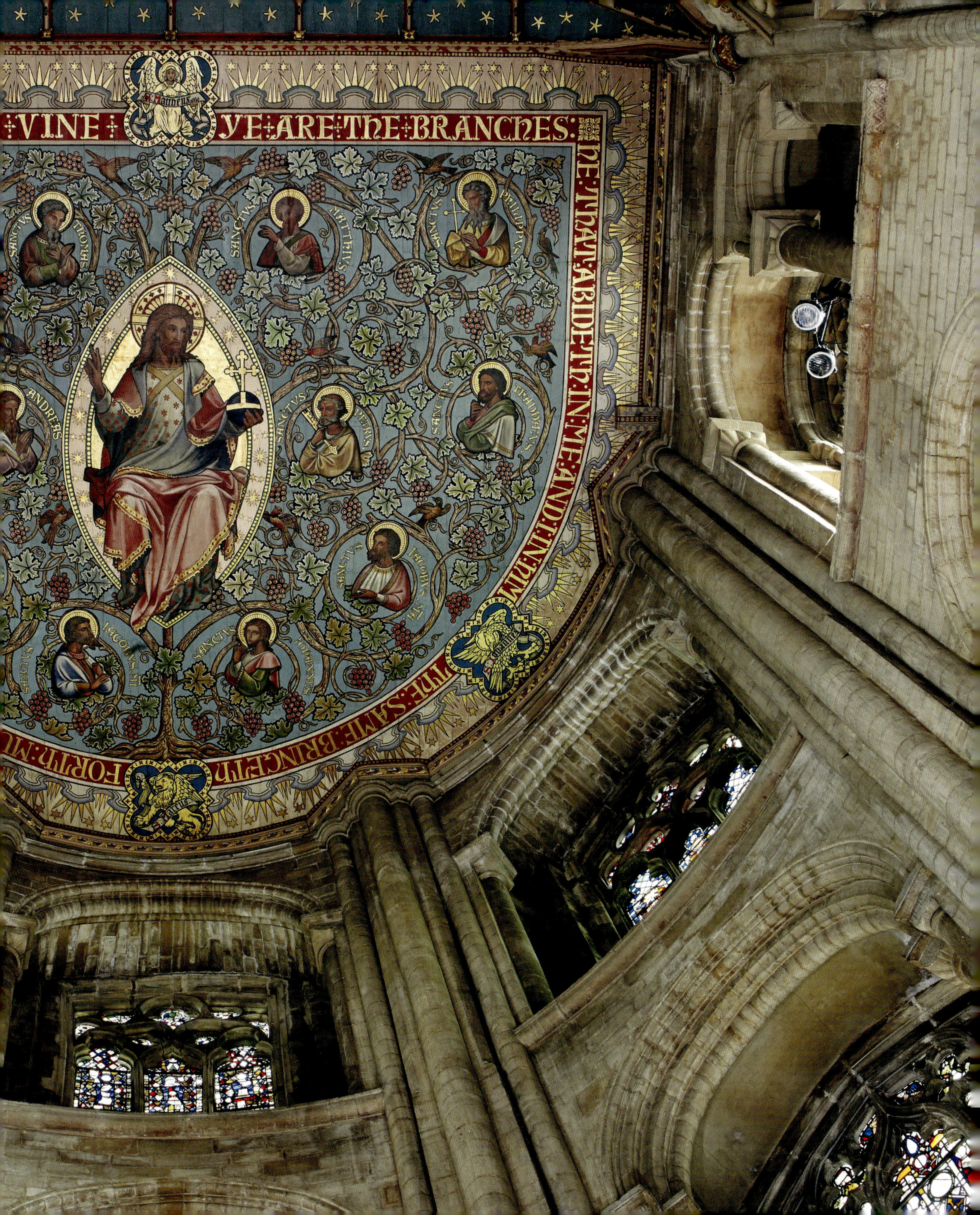
VINE YE ARE THE BRANCHES:
HE THAT ABIDETH IN ME AND I IN HIM
THE SAME BRINGETH IN FORTH MU
SANCTUS THOMAS
SANCTUS MATTHEUS
SANCTUS PHILIPPUS
SANCTUS ANDREAS
SANCTUS PETRUS
SANCTUS THADDEUS
SANCTUS

APPENDIX

LIST OF ABBOTS AND BISHOPS OF PETERBOROUGH CATHEDRAL

ABBOTS

Saxulf 654
Cuthbald 675
Egbald before 716
Pusa
Beonna
Ceolver
Hedda 870
Adulf 972–92
Kenulf 992–1005
Elsin 1006–55
Ernwin, 1055–57
Leofric 1057–66
Brand 1066–69
Thorold de Fécamp 1069–98
Godric, abbot for four days
    1099
Matthias 1103–04
Ernulf 1107–14
John de Séez 1114–25
Henry de Angeli (banished
    1133) 1128–33
Martin de Bec 1133–55
William Waterville 1155–75
Benedict 1177–94
Andrew 1194–99
Acharius 1200–10
Robert of Lindsey 1214–22
Alexander of Holderness
    1222–26
Martin of Ramsey 1226–33
Walter of Bury St. Edmunds
    1233–45
William of Hotoft 1246–49
John de Caux 1250–62
Robert of Sutton 1262–73
Richard of London 1274–95
William of Woodford 1295–99
Godfrey of Crowland
    1299–1321
Adam of Boothby 1321–38
Henry of Morcot 1338–53
Robert of Ramsey 1353–61
Henry of Overton 1361–91
Nicholas of Elmstow 1391–96
William Genge 1397–1408
John Deeping 1409–39

Richard Ashton 1439–71
William Ramsey 1471–96
Robert Kirkton 1496–1528
John Chambers 1528–39

BISHOPS

John Chambers 1541–56
David Pole 1557–59
Edmund Scambler 1560–85
Richard Howland 1585–1600
Thomas Dove 1601–30
William Piers 1630–32
Augustine Lindsell 1633–34
Francis Dee 1634–38
John Towers 1639–46
(Interregnum 1646–60)
Benjamin Lany 1660–63
Joseph Henshaw 1663–79
William Lloyd 1679–95
Thomas White 1685–90
Richard Cumberland
    1691–1718
White Kennett 1718–28
Robert Clavering 1729–47
John Thomas 1747–57
Richard Terrick 1757–64
Robert Lamb 1764–69
John Hinchcliffe 1769–94
Spencer Madan 1794–1813
John Parsons 1813–19
Herbert Marsh 1819–39
George Davys 1839–64
Francis Jeune 1864–68
William Connor Magee
    1868–91
Mandell Creighton 1891–97
Edward Glyn 1897–1916
Frank Woods 1916–23
Cyril Bardsley 1924–27
Claude Blagden 1927–49
Spencer Leeson 1949–56
Robert Stopford 1956–61
Cyril Easthaugh 1961–72
Douglas Feaver 1972–84
Bill Westwood 1984–95
Ian Cundy 1996–2009
Donald Allister 2010–

NOTES

1   Through archaeological digs directed by Francis Pryor after 1982, pre-Roman life was uncovered in spectacular detail beneath the clays of Flag Fen. From 1999 came the separate discovery of the Must Farm site four miles east-south-east of the cathedral, where a Bronze Age waterside settlement revealed a sophisticated culture 3000 years ago, long before the watery expanse of the fens was drained to gain the land we know today. Beads, fine textiles and swords testify to lives settled enough for refined crafts, but also a society facing the threat of violence. They knew ancient rivers and marshes teeming with fish and fowl, while serving as the main transport routes in an age of boat travel. What we regard as a marginal landscape was in fact highly connected, a meeting place of peoples and their resources.

2   'A relief depicting two dancing deities and other Roman stonework from Peterborough Cathedral', B.A.A. Conf. Trans., *Peterborough Cathedral*, ed. J. Hall (forthcoming)

3   'Roman Buildings in the Lower Nene Valley', B.A.A. Conf. Trans. *Peterborough Cathedral*, ed. J. Hall (forthcoming)

4   The underground practice of Christianity was marginalised up to the end of the third century, when believers faced severe persecution under Emperor Diocletian (284–305).

5   Constantine endowed bishops with many favours, such as tax exemptions, and outlawed Christian persecution. He also ensured that worship was maintained to his standards, for this religious policy was a personal decision and the crucible for a Christian empire was his own city, Constantinople.

6   It took decades to accrue sufficient wealth to become institutionalised, while late Roman society remained a polytheistic world. To augment its message, Christian culture needed a current literature and charismatic proponents, a status it reached by the early fifth century when St Augustine of Hippo wrote *The City of God*, his great work of Christian philosophy. In 22 volumes, he refuted the accusation that Christianity had, through abandoning the old classical gods, caused the fall of Rome to the Visigoths in 410. The world was divided between Christianity and paganism, said Augustine, and believers should be concerned with the heavenly city – the New Jerusalem. Their lives on earth should be spent glimpsing the world beyond. This leap of imagination depended on contemplation, but also on the symbolic and theatrical power of art and architecture.

7   The biblical Book of Revelation promised that through death came the promise of life and, if Christ had paved the way, then the saints built the bridges for mankind to follow. This needed a culture shift, for ancient Romans had buried human remains outside cities for better sanitation: Rome's other major saint, St Paul, was interred at S. Paolo Fuori le Mura (literally, 'outside the walls'). As martyrs' graves became vulnerable to the menace of relic hunters, saintly relics needed protection. The Latin church saw many of these bones brought into cities and the architecture of public gathering and circulation built around them for greater protection.

8   F. Bond, *Dedications & Patron Saints of English Churches* etc.,
     London, 1914

9   In the late sixth century, pilgrims to the sunken shrine of St Peter
     in Rome took strips of cloth (*brandea*) and string. Gregory of Tours
     explains that they lowered the cloth over the grave, like fishing bait,
     and when drawn up the next morning it was purportedly heavier,
     laden with holy power. Pilgrimage needed practical management,
     and Pope Gregory the Great sought to organise the presentation
     of saintly relics. Otherwise the irreplaceable relics of Rome's martyrs
     would be lost, distributed, by limb or dust. He wrote *Moralia in Job*,
     explaining the obtuse, frequently astronomical, references in the
     Book of Job, the first poetic book of the Old Testament.

10   The Irish church emerged from *c*.431 and monasteries that
     embraced isolation were founded there during the sixth century,
     spreading the faith thence to Iona in 565, north Wales, and
     Northumbria.

11   Hugh Candidus explained that they occupied the banks and
     marshes, as 'those men are called Gyrwas who dwell in the fen,
     or hard by the fen...'

12   *Anglo-Saxon Chronicle* [E] for 653 AD ed. M, Swanton, London
     1998. Hugh Candidus could have had no understanding of the lost
     Roman settlement, with its temple to other gods. He was inclined
     to believe that the abbey emerged afresh, as every medieval church
     foundation myth represented God's will: 'In the region of the men
     of the Gyrwas stands a famous monastery [which was] once called
     Medeshamstede [...] From flooding or the overflowing of rivers
     the water standing on flat ground makes a deep swamp, save on
     certain higher ground, which I believe God himself raised, with the
     intent that it should be the habitation of those servants of God
     who had chosen to dwell there.'

13   The central episcopal seat for the Mercian diocese was founded
     in 656 at Repton in Derbyshire and from there came St Guthlac,
     founder of Crowland Abbey. The Northumbrian St Chad, the fifth
     bishop of Mercia, transferred the seat to Lichfield in 669, with
     oversight of Lindsey in North Lincolnshire. See Foyle, *Lichfield
     Cathedral: A Journey of Discovery*, London, 2016. Seaxwulf of
     Medeshamstede became the seventh Mercian bishop and the
     second bishop of Lichfield in around 676.

14   Many suspected this was the vengeance of their abandoned
     old Norse gods, which threatened the stability of the Church,
     a challenge to Medeshamstede's next abbot, Cuthbald.

15   Bede described stone buildings '*in more Romanum*' (in the Roman
     style). To seventh and eighth-century builders, Roman style meant
     masonry, alien to a rustic society's need for timber.

16   Personal communication

17   '*Ne fand peer nan ping buton ealde weallas & wilde wuda*',
     Anglo-Saxon Chronicle [E] for 963.

18   *Anglo-Saxon Chronicle* for 963.

19   The historian Simon Gunton offered a reason for Ealdwulf
     (Adulphus or Edwulf) becoming abbot: 'He being Chancellor to
     King Edgar, changed his Court life for a Monastical in this place;
     the reason of which change was this: He had one only son, whom
     he and his wife dearly loved, and they used to have him lie in bed
     betwixt them, but the parents having over-night drunk more wine
than was convenient, their son betwixt them was smothered to
death. Adulphus the father being sadly affected with this horrid
mischance was resolved to visit St. Peter at Rome, after the
manner of a penitent for absolution, imparting his intent to Bishop
Athelwoldus, who dissuaded him from it, telling him it would be
better if he would labour in the restoration of St. Peter's church
in this place, and here visit him. Adulphus, approving this advice,
came with King Edgar to Burgh, where in the presence of the King
and the rest of that Convention, he offered all his wealth, put off his
Courtly Robes, and put on the habit of a monk, and ascended to
the degree of Abbot in the year 972.'

20   'For a price obtained from the king [Edgar] and the nobles of the
     land another place, in the region of the Gyrwe and located on the
     bank of the River Nene, which in the language of the English once
     bore the name 'Medeshamstede', but which is now usually called
     'Burh'. The basilica of this place, adorned with the appropriate
     structures of buildings ['*domus*': houses] and endowed copiously
     with adjoining estates, he consecrated in honour of blessed Peter
     Prince of the Apostles. And there in like manner he gathered a
     company of monks [...]'

21   R. Gem, 'The Anglo-Saxon Abbey of Peterborough: A Review of
     the Evidence', B.A.A. Conf. Trans. *Peterborough Cathedral*, ed. J. Hall
     (forthcoming).

22   R. Gem, 'The Anglo-Saxon Abbey of Peterborough: A Review of the
     Evidence' B.A.A. Conf. Trans., *Peterborough* Cathedral, ed. J. Hall
     (forthcoming).

23   According to Hugh Candidus, they 'went into the minster, climbed
     up to the holy rood, took away the diadem from our Lord's head, all
     of pure gold, and seized the bracket that was underneath his feet,
     which was all of red gold. They climbed up to the steeple, brought
     down the table that was hid there, which was all of gold and silver,
     and took away fifteen large crucifixes, of gold and of silver; in short,
     they seized there so much gold and silver, and so many treasures, in
     money, in raiment, and in books, as no man could tell another.'

24   From Matthew 9:36. Scale. H., *Hugo Candidus' Peterborough History*,
     London, 1830

25   E. King, *Landlords, Peasants etc*, T.H. Aston (ed.) Cambridge, 1988,
     p.144

26   Bridges, the historian of Northamptonshire (vol. ii, p.368) relates that
     'of Dionisia the second daughter of Walter de Grauntcourt it is
     recorded that when a maiden, clad in a tunic, with a hat upon her head
     and armed only with a hollow shield, about the seventeenth year of
     King Stephen [1151/2] she attacked a certain knight, with one blow
     of her spear bringing him to the ground, and carried off his horse'.

27   The focus of this mythology was the powerful King Wulfhere,
     an authority figure likely to win the esteem and acquiescence of
     contemporary monarchs, who would otherwise exercise power to
     their own political gain and financial advantage.

28   See J. Paxton, 'Memory and Identity in Post-Conquest England',
     Haskins Society Journal 2002, pp.92–112

29   An approach seen at Norwich Cathedral Priory, for example.

30   It seems inconceivable that huge blocks freshly quarried at Barnack
     were carted, craned and floated along the Nene, only to be
     shackled to a hapless team of oxen at a wharf at Peterborough.

31 Norwich Cathedral retains an aedicule in which to set a holy relic beneath the bishop's throne in its ambulatory apse.

32 Gervase of Canterbury. See W. Stubbs, ed. *The Historical Works of Gervase of Canterbury*, Rolls Series 73, London, 1879, p.38, n.42.

33 By contrast, Canterbury was being rebuilt to represent a spiritual plane of justice and reward to a broader audience. As countless churches before, the cathedral manifested a convincing promise that paradise lay beyond earthly suffering through intercession enabled by prayer and tributes, a story now being enthusiastically backed by a written narrative of its early saints. It blended high French fashion with classically-proportioned columns and the circular plan of a Roman martyrium church to tell an old story ultimately leading back to St Augustine, who had imported the authority of Rome to Canterbury in 597.

34 Having tried to sanctify its founding by Bishop Rémi in vain, Lincoln created its own bishop St Hugh (d.1200). He most unusually built his own shrine church when, in 1192, he took responsibility for rebuilding the east end of Lincoln cathedral after an earthquake seven years previous. Strikingly, his burial emulated Becket's, set within an eastern tower-chapel similar to that in which Becket's scalp was displayed.

35 Technically, French verticality was turned horizontal; thin and skeletal walls were rejected for the usual thick mass of Norman building, a depth exploited by sunken arcades; the simple forms of French arch mouldings became multiplied and varied. But as importantly, English architecture was highly inventive, manifesting issues of history and allegiance, for each church held its own concerns, its own histories and loyalty to its titular saints.

36 In eighth-century England, the Venerable Bede associated Irish monks with the tonsure of Simon Magus, the Benedictine tonsure (worn at Peterborough) more favourably with the Apostle John.

37 '*Hic Petrus et Paulus in Romam ante Neronem disputaverunt cum Symone Mago. Hic praecepto Petro, et orante Paulo, Symon Magus caecidit in terram.*' See also recent sculpture in Spain (Ripoll, Catalonia) and France (Nave of Autun, but seated at the Miègeville Gate of Saint-Sernin in Toulouse).

38 In 1897, M.R. James first published the attribution to Simon Magus and noted the relationship between this stone and St Peter in the gable above.

39 Peterborough's lozenge-boarded transepts are comparable to the nave, and a further similar ceiling probably hung over the presbytery before the present fourteenth-century replacement.

40 P. Binski 'The Painted Nave Ceiling of Peterborough Abbey', in *The Medieval English Cathedral* ed. J. Backhouse, Harlaxton Medieval Studies, vol. X, 2003, pp.41–62.

41 The tree rings reveal that the timber was probably stockpiled rather than being felled as the work progressed.

42 In the *Recognitions* and *Pseudo-Clementine Homilies*, Helena is called Luna.

43 The same text suggests that her proximity to the western block with integral bell-towers may be deliberate. 'Once, when this Luna of his was in a certain tower, a great multitude had assembled to see her, and were standing around the tower on all sides; but she was seen by all the people to lean forward, and to look out through all the windows of that tower.'

44 This is the avatar of St John the Apostle, the author of the Book of Revelation that concludes and resolves the Bible. He describes both the threat of hell and the opportunity for the faithful to crush the devil's intent and return to paradise where Christ and the Virgin reign, and where the tree of life redeems. St Peter's central role is holding the keys to both.

45 The Victorian lithographer W. Strickland recorded the ceiling in an illustration.

46 The most influential medieval book on astronomy was written by John of Sacrobosco, a northern Englishman working in Paris about 1220, when universities promoted discussion across Europe and just as Peterborough's ceiling was being conceived. He represented the theory of the fourth-century Heraclides of Pontos, who supposed Mercury and Venus rotated around the sun, which in turn revolved around the earth. Yet while John of Oxford, bishop of Norwich from 1175–1200, reflected that idea, the scientist-bishop of Lincoln, Robert Grosseteste, did not. Grosseteste arrived at Lincoln in 1235, after the ceiling was begun.

47 See the north aisle of the choir at Lincoln Cathedral, where whirls representing the sun are presented in tandem with stiff-leaf carving.

48 A similar convention can be seen in a south aisle boss of the Angel Quire at Lincoln Cathedral *c*.1260.

49 W. Newburgh, *A History of English Affairs*, Book 1, ed. & transl. P.G. Walsh & M.J. Kennedy, 1988, p.105

50 The old monastic curriculum centred on the *trivium* alone: grammar and rhetoric in the service of logic as biblical authority.

51 A.J. Duggan, 'Henry II, The English Church and Papacy, *c*.1154–76', in *Henry II: New Interpretations*, Cambridge, 1988, 2007, pp.154–183, p.179

52 *Conservation and Discovery: Peterborough Cathedral Nave Ceiling* (etc), eds. J. Hall and S.M. Wright, 2015, p.95. The Canterbury vault in *c*.1220 portrayed Henry III in his minority, an aspirational presentation rather than an appeal to his authority.

53 The status of God's appointed as royal priest and Christ-figure became increasingly literal as the thirteenth century wore on, after King John inaugurated the Maundy ceremony wherein he imitated Christ washing poor men's feet. In France, the late 1230s witnessed the start of the Sainte-Chapelle for Louis IX, a super-shrine for purchased relics supposed to include those of the crown of thorns, to which Henry III would soon respond by rebuilding Westminster Abbey to house a phial of Christ's blood.

54 Medieval kings carried orbs in imitation of the spherical earth, as often portrayed in Christ's hands, wherein Asia occupied the north, Europe and Africa the south in an arrangement that made a 'Tau' (T-shaped) cross. As Christ was crucified to save the earth, so the notional form of this world map revealed its manifest destiny.

55 It has been noted that at Canterbury Cathedral, a similar *agnus dei* was the chosen subject for the vault boss set in the eastern crossing (*c*.1178) that divided the choir from the presbytery; a junction between realms. Perhaps more relevant at Peterborough was this painted lamb's position, as seen from the nave, to be over the rood screen surmounted by a crucifixion, which divided the

56 laity in the nave from the monks' choir. Set before this screen was the nave altar at which eucharistic wine was taken.

56 As the imp and serpents in the Angel Quire of Lincoln Cathedral of after 1256 went on to brilliantly portray.

57 A fish and a lion might be argued to be symbolic of Christ, but he was not represented as a fish for the acrostic '*Icthus*' at this date – nor by a female lion, let alone four of them.

58 In his illustration of the ceiling, the Victorian lithographer W. Strickland coloured them neither yellow nor gold but grey, following an eighteenth-century overpainting. However, he also painted the rampant lion a similar colour.

59 The Vercelli Acts of St Peter, XII–XIII.

60 We might ask whether other great English churches dedicated to St Peter – Westminster Abbey, Exeter Cathedral, Gloucester Abbey among them – may have had similar imagery before the 1230s. The fact that all their high vaults were rebuilt after this date and their furnishings replaced has surely lost us the opportunity to judge Peterborough's context, unimpeachable though it is as a surviving painted ceiling of the grandest scale, interest, and eloquence.

61 Before a fire in 1834, one tantalising similarity used to exist in the 'Painted Chamber', the innermost sanctum of the king's chambers at Westminster, where a fictive architectural framework painted for Henry III in about 1263 portrayed a narrow central arch flanked by two broader arches, bookended by spirelets. It is too much to speculate that Henry III may have cast an eye on Peterborough, where he was depicted in flattering terms on the ceiling. He was certainly interested in his own patronage at Lichfield, which he emulated at Windsor.

62 Lincoln's popular focus for pilgrimage to the shrines of two saints called Hugh was built 1256–80, to promise salvation for the faithful of spirit and generous of pocket. The sculpture in the triforium level showed St Mary recovering paradise while somehow renewing the infancy of Christ after his death, her breast milk regarded as the antidote to the devil. This Marian paradise was the first major regional response to the French bar tracery imported at Westminster Abbey from 1245, even if Binham Priory's west window was earlier. A separate Lady Chapel was built to the north of the Angel Quire.

63 Boniface decreed in 1302 in his *Unam Sanctam* that 'it is necessary to salvation that every human creature be subject to the Roman pontiff'. His confidence in side-stepping royal authority was misplaced; in 1303, a French delegation forcibly took the papacy to Avignon.

64 *The Heads of Religious Houses in England and Wales, II: 1216–1377*, eds D.M. Smith, V.C.M. London, p.58

65 Paul Binski's observation, developing a comparative method that stems from Richard Krautheimer's essay 'Introduction to an 'Iconography of Mediaeval Architecture', *Journal of the Warburg and Courtauld Institutes* 5, 1942, which argues that medieval architectural emulation of distant prototypes was more to do with respecting the simple data of number (e.g. columns, polygons) and metrics (measurements, matched or exceeded) than achieving verisimilitude.

66 It was dropped to St Thomas, a neat parallel to his doubting Christ's return to life unless he felt the wound made by Longinus' spear (John 20:24–9). The girdle, or *sacra cintola*, was popular with pregnant women.

67 I am grateful to Dr Jackie Hall for sharing her paper prior to publication. The deduction that the nave of St Thomas's chapel was taken from the site by the abbey gate was made by Owen W. Davys in *An Historical and Architectural Guide to Peterborough Cathedral*, 1842, Appendix note A.

68 That claim included his 'uncle', Henry VI (1422–61; 1470–71), a candidate for sainthood rejected by Rome.

69 As the flowers of heaven, roses represent the realm that St Peter's keys protect. It is a convention used in royal manuscripts of the period to show that England (called 'Mary's Dowry') was ruled in the stead of Christ and the Virgin.

70 He also went hunting with Richard Empson, Henry VII's financier, in the royal forest, albeit illegally. W.T. Mellows, *The Last Days of Peterborough Monastery*, 1940 p.x

71 As used with a cross florey by Bishop Tunstal on Durham Castle after 1530.

72 The others were Westminster, Oxford, Gloucester, Chester and Bristol.

73 At Winchester medieval pages were turned into kites for the recreation of soldiers.

74 Having lived at nearby Northborough Manor, Elizabeth Cromwell (Oliver's wife), was buried in that church in 1665, 'lacking any monument or inscription'.

75 *The Collected Letters of William Morris* Vol. III: 1889–1892

INDEX

NOTE: Page numbers in
italics refer to illustrations or
information in a caption.

accommodation buildings 37–8
Ælfric Puttoc, Archbishop of
York 26–7, 35
Ælfsige, Abbot 25
Æthelric, Bishop of Durham 25
Æthelwold, St, Bishop of
Winchester 22, 23, 24, 25,
26, 31
Alexander of Lincoln (the
Magnificent) 79
Alwalton marble effigies 85
Anglo-Saxon Chronicle 30, 36
Anna, king of East Anglia 19
apse 28, 42, 42, 120–1
arches/arcading 42, 42–3, 48–9
Roman influence 45, 45,
57, 59
Arthur, Prince 103–4
Augustine of Canterbury 19, 54
Austin, Humphrey 112, 113

baldacchino 108, 117
Barnack stone 41
Becket, Thomas 46, 48, 52, 79
Becket Chapel 54, 55, 88–9,
91, 95
Bede, the Venerable, St 19, 36
Benedict, Abbot 55, 70, 71
Benedictine Rule 32–3
Bernard of Clairvaux, St 84, 86
Black Death 92
Bloet, Robert, Bishop of Lincoln
79
Boniface VIII, pope 88
Boothby, Adam de, Abbot 91
bosses 94, 95, 103, 104
bowl from Saxon period 23
Brand, Abbot 30, 31
Burgh (Gildenburgh) 23, 34
see also Medeshamstede

Candidus, Hugh *see* Hugh
Candidus
Canterbury Cathedral 19, 36, 37,
42, 52, 53, 102
and Peterborough 54–5,
71
Car Dyke 13–14, 13, 16
ceilings
apse 120–1
bosses 94, 95, 103, 104
nave 10, 68, 70–84, 72,
74–83
quire 91

retroquire 98, 101, 102–3
see also vaulted ceilings
central tower
octagonal plan 91–3, 93,
96–7
rebuilding in late 1800s
117, 119
Chambers, John, Abbot 105,
106, 107
chapter house 45
choir 42, 84, 88, 117, 117
choirboys in west front 60,
62–3, 71
Christianity
Hedda Stone 22, 23
nave ceiling symbolism
71–84
in Roman times 14, 16–17,
18, 19
west front porch
symbolism 94–5, 95
Civil War 111–14
clerestory 45, 55, 57
cloister 37, 38, 39
Constantine, Roman emperor
16, 17
Arch of Constantine 59
Cromwell, Oliver 111–12
Cromwell, Thomas 107
Cynesige, Archbishop of York 27

devil in nave ceiling 83
dissolution of the monasteries
106–7, 110
dogs in nave ceiling 84
Dugdale, William 114
Durham Cathedral 30–1, 39,
42, 44
Durobrivae (Water Newton)
13, 18

eagle and St John 74, 75
Ealdwulf, Abbot 23
Earnwig (monk) 25
ecclesiastical imagery 74–5,
76–81
Edward I, king of England 88
Edward II, king of England 88
Edward III, king of England 91,
92
Edward the Black Prince 92
Ely Cathedral 23, 30–1, 36, 39,
41, 55
Lady Chapel 87, 91
octagonal tower 91, 92
west front 25, 27
Ernulf of Canterbury, Abbot
36–8, 39, 52, 71

famine in 1300s 88–9
fan vaulting 98, 101, 102–3
Fenland monastic cells 20, 20
fires 30, 34, 37, 38–9, 119
fish imagery 84, 118
foliage motifs 72, 73, 75, 84,
120–1
font 118
Fourth Lateran Council 70,
83
funerary monuments 114, 115,
116
Katherine of Aragon's
tomb 106, 107

Gaveston, Piers 88
Genge, William, Abbot 95
Gildenburgh *see* Burgh
goat in nave ceiling 81, 82
Godfrey of Croyland, Abbot 88,
90, 91
Godiva, Lady 25, 26
Gothic architecture 46, 94
Gregory the Great, pope 19
Grosseteste, Robert 66, 78,
81
Gunton, Simon 114

Hedda Stone 22, 23
Henry de Angeli, Abbot 48
Henry I, king of England 79
Henry II, king of England 48, 52,
54, 55, 78, 79, 80
Henry III, king of England 54, 66,
78, 78, 81, 87
Henry VII, king of England 100,
103–4
Henry VIII, king of England 104,
105–7
Hereward the Wake 31, 34, 35
hospital 37
Hugh Candidus 12, 12, 31, 34, 35,
38–9, 41, 76
Hugh de Spalding 92
Hugh of Lincoln 79, 80
Hugh of Wells *see* Wells, Hugh
of

illuminated books 25
Peterborough Psalter 90,
90
infirmary 37
Irvine, J. T. 117

James, M. R. 114
John, St 74
John, king of England 54, 59, 70,
78, 81

John de Séez, Abbot 38, 39,
41, 48
John of Salisbury's *Policraticus*
46, 46, 57, 66, 79
and nave ceiling 72, 74, 75,
76–7, 81–2, 84
Judas in nave ceiling 83–4

Katherine of Aragon 103–4,
105–6
tomb 106, 107
King's College Chapel,
Cambridge 103, 103
kings in nave ceiling 74–5,
76–81, 78, 80
Kirkton, Robert, Abbot 100, 102,
103, 104–5

Lady Chapel 86–7, 86–7, 110,
112
lamb of God imagery 82–3, 83
Langton, Stephen 59, 81
lectern 100
Leofric, Abbot 25–6, 30
Liber Niger 36
Liberal Arts imagery 74–5,
76–81, 77
Lichfield Cathedral 21
Lincoln Cathedral 34, 34, 36, 39,
44, 45, 57, 87
lion/lioness imagery 75, 84
liturgy and west front 60, 61,
62–3
Longthorpe Roman fortress 13
Luna figure 72, 72, 74, 75, 76

Magna Carta 54, 70
marble effigies 85
Martin of Bec, Abbot 48
Mary, Virgin 84, 86–7, 94–5, 95
Marian rose 100, 103, 104,
105
Mary, Queen of Scots 110
Medeshamstede abbey and
church 9, 19–21, 38–9, 48
destruction by Vikings 22,
23
rebuilding as Peterborough
Abbey 22–7
Roman origins 12–18, 14
survival of church building
14, 14, 25, 34, 36, 38–9,
48
treasures 26
see also Peterborough
Abbey
Medeshamstede (Burgh) 9, 15,
19–20, 23

Mercia 19–20, *19*
monastic life 32–3
monkey in nave ceiling 81, *82*
Morris, William 119
Mount Thorold 35, *35*
music in nave ceiling 81–2

nave 48, 55, *55*
    painted ceiling *10*, 68, 70–84, *72*, *74–83*
    screen *41*, 100, 110
New Building 98, 100, *101–2*, *102*, *104*
Norman Conquest (1066) 30

Oswald, St, relics 25, 31, 42
owl in nave ceiling 81, *82*

Paris, Notre-Dame 46, *47*
Paul, St 82–3
Peada, sub-king of the Middle Angles 19–20
Pearson, J. L. 117
Peasants' Revolt (1381) 92–3
Perpendicular tracery 94
Peter, St 8, *10*, 12, 17–18
    in nave ceiling 82–3
    and Simon Magus 63–6, 74, 84
    on west front 66, *67*, 73
Peterborough (city) 9, *13*, 48
    Guildhall 112, 114
    Knights' Chamber and abbey gate 88, *88–9*
    rebuilding after Civil War 112, 114
    St John's church 95
Peterborough Abbey 22–7, 30–8, *39*
    fires 30, 34, 37, 38–9
Peterborough Cathedral 9
    abbots and bishops 122
    Anglo-Saxon buildings 12–27, 30–8
    education and learning 46
    fire in 1116 and rebuilding 38–48, *40–1*
    gaps in documentary evidence 9, 12
    historical accounts 114
    New Building and Tudor period *98*, 100–7, *101–2*, *104–7*
    parliamentarian destruction 111–12
    survival and later renovation 114–19

see also Medeshamstede abbey and church
Peterborough Psalter 90, *90*
plague 92
porch 94–5, *94–5*
Prior's Gate 104, *105*

quarries 41
quire ceiling *91*

Raunds parish church *62*, 63
relics 17, 25, 31, 48
    see also Becket Chapel
'Renaissance' culture 46–7
Repton, Derbyshire 21
retroquire ceiling *98*, *101*, 102–3
rib vaulting 42, 44, 55, *55–6*, 57, 70
Richard I, king of England 79, 80, 81
Richborough, Kent, Roman arch 16, *16*
Roman influences 44, 45, *45*, 46
    see also triumphal arches
Roman settlements 12–18
Rome 54–5
    Old St Peter's 17, *17*, 70–1
Royal Albert Hall, London 115, *115*

St John, Oliver, Lord Chief Justice 112
Salisbury, John of, *Policraticus* 46, *46*
Salisbury Cathedral 60, 63
Sarum Use liturgy 62–3
Scarlett, Robert 110, *110*
Scott, George Gilbert *120–1*
screens
    nave screen *41*, 100, 110
    presbytery screen 110
Seaxwulf, Bishop of Lichfield 20, 21
Sedgwick, William 114
shrine of St Oswald 42
Simon Magus 63–6, *65*
    and nave ceiling *72*, *72*, 74, 76, 83, 84
Spalding, Hugh de 92
Staffordshire Hoard 21
Stephen, king of England 79
'stiff-leaf' motifs *73*, 75, 84
stone carvings
    baldacchino *108*, 117
    Hedda Stone 22, *23*
    marble effigies 85
    Roman deities 14, *14*

tracery in 1400s *94*, 100
west front figures 63–6, *65*, *67*, *73*, *75*
west front and liturgy 60, *61*, 62–3
west front porch 94–5, *94–5*
Stukeley, William 114–15
sun imagery 75
Sutton, Robert, Abbot 87
Swaffham cartulary 112, *113*
Swein, king of Denmark 31

Tarrant, Dean 115
Thorold, Abbot 31, 34–5, 37, 63
Thorpe family of Longthorpe 88
tombs *see* funerary monuments
Tout Hill 35, *35*
towers *see* central tower
transepts 48, *48–9*, 100
    and early buildings 14, 25, *40–2*, 44–5, *45*
    western transept 55, 56, 57, 70, *71*
triumphal arches 16, *16*, 45, *45*, 57, *59*
Tudor iconography 100, 103, 104, *104–6*, 105
tympana 42, *43*, 44

unclean beasts imagery 81, *82*

vaulted ceilings 42, *44*, 55, *55–6*, 57, 70, *101*, 102–3
vegetation motifs
    foliage motifs *72*, *73*, *75*, 84, *120–1*
    Tudor iconography 100, 103, 104, 105, *105*, *106*
Venus image 75
Viking invasions 22

Walter, Hubert, Archbishop of Canterbury 80, 81
Walter of Bury St Edmunds, Abbot 72, 84
Wastell, John 102–3
Water Newton *see* Durobrivae
Water Newton Treasure 18, *18*
Waterville, William, Abbot 48, 52, 79
Wells, Hugh of, Bishop of Lincoln 59, 63
Wells Cathedral 59, 60, *60*, 63
west front 8, *8*, 50, 52, 57–63, *58*, *61*
    choirboys in 60, 62–3, *71*
    lack of imitators 84

porch 94–5, *94–5*
repair in 1890s 117, *119*
on Royal Albert Hall 115, *115*
St Peter figure 66, *67*, 73
Simon Magus figure 63–6, *65*
Westminster Abbey 103
wheel windows in west front 8, *59*, *61*, 73
William I (the Conqueror) 30, 35, *36*
William of Ramsey, Abbot 100
windows 91, 110, *111*, 112, 115
    Spencer Leeson memorial window *12*, *24*, *113*
    stone tracery in 1400s *94*, 100
    west front 8, 57, 59–60, *61*, *73*
Wolsey, Cardinal Thomas 105
Wulfstan the Cantor 23

ACKNOWLEDGEMENTS

I am grateful for the opportunity presented by the
then Dean of Peterborough, the Very Reverend Charles
Taylor; for the encouragement of the Reverend Canon
Jonathan Baker; and for the guidance and care of the
cathedral's Head of Operations, Stuart Orme, a venerable
historian and man of the city. My fourth cathedral
monograph with Scala revisited the now customary
skill and efficiency of commissioner Rosemarie McCabe
and editor Jessica Hodge.

It is a privilege to write a volume on any great building;
more so to have the opportunity to rethink the narrative
of a church as fine as Peterborough Cathedral. This is an
oasis of medieval culture I thought I knew well, having
spent my teenage years exploring here, but have come to
understand much better by revisiting a familiar scene
with new eyes.

This is in part due to others' efforts and insights.
It takes a special generosity for scholars to share
unpublished work, and this book was much improved
by contributors to the British Archaeological Association's
Peterborough conference in 2015, who entrusted their
draft papers for the forthcoming volume edited by Jackie
Hall. They are Richard Gem, Ron Baxter, Sandy Heslop,
Stephen Upex, Martin Henig, Lisa Reilly, Harriet Mahood,
Cathy Oakes, Stuart Harrison and Jackie Hall herself, who
also shared her expertise on the built fabric.

Lastly, I would like to thank my mother, for having
opted to give birth to me at Maxey, seven miles or
so north of the city, so that I have forever carried
'Peterborough' on my passport. Returning was only
a matter of time. This book is for her.

Supported by generous funding from the
Heritage Lottery Fund.

First published in 2018 by
Scala Arts & Heritage Publishers Ltd
10 Lion Yard
Tremadoc Road
London SW4 7NQ, UK
www.scalapublishers.com

In association with
Peterborough Cathedral
Minster Precincts, Peterborough PE1 1XS

ISBN 978-1-78551-080-9

Edited by Jessica Hodge
Designed by Bobby Birchall
Index by Jane Horton
Printed and bound in China

10 9 8 7 6 5 4 3 2 1

Front cover: The west front
Back cover: The east end
Frontispiece: One of the Seven Liberal Arts from the
fourteenth-century nave ceiling
p.2 The quire vault, as repainted in the mid-Victorian era. The capitals bear
the crossed keys of St Peter, and bosses include many roses of heaven.
p.3 Peterborough's rib vaults are early examples of England's inventive
vaulting design, one of the nation's great architectural legacies in which
the vault was a metaphor for the heavenly veil.

PHOTO CREDITS

© Historic England Archive: pp.1, 10, 16, 72, 74/5, 76, 77 both,
78, 80, 82, 83
Angelo Hornak: front cover, back cover, back cover flap, pp.2, 4, 8, 14 below,
23 below, 28, 37 both, 40, 41, 42, 43, 44, 48, 49, 50, 56, 61, 64 left, 68, 85
both, 91, 96/7, 98, 101, 102, 105, 107, 108, 114, 116, 117, 120/1
Matthew Roberts: pp.6/7, 12, 14 (top), 23 (top), 24, 45, 54, 55, 73, 94, 95, 103
(top), 104, 110, 111, 113
[Alamy] p.9
[British Museum] p.18
© Birmingham Museum Trust: p.21 top
Dr Jonathan Foyle: pp.27, 62, 89, 92, 106 both, 118
James Newton: p.34
Robert Greshoff Photography: p.53
[Bridgeman] p.90